DAILY LIFE IN ANCIENT CHINA

In this volume, Mu-Chou Poo offers a new overview of daily life in ancient China. Synthesizing a range of textual and archaeological materials, he brings a thematic approach to the topic that enables a multifaceted understanding of the ideological, economical, legal, social, and emotional aspects of life in ancient China. The volume focuses on the Han period and examines key topics such as government organization and elite ideology, urban and country life, practical technology, leisure and festivity, and death and burial customs. Written in clear and engaging prose, this volume serves as a useful introduction to the culture and society of ancient China. It also enables students to better understand the construction of history and to reflect critically on the nature of historical writing.

Mu-Chou Poo is Chair Professor of History at the Chinese University of Hong Kong. His research interests include society and religion in ancient Egypt and China and comparative ancient history. He is the author or editor of five books in English, most recently *Old Society, New Belief: Religious Transformation of China and Rome, ca. 1st–6th Centuries*.

DAILY LIFE IN ANCIENT CHINA

MU-CHOU POO
Chinese University of Hong Kong

CAMBRIDGE
UNIVERSITY PRESS

CAMBRIDGE
UNIVERSITY PRESS

University Printing House, Cambridge CB2 8BS, United Kingdom

One Liberty Plaza, 20th Floor, New York, NY 10006, USA

477 Williamstown Road, Port Melbourne, VIC 3207, Australia

314–321, 3rd Floor, Plot 3, Splendor Forum, Jasola District Centre, New Delhi – 110025, India

79 Anson Road, #06-04/06, Singapore 079906

Cambridge University Press is part of the University of Cambridge.

It furthers the University's mission by disseminating knowledge in the pursuit of education, learning, and research at the highest international levels of excellence.

www.cambridge.org
Information on this title: www.cambridge.org/9781107021174
DOI: 10.1017/9781139108621

First published 2018

Printed in the United States of America by Sheridan Books, Inc.

A catalogue record for this publication is available from the British Library.

ISBN 978-1-107-02117-4 Hardback

CONTENTS

FIGURES AND MAPS

PREFACE

This book was written at the invitation of Cambridge University Press, for which I am very grateful. It gave me an opportunity to venture into areas of Chinese history that I had been interested in but had never really had the chance to explore deeply enough to form any perspective. I have of course read a number of books on daily life in various cultures and histories since my school years, and have always been interested in looking at history from a bottom-up angle. But when the time came to write this book, the question that immediately came to mind was not how to write it, but why to write it. I have attempted to answer this in the Introduction. As to how to write it, indeed I had so many samples to consult and emulate that it should not have been a problem. For the period that I was going to write about, there are abundant literature as well as archaeological sources to support an account of the daily activities of the people of early imperial China: food, drink, dress, house, entertainment, family life, education, social engagement, festivities, transportation, agriculture, medicine, technology, etc. Many of these were written by earlier scholars, including Michael Loewe, whose *Everyday Life in Early Imperial China during the Han Period, 202 BC–AD 220* remains the most important work on this subject in the English language. As I try to suggest in the Introduction, the present volume is not meant to repeat or replace Loewe's book. What I wish to do is to provide readers with a historical framework that could allow them to appreciate the general conditions that people had experienced in their daily lives. In other words, I tried to make sense of the daily experience of the people of that bygone time by providing a historical framework: why their life evolved the way it did, and what structural sources influenced it.

Some reflections on the historian's craft arose after I had finished the manuscript. Historians who are eager to understand and reconstruct the past – and, therefore, produce "historical knowledge" as opposed to mere "historical fact" – can usually do two things: (1) select sufficient facts to describe an event according to one avenue of thought – of human nature, of political or economic necessity, or of "the law of history," and thus create meaningful "historical knowledge" through which facts can be understood in a logical fashion; and (2) include as many facts as possible in the description of an event, hoping that the more we know about them, the clearer the picture of the event will be. The two are not mutually exclusive, but there might be certain differences as to whether the historian constructed the event with explicit lines of interpretation.

There are, moreover, two aspects to the studying and writing of history: the private and public. A person may read history in private moments and find personal satisfaction or revelation. When the reader later wishes to make use of historical knowledge, however, it may or may not be a private act, since historical knowledge is often the motivating factor behind human actions, private or collective. Similarly, the writing of history, though it may be defined as a private act, is actually also a public act, as historical works are expected to be published and read by the public. As a creator of historical knowledge, the historian should ideally abide by the rule that he or she is creating historical knowledge based on facts, not fabrication, even though it is entirely possible that a historian can get every fact right but write a history that is fictitious. In reality, of course, there is probably no absolute, objective, historical knowledge, since all historical knowledge derived from facts and interpretations is created by the historian, who is bound to have certain personal biases. Even simple lists of events, such as the chronicles of the emperors in traditional Chinese historiography, were deliberate selections of facts, and certainly not all the facts were known to the historian. As is often the case, a historian with ideological missions may use his or her craft to manipulate the facts to create a historical memory that fits a specific purpose. The historian, however, might not be responsible for how the reader uses the historical knowledge provided.

What is more dangerous is the claim that the historian had told the whole or the true story. We are constantly reminded of that ironic comment, not without a certain grain of truth: in history everything except dates, places, and names is false; in novels everything except dates, places, and names is true. Most historians would like to steer away from being novelists, the reason being that historians consider their work to be of a special nature; that is, historical works are supposed to record past events as closely as possible to what really had happened in history. The function of historical works is not, primarily, for entertainment (though that may be one of the reasons), or for philosophizing (though many historians may secretly hope that their magnum opus would have that quality), but to provide responsible accounts (which are not necessarily equal to "true accounts") of our past and to construct a reliable foundation for our whole existence. Historical works, in our view, provide human society with a "relatively reliable memory" that may allow society to navigate through a myriad of "facts," true and fabricated, that float in the collective memory of society, and find a better way to the future. Most importantly, such relatively reliable memories could and should be responsibly examined and corrected by the community of historians so that individual prejudice may be reduced to a minimum. But if historians do not try to find out what really happened in history to the best of their ability, and allow fellow historians to cross-check the result, then they may as well claim to be novelists.

Rereading the pages of this volume, certain shortcomings in the interpretation and organization of the source materials become obvious to me. While dissatisfied with the limited amount of historical evidence at one's disposal, simultaneously, one also regrets one's inability to do justice to the evidence that is available. The reader is, therefore, the sole judge of the work if he or she is generous enough to spend time reading through the pages.

Finally, I would like to acknowledge the support of many colleagues, among whom Professors Robin Yates, Ping-chen Hsiung, and Lothar von Falkenhausen had contributed the most by making critical comments and suggestions on the manuscript. The anonymous reviewers also provided some very useful comments and suggestions, which are highly appreciated. Any mistakes and misinterpretations are of course my responsibility.

WEIGHTS AND MEASURES

Equivalents

Length	1 cun		23.1 mm
	1 chi	10 cun	23.1 cm
	1 bu	6 chi	1.38 m
	1 zhang	10 chi	2.31 m
	1 li		0.415 km
Capacity	1 ge		19.968 cc
	1 sheng	10 ge	199.687 cc
	1 dou	10 sheng	1.996 L
	1 shi (also 1 hu)	10 dou	19.968 L
Weight	1 shu		0.64 g
	1 liang	24 shu	15.36 g
	1 jin	16 liang	245 g
	1 jün	3 0 jin	7.37 kg
	1 shi	4 jün	29.5 kg
Area	1 qing	100 mou	11.39 English acres

The chart follows Denis Twitchett and Michael Loewe, eds., *Cambridge History of China*, Vol. 1 (Cambridge University Press, 1986), p. xxxviii.

JOURNALS AND ABBREVIATIONS

AEPHE	*Annuaire de l'Ecole practique des Hautes Etudes*
AM	*Asia Major*
BIHP	*Zhongyang yanjiuyuan lishiyuyan yanjiusuo jikan* 中央研究院歷史語言研究所集刊
BMFEA	*Bulletin of the Museum of Far Eastern Antiquities*
CEA	*Cahiers d'Extrême-Asie*
Dalu zazhi	大陸雜誌
EC	*Early China*
Hanxue yanjiu	漢學研究
Huanan shifan	*Huanan shifan daxue xuebao* (*Ziran kexueban*) 華南師範大學學報 (自然科學版)
JAH	*Journal of Asian History*
JESHO	*Journal of the Economic and Social History of the Orient*
Jianbo yanjiu yicong	簡帛研究譯叢
Jianghan kaogu	江漢考古
Jiuzhou xuelin	九州學林
Kaogu tongxun	考古通訊
Kaogu xuebao	考古學報
Kaogu yu wenwu	考古與文物
KG	*Kaogu*考 古
Late Imperial China	
Lishi yanjiu	歷史研究
Nature	
Nongye kaogu	農業考古
Numen	
Qilu xuekan	齊魯學刊
Qinghua daxue	*Qinghua daxue xuebao* (*Zhexue shehuikexue ban*) 清華大學學報(哲學社會科學版)
Shixue yuekan	史學月刊
Shoudu shifan	*Shoudu shifandaxue xuebao* (*Shehui kexueban*) 首都師範大學學報(社會科學版)
Sichuan daxue	*Sichuan daxue xuebao* 四川大學學報

TP	*T'oung Pao*
TR	*Taoist Resources*
Wenshizhe	文 史 哲
WW	*Wen Wu* 文 物
Yanyeshi yanjiu	鹽業史研究
Zhengzhou daxue	*Zhengzhou daxue xuebao* (*Zhexue shehuikexue ban*) 鄭州大學學報 (哲學社會科學版)
Zhongguo dianji yu wenhua	中國典籍與文化
Zhongguo jingjishi yanjiu	中國經濟史研究
Zhongguo nongshi	中國農史
Zhongguo shehui jingjishi yanjiu	中國社會經濟史研究
Zhongguoshi yanjiu	中國史研究
Zhonghua wenshi luncong	中華文史論叢
Zhongyuan wenwu	中原文物
Zhongzhou xuekan	中州學刊

INTRODUCTION

WHY DAILY LIFE?

Why do we need to know about the kind of daily life people in the ancient world, including ancient China, had? Several reasons spring to mind. To begin with, it is inherently interesting for those of us with an inquisitive nature to want to know what was happening in the world, including how people lived their lives. This may be a way of reflecting on the quality and meaning of our own existence. The study of history may be said to consist, although not exclusively, of the study of the lives of others, as individuals, groups, ancient or modern, young or old, male or female. Yet, professional historical studies with which we are familiar usually deal with the so-called "big events," that is, events that happened to large numbers of people, such as a change of dynasty, war, famine, or the rise and fall of empires. These continue to interest most historians and readers, with good reason. When we focus on the daily lives of people, however, we are looking at history from a different perspective. Ever since the early twentieth century, the Annales School of historical research had already demonstrated with their works the long-neglected aspects of the past, the process of social and cultural change on the basis of *longue durée*, and the structure of daily life that was not in the picture of traditional history, which focused mainly on political change. Here there are no big events, no prominent figures, but simply descriptions of how people lived in a certain period. Yet, of course, the big events could, and indeed did, exert a certain influence on people's lives; thus they serve as the backdrop to daily experience.

Our intention in this volume, simply put, is to try to re-create for the reader glimpses of life experiences of people in a past era. Yet, we need to be realistic about what we can expect from such an undertaking. It is nearly impossible, given the material at our disposal, to reconstruct the details of the daily life of any individual in the past, even though we may occasionally have access to records of someone's thoughts and emotions that survived through chance preservation. Thus, the kind of daily life we can study is not the life of any individual person, but the general conditions of life that may have been experienced by many.

Furthermore, to see how people fared in their lives is one thing; to understand why their lives proceeded or developed the way they did is another. To achieve this, we decided to investigate the various social, economic, ideological, political, and physical factors that constituted the framework within which people of different social strata conducted their lives. The archaeological discoveries of the last half century in China had provided us with quite a large amount of texts and artifacts that could allow us to discuss these factors with new materials unavailable to our predecessors. Our aim is not to provide any theory to explain the course of history, but only to suggest reasonable ways to understand, with hindsight, the possible circumstances that generally shaped the lives of individuals.

Despite our interest in the details of daily life and its underlying structure, we still have to ask ourselves what the value is of such an undertaking besides personal enjoyment. The purpose is not to find a moral justification – though it may be a legitimate one – for doing, perhaps, what one enjoys doing, that is, to satisfy one's curiosity. We are essentially asking about the nature and value of historical knowledge.

This is hardly the place to discuss subjects such as "what is history?," whether to choose sides with positivism or relativism, or whether to concede that all histories are "constructions" and no "reconstruction" is possible.[1] Our position here is relatively simple. The content of historical knowledge can be described as consisting of two parts: facts and interpretations. Events happened only once. Therefore, there is only one objective historical fact about everything in the past. How to obtain and ascertain the facts is part of the work of professional historians. The truth about a past fact, moreover, may be accessed and verified at different levels, depending on what kind of questions the historian wishes to ask. "The Past" as an abstract idea referring to an all-encompassing

[1] The famous book by E. H. Carr 1986 (*What Is History?*) touches on some of the fundamental questions about historical studies in the modern era. For a useful overview of the subsequent development of the debates over constructionism, deconstructionism, postmodernism, etc., see Alun Munslow (1997).

entity may, indeed, be unknowable, yet the "past" (with a small "p") may still be possible to investigate as long as we clearly define the level of truth that we are interested in. Needless to say, the process of finding and ascertaining facts already involved the historian's interpretation. Interpretation based on the knowable facts, moreover, is really what gives meaning to the facts. In search of meaning is what history is about; even meaninglessness is a form of answer that may be acceptable.

The human mind, though incredibly complex in terms of its biological structure, is still far from being able to comprehend the significance of the sum of all knowable facts and, thus, has to select from the myriad facts those that fit within its comprehension, to create a narrative of an event that may have consisted of many known and unknown facts. Most of the facts in history, needless to say, are lost to us. These are not merely the deeds of deceased people and their material remains, but the thoughts and emotions, likes and dislikes, happiness and sorrow, joy and remorse, desire and despair that each human being would have experienced. It was these daily experiences that drove human beings to act, or refrain from action, and, finally, to create history.

The value of the knowledge of daily life in history, therefore, lies in the fact that such knowledge may attract our attention and help us to understand what people experienced on a daily basis. Such historical knowledge may be placed side by side with the "grand narratives" that are often seen in standard historical works, and allows the readers to imagine the process of history of a certain period with a more down-to-earth view, to flesh out the skeleton of historical events. Since interest in daily life is a modern phenomenon that reflects democratic values, the lack of ancient discourse on daily life may actually point to a different collective mentality. That is to say, even though we can find evidence that may allow us to have access to certain aspects of daily life in the past, that evidence was most likely not originally meant to serve such a function. This, of course, is not to say that people in the past did not pay attention to their daily lives. In fact, we have quite a lot of evidence that points to the institutional and individual concerns of people's daily lives in various manifestations. We can predict that, for most people, a "comfortable" daily life was probably what they hoped for. That we are now consciously interested in examining the daily lives of people in the past, therefore, is not only to satisfy our curiosity, but also, as historians, to demonstrate how the grand narratives of history may have overlooked most of the ordinary people for whom the rigors of daily life were their sole focus. The preconceptions or biases of our historical knowledge, therefore, are exposed and, at the same time, partially redeemed when the agenda of daily life in the past is revealed. It is an opportunity to regain some portion of the holistic image of the past, a methodological countermeasure for a balanced view of history.

In the field of Chinese history, previous works have of course studied daily life during a certain period.[2] For the ancient period that concerns us in this volume, it has been fifty years since Michael Loewe published his *Everyday Life in Early Imperial China*.[3] While the main contour of his description of life in early imperial China may still be valid, the enormous progress both in terms of research and archaeological discoveries that had ensued since his work dictates that a new overview of the subject, incorporating the latest scholarly achievements and utilizing the exciting new archaeological as well as textual materials would be useful in obtaining an understanding of not only the life experience of the people in ancient China, but also the state of the field of the study of early China. To be sure, individual works on various aspects of material and spiritual life have continuously been published: Michael Loewe's own works pioneered the study of the intellectual and religious traditions as well as the operation of the government of the Han period, which provided a sound foundation for the construction of an overall understanding of life during that time.[4] A recent monographic study by Anthony Barbieri-Low explored the trades and lives of the artisans of the Han period, which amply demonstrates that with the help of newly available material there can be substantial progress in the understanding of history from a bottom-up and daily operational perspective.[5] One very useful book, with abundant illustrations of archaeological discoveries and artifacts that far surpass what the present volume could have included, and therefore a must read for anyone with an interest in the material life of the Han, is Wang Zhongshu's *Han Civilization*.[6] In this book the reader may find all sorts of illustrations that could supplement what we have discussed in the present volume.

What we hope to achieve in this volume is to provide a historical framework that may assist the reader to access the material as well as spiritual life of the ordinary (and some not so ordinary) people, and to be able to understand and appreciate their lives and experiences, their hopes and fears, likes and dislikes, and purpose in life. By learning how people lived thousands of years ago, and thereby gaining an understanding the human condition, however incomplete, the reader is given a chance to reflect on his or her own condition of life. The guiding principle in the writing of this volume, therefore, has been a close reading and analysis of the materials that are relevant to the formation of a view of the life experience of the people of early China. Such a view, which no doubt reflects our modern concerns, will give the reader a fresh perspective for examining the history and culture of early China, one that goes beyond the

[2] Gernet (1962); Benn (2002); Dikötter (2007).
[3] Loewe (1968).
[4] Loewe (1982, 1994, 2006).
[5] Barbieri-Low (2007).
[6] Wang Zhongshu (1982).

usual façade of various "great achievements" that are often self-aggrandizing for historians and their modern readers, yet removed from our sentiments and passions for getting to know a people.

A few words about the sources used in this volume may also help the reader to understand the conditions under which scholars now conduct research of this period. The study of early China, especially the late Warring States period and the Qin-Han Empires, had been given new opportunities in the last half century with the discovery of new archaeological materials, including artifacts and texts found in tombs and ancient sites. These new materials provide evidence for us to study the material life of the people, and to obtain new information on many aspects of the intellectual development of the period. Notable types of texts include legal texts, bureaucratic records, hemerological texts, funerary texts, and literary and philosophical texts, some of which were variants of traditional texts such as the *Book of Poetry*, the *Confucian Analects*, *Laozi*, and some of which were "new" – that is, unknown to the world until their discovery, such as the medical texts found in the Mawangdui tomb no. 3.[7] These new materials, together with traditional texts transmitted throughout the centuries, shall be utilized to illuminate our subject whenever appropriate. This, of course, is not to say we have most of what we need, but only that we are better informed than our predecessors half a century ago. However, because this volume is written for English-speaking readers who are not necessarily familiar with Chinese, we kept the Chinese sources to a minimum.

THE SYNOPSIS

The main period of focus in the present volume is the Han dynasty (202 BCE–220 CE), with background coverage of the previous Shang and Zhou periods (including the brief period of the Qin Empire), with extension into the early medieval period after the fall of the Han. The reason for making such a choice is as follows. As the Han was the first enduring and "successful" regime that had inherited and consolidated a form of political structure developed by the previous Qin dynasty and lasted for 2,000 years, there is good reason to see the Han as the beginning of a new phase in the history of China, not only in terms of political development, but also in various other aspects such as social structure, economic institutions, religious and intellectual growth, and technological advancement. Much of what we know of the "traditional Chinese state" had its roots in the Han dynasty. An understanding of the life of people at this important juncture of the development of Chinese civilization, therefore, is a crucial part of any attempt to understand China and Chinese history in general. Needless to say, since history exists in a continuous

[7] Shaughnessy (1997).

flow of time, a description of the Han period could neither be the beginning nor the end of a larger picture of Chinese civilization. We need to trace some of the characteristics observed in the Han period back to the earlier periods, the Shang, Zhou, and Qin, in order to present a contour of various elements that became prominent in the Han period. Similarly, we should also note some of the salient aspects of daily life that were passed on to successive generations, so that a continuum of cultural development and change may be appreciated.

With the foregoing background in mind, Chapter 1 sets out to describe briefly the historical development of various cultural centers or regimes, from the late Neolithic period to the end of the Zhou dynasty, in the land that was later called China.[8] One of the main points that needs to be emphasized is the multiple origins of the various prehistorical cultures that later interacted and merged with each other to form what was later known as the "Chinese" culture. The reader is introduced to the reality of early societies: physical conditions and relative locations of various communities constituted major factors for cultural development on this vast land. The chapter aims to help the reader gain a sense of the physical environment in which literacy, practical knowledge, lifestyles, modes of production, political and social organizations, religious traditions, and value systems combined to form certain cultural characteristics. In summary, this chapter provides an overview of the historical and cultural development of China before the Han, in order to give the reader a diachronic and synchronic orientation of what will be discussed in the following chapters.

Chapter 2 first sets out the political stage on which the players performed. As the Qin-Han Empire took control of the land, and instituted a vast bureaucracy to manage it, it makes sense to have an idea of this basic structure in which all the people, from the emperors to the peasants, organized their lives. Thus, we describe the government organization from the court in the capital, to the regional government, the county magistrates' offices, and down to the village household level organizations, in order to set the stage. It is important to understand, for example, how the state extended its power and control through various levels of local governing bodies, enabling a population census to be taken, corveés to be organized, and taxes imposed and collected. The government was not daily life itself, but the hard reality that conditioned the daily lives of the multitudes.

The art of governing, however, was not the invention of the Han. The political philosophy – or ideology – that the Han regime relied on had been gradually forged during preimperial times, and could be traced to the teachings of Confucius (c. 551–476 BCE) and beyond. A brief account of this most important system of thought will help to explain many features of the daily

[8] Loewe and Shaughnessy (1999).

lives of the people, though certainly not their entirety. It is important to know, for example, how an "elite ideology," such as Confucianism, could have penetrated to the lower social stratum, and what the practical implications were for the lives of the people. In particular, social institutions, such as family ethics and kinship organization, or funeral customs, have been deeply imprinted with this ideology. It is also necessary to emphasize that Confucianism, or Ruism as some scholars now prefer to call it, at this time was not the only ideology that was accepted among the elite class. Philosophies such Daoism and Legalism were also strong competitors of – but were also sometimes complementary to – Confucianism.[9] On the other hand, as the majority of traditional, textual sources passed down to us are now heavily influenced by such ideologies, the reader needs to be informed of the possible biases that the information from these traditional sources may have created. It would also be useful to allow the reader to have a balanced perspective when introduced to the newly discovered texts, especially those that pertain to the more mundane aspects of life, which were considered to be relatively "uncontaminated" by the later processes of redaction and revision.

Having discussed the political as well as the ideological construction of society, Chapter 3 ventures to describe the social structure of the Han, and the common rules of behavior under which social interactions took place. The traditional Chinese partitioning of society into the four types of people, that is, gentlemen, farmers, craftsmen, and merchants, though useful to a certain extent, cannot represent the complicated reality of the day. Since the Han society had it's roots in the past, we need to trace the composition of the various social groupings back to the earlier, preimperial, period. Thus, we will provide a brief account of the social structure of the Shang and Zhou, including the Spring and Autumn and Warring States periods, and move on to the Han social structure and the law. Using recently discovered texts, the reader is given a chance to see how the rule of law affected social life in many ways: household registration, movement of people, taxation, marriage, family relations, commerce, and even farming activities.

Chapter 4 deals with the agricultural cycle of the farming community, and discusses various aspects of farming technology, and all sorts of natural and social problems that challenged the farmers. They are the disruptive forces of regular life: natural disasters such as flood, drought, locust plague, and earthquake, or manmade disasters such as war and corruption, which caused dislocation of communities and the abandonment of farm land. It is particularly important that we should not intentionally provide an "idyllic" view of country life, but try to gain a closer look at the reality of the farmer's lot.

9 Schwartz (1985).

Yet, much as we like to portray the lives of the ordinary people, who were mostly farmers, the physical remains of village settlements of this time are extremely rare. Some glimpses may be gained in certain paintings, reliefs, and even funerary objects found in tombs, though hardly sufficient to paint a whole picture. On the other hand, archaeologists have been able to locate and reconstruct the most important cities, Chang'an, and Luoyang, the capitals of Western and Eastern Han, respectively. With a basic understanding of the different neighborhoods and areas of the capitals, we are able to describe the lives of the city dwellers in more realistic terms: the distances they had to travel to get from one part of the city to another; the different kinds of neighborhood the city had; and how the city functioned as a ritual center, a bureaucratic center, a military garrison, a commercial center, a place of recreation, a center for education and, ultimately, a symbol of luxury and prosperity and the power of the empire. With the basic physical structure laid down, Chapter 5 uses various kinds of textual evidence to trace the life of the people in the city by attaching stories and anecdotes to the various elements of this physical structure. There is abundant textual evidence that attests to various aspects of life in the cities, or events that happened in the cities.

Production, consumption, income, and expenditure are some of the hard facts of people's daily existence. With the help of texts that dealt with economic issues, it is possible to understand to some extent the factors that formed the basic structure of economic life of the people. Chapter 6 discusses examples of basic production industries such as weaving, lacquer ware, wine, salt, and iron. We also discuss the commodities' prices in relation to people's income and expenditure, and explore the underlying ideological constraints and shared values that might somehow have limited or assisted the development of one or other aspects of these factors.

Complementing or supplementing the economic structures are the technological factors that assisted the operation of the economic system, thus, the process of daily life. Without engaging in technological details and scientific theories, we intend to see how practical technology materialized in daily operations. Factors to be considered in Chapter 7 are the transportation and various measuring systems of length, weight, volume, time, and the calendar, all of which are fundamental guidelines for any kind of activities that involve the transportation and exchange of information and goods over a period of time. Finally, medical knowledge is one factor that directly influenced people's lives to a great extent, for which the Han period already held some very interesting records.

Chapter 8 discusses subjects that are more popular in traditional accounts of daily life, such as leisure and entertainment, games and festivals. Many of the festivals were ancient customs developed in rural society, passed down through history, further developed during this time, and passed on to later generations.

There is abundant textual, as well as archaeological, evidence that bears witness to all sorts of activities, entertainments, or banquets in connection with various seasonal festivals celebrated at all levels of society. Often, symbolic rituals would evolve into public celebrations or dramatic performances. Thus, by giving accounts of the festivals we can help convey a sense of the ebb and flow of popular sentiments throughout the year. As many of the annual festivals celebrated during the Han period are still celebrated in modern times, connections between the modern reader and the Han society may serve as important reminders of the continuation of Chinese cultural tradition. Entertainments, games, and pastimes, in addition to annual festivals, that people enjoyed in their lives as ways of alleviating the drudgery and pressure of daily work (for the commoners), or to show off wealth and power (for the rich), are also worthy of our attention. By studying records of such activities, it may allow us to have access to the private sentiments and, perhaps, the character of the people at certain moments. This, then, leads us to Chapter 9 on emotional life.

After the previous discussions of the various practical aspects of daily life, it is time to focus on the feelings of people in specific situations. Chapter 9 attempts to explore the feelings that manifested in various social and ethical relationships between people of all walks of life. Whether women were respected and had control of their own lives, whether filial piety was innate in a person or enforced externally, whether gender relationships between men and women could reveal the nature of social ethics, whether we can assess the value of friendship, and whether the lives of children and the elderly in society constituted any conscious reflections and concerns are all issues that we explore in this chapter. Yet we need to remind ourselves that as much as we like to know about the emotional lives of people long gone, we may capture only some very cursory glimpses of emotions that left their imprint on the sources we have. Instead of having access to detailed accounts of the life history of an individual, we should consider ourselves fortunate to be able to look at some special, or even mundane, moments in the life of the ancient, and reflect on what life would have felt like in a bygone age.

With life comes death. An account of daily life would, therefore, inevitably have to deal with how death featured in people's lives. How the dead were buried, what kind of rituals or funerary paraphernalia were provided for the deceased, as well as how people imagined a life hereafter, in fact, are all important pieces of information to help us reconstruct people's views of what constituted a worthwhile life on earth, what ethical standards or religious beliefs people held to sustain their lives. In summary, Chapter 10 discusses how people dealt with death physically and spiritually. Through this, we gain some understanding of their ultimate goal in life.

As this account of the daily life experience of the Han people comes to a close, it is important to emphasize the continuation as well as the transformation of this experience in later eras. The conclusion of this volume provides an overview of the historical development of Chinese history after the establishment of the Han in order to bring the reader back to the grand historical process that began before the Han and continued after it ended. Yet, we do not plan to give a conventional general account of all the important events, of the various dynastic changes and wars that created the division of the north and the south, which can be found in many standard accounts. Instead, we first provide an interpretation of the fall of the Han, followed by an account of the cultural transformation in North China following the inroads made by the nomadic groups who established various regimes there. A brief note on the continuation and transformation of life experience after the fall of Han concludes this survey. Although it is outside of the coverage of this volume, it is important to recognize that the process of cultural integration, including that of lifestyle, religious belief, and dietary habits in North China, during the time between the fall of the Han and the reunification under the Sui and Tang was a major factor that contributed to the formation of a new cultural spirit and lifestyle in the years to come.

ONE

THE STAGE

THE LAND

When Ban Gu 班固 (32–92 CE) set out to write the *History of Han* (*Hanshu* 漢書), he planned a chapter titled "Treatise on Geography" (*Dili zhi* 地理志). He began by quoting legends about the earliest period of history known at that time, the era of the Yellow Emperor. It was a favorite practice of the authors of the Han dynasty, and, for that matter, of most of Chinese imperial history, to begin a treatise by quoting from ancient sources. The idea of antiquity seemed to have an authenticating effect, in most cases, rendering support and giving authority to what the author was about to write and argue.[1] Ban Gu was no exception:

> The Yellow Emperor invented ships and wagons to assist with travelling so that people were able to move all over the country. He set up institutions across ten thousand *li* and drew lines to divide the provinces, and this resulted in ten thousand states, each being one hundred *li* square. This is why the *Book of Change* (*Yijing* 易經) states, "the former king established ten thousand states, and formed an alliance with the vassals," and the *Book of Documents* (*Shujing* 書經) states, "[the Yellow Emperor worked] to harmonize the ten thousand states." During Emperor Yao's time there was a flood that flowed over the mountains and hills and separated the

[1] Poo (2007: 85–101). For a standard survey of early Chinese history, see Loewe and Shaughnessy (1999).

> country into twelve provinces, and Yu was assigned to manage the flood. When the flood was under control, he re-divided the state into nine provinces, established the five levels of officials and instituted the taxation system.[2]

As one follows the pages of the "Treatise on Geography" further, it is difficult not to get the impression that Ban Gu was actually writing about the historical evolution of the administrative units of the state; even the statistics about the households and residents of each of those units were all recorded. For example,

> The Commandery of Hongnong, established in year four of Yuanding era (113 BCE) of Emperor Wu. It was known as Youdui by Wang Mang's time. It has 118,091 households, with a population of 475,954. There is an office of iron production at Minchi. There are 11 counties: Hongnong County, formerly the Hangu Pass. Mount Ya presides over Xiagu, from which the River Zhu flows northward into the Yellow River; Lushi county, with the Xionger mountain to the east, where the River Yi flows towards the northeast and enters the River Luo, passes by one commandery and continues for 450 li. There is also the River Yu that flows southward until it enters the River Mian at Shunyang...[3]

The geographic regions that he described in the "Treatise on Geography" encompassed most of the territory of the modern state of China, except for the Northeastern Provinces, Inner Mongolia to the north, Xinjiang and Qinghai to the west, and Tibet to the southwest. In a word, the world known to him as belonging to the rule of the Han regime roughly corresponded to the area that people lived in throughout later Chinese history. It is quite impressive that he was able to collect this detailed geographic information, although his position as the Director of the Royal Archives (*Lantai lingshi* 蘭台令史), did give him access to some of the most important documents and maps pertaining to the operation of the government. But why did he want to write this treatise, and to what purpose? Ban Gu's main interest was, of course, not only the geography of the country, but also the entire history of the Former Han. It is nevertheless remarkable that he should have included such a chapter in his *History*, which strongly suggests that there was an interest in collecting the kind of information that could be useful in providing a bird's eye view of the entire empire for people with a managerial mindset. The fact that such information was available at all, moreover, presupposes a society in which records of a massive scale were collected and archived on a regular basis by certain government agencies such as the Royal Archives that Ban Gu worked for. The recent discovery of a set of statistics concerning personnel and armory that was supposedly

[2] *Hanshu* (henceforth *HS*) 28:1523; Lewis (2006).
[3] *HS* 28: 1548–49.

part of the annual report sent to the central government from the Donghai Commandery may corroborate this point.[4] Therefore, let not the 2,000 years between his time and ours veil the fact that at the beginning of its imperial history China was already a highly bureaucratized state, with managerially minded intellectuals who constituted the backbone of the government.[5] We shall have ample opportunity to witness this character throughout the study.

Ban Gu was particularly interested in describing the historical evolution of the hydraulic system of the land, as the taming of the flood water by the legendary King Yu was considered in most early sources a decisive episode and a common memory of ancient Chinese history. Unlike the biblical flood that was sent down by God, in China the flood was a natural disaster that people were expected to conquer. Since the management of water was essential to agriculture, the issues of flood and drought were constant and serious factors that affected the livelihoods of myriads of farmers, and ultimately everyone in the country. According to legend, when Shun was emperor, an enormous flood spread throughout the land. Shun first entrusted Yu's father, Gun, with the task of managing the flood. Nine years on, he still had not completed the task, as he was using the strategy of damming up the water, which was ineffective. Shun thereupon appointed Yu to continue the work. Fearful of another failure in completing the job, he put all his efforts into the task, did not return home for thirteen years, and finally succeeded in channeling the flood into the ocean, thereby managing to save the ravaged land. Yu's son, Qi, succeeded him and became the first sovereign of the Xia dynasty, the chronicle of which was preserved in the *Records of the Grand Scribe* (*Shiji* 史記) by the Western Han dynasty historian Sima Qian (司馬遷 c. 140–86 BCE). Some modern scholars view the story as wholly fictional and see Yu as no more than a sort of cultural hero who epitomized the ancient memory of an era of natural disasters.[6]

Certainly, the legendary history of early China began earlier than the reign of King Yu, as the interest in historical writing and in managing the state also preceded Ban Gu. Sima Qian gave an account of the early history of China in the early chapters of his *Records of the Grand Scribe* by piecing together stories about the rulers of the remote past, beginning with the Yellow Emperor; continuing up to the sage rulers Yao, Shun, and Yu; down to the kings of the Shang and Zhou dynasties. This chronological account of the succession of the rulers is, of course, not to be taken literally, as we know from modern archaeological studies that during the period between 3000 and 300 BCE (roughly before the unification of the Qin dynasty in 221 BCE), the East Asian subcontinent was never ruled by a single regime, despite the claims of the dominion of the Shang and the Zhou. The vastness of the land itself and the diverse

4 Lianyungang bowuguan (1997). See Chapter 2.
5 Loewe (2006); ibid. (1967).
6 Lewis (2006: 79–85).

geographical features speak forcefully of the natural division of the land into smaller units.

Sima Qian was well aware of this situation, which he described in the "Treatise on Food and Merchandise" (*Huozhi liezhuan* 貨殖列傳) in his *Records of the Grand Scribe*:

> The area within the Pass, from the Qian and Yong rivers east to the Yellow River and Mount Hua, is a region of rich and fertile fields stretching for a thousand *li*. Judging from the tribute exacted by Emperor Shun and the rulers of the Hsia [Xia] dynasty, these were already considered to be among the finest fields available at that time ... In fact, the people of this region still retain traces of the customs they learned under these ancient rulers. They are fond of agriculture, raise the five grains, take good care of their fields, and regard any wrongdoing as a serious matter.
>
> Later, Dukes Wen and Mu of Qin established the capital of their state at Yong, which was on the main route for goods being brought out of both Long and Shu and was a center for merchants. Dukes Xian and Xiao moved the Qin capital to the city of Yue ... It, too, was a center for great merchants. Kings Wu and Zhou established their capital at Xianyang, and it was this site that the Han took over and used for their own capital, Chang'an. People poured in from all parts of the empire to congregate in the towns established at the imperial tombs around Chang'an, converging on the capital like the spokes of a wheel. The land area is small with a large population, and therefore the people have become ever more sophisticated and ingenious and have turned to secondary occupations such as trade to make a living.[7]

Sima Qian's account could be seen as a kind of "cultural geography" in the modern sense; he was interested in the interactions between various factors such as the geographic features of the land, the resources of each area, the character and temperament of the people, and the local customs. Again, from a different angle, he demonstrated a kind of managerial interest in describing the composition of various sectors of the state. It was his way of giving a historical explanation to the social and cultural development of the country by observing the multifarious characteristics of different regions. Such an interest, therefore, received further development in Ban Gu's "Treatise on Geography," where cultural geography can be seen in the account of administrative registers.

THE RIVERS

In looking at a map of China, it is clear that the land of the East Asian subcontinent has been carved out by two river systems – the Yellow River and the Yangzi River – into several smaller areas.[8] The Yellow River to the north was

7 Watson (1993: 484–85).

8 See Li Liu (2012: 26–29).

known to the people in ancient times simply as "The River." Its power to give life but also bring about destruction was likely the reason for its divine status in the belief systems of these ancient peoples. In the Shang dynasty oracle bone inscriptions, the river was one of the deities to which the Shang king offered sacrifices and prayed for blessings.[9]

The famous Tang dynasty poet Li Bai (711–762 CE) opens his most renowned poem, "Wine Drinking (*Jiang jinjiu* 將進酒)," with these lines:[10]

> Have you not seen the Yellow River waters falling from the sky?
> Racing towards the ocean, never to return.
> Have you not seen elders looking into the bright mirrors as they mourn
> their white hair?
> Dark silk in the morning, by evening turned to snow.

Usually readers of this poem appreciated the use of the constant flow of the Yellow River as an allusion to the passing of time. Less noticed is that the Yellow River was, by Li Bai's time, no less a source of life than it was in the Shang dynasty. The phrase "falling from the sky" was not only a literary expression to describe its source, but also carried some implicit reference to its divine status. It originates in the high mountains of modern Qinghai Province, rushing down from an elevation of 4,800 meters toward the eastern sea for a distance of 5,460 kilometers. Along the water course, areas suitable for agriculture were formed, notably around the middle reaches of the area of the Wei River (a tributary of the Yellow River) basin, where the Han capital city Chang'an (modern Xi'an) was located, and further downstream to the east, the Central Plain area, where the city of Luoyang had been the center of political and economic power since the time of the Zhou.

Owing to the lower elevation of the plain and the high sedimentation level of the river, the river bed below its middle reaches actually rose higher than the plain through centuries of sedimentation; thus the river was prone to bursting its banks and causing flooding from time to time. In the two and half millennia of recorded history, the Yellow River flooded its area more than 1,500 times and changed its course 26 times, which indicates that King Yu's celebrated achievement was nowhere near a complete success.[11]

In the ancient period, during the fourth and third millennia BCE, the average temperature of North China was a few degrees higher than it is in the modern era, and lush forests were part of the landscape. The loess plateau encircled by the Yellow River, which comprises present-day Shaanxi Province, was greener than in its present state and boasted abundant natural resources. It was allegedly through thousands of years of human development that the area

[9] Eno (2009). See Elvin (2004); Li Liu (2012: 22 ff.); Feng Li (2013: 1–13).
[10] *Li Taibai ji*: 14.
[11] Sato (1993).

lost its vegetation and became impoverished. The Wei River basin south of the loess plateau was nevertheless suitable for agriculture and, being encircled on all sides by mountains, was the power base of the Qin-Han and later the Tang Empires. A Western Han scholar, Jia Yi (200–168 BCE), once pointed out the strategic importance of this area:

> The land of Qin was surrounded by mountains with rivers running through, and it was secured on four sides. Since the time of Duke Miu, until the First Emperor, there were more than twenty rulers who often were leaders of the vassals of Zhou. Could this mean that every generation of rulers was good? It was in fact due to the geographic superiority of the region.[12]

Passing through the Hangu Pass (*Hangu guan* 函谷關) at the eastern end of the Wei River basin, therefore, the Yellow River faced no further obstacles to the east, and the entire Central Plain was practically the beneficiary – or the victim – of the river system. The city of Luoyang was the power center, located at a strategic position west of the Central Plain, flanked on both sides by mountain ranges, taking command of the land to the east. It was the capital of the Eastern Zhou and Eastern Han, and of many later dynasties.

The Yangzi River is the longest river in China, also originating, as does the Yellow River, in the high mountains of Qinghai Province. To the ancients, it was known simply as the "Jiang" (river), a name probably derived from a language of the ancient Austroasiatic people.[13] Modern Chinese refer to it as the Long River (Changjiang 長江). Its 6,300-kilometer journey across the middle of the East Asian subcontinent passes through some of its most fertile agricultural regions, with no fewer dramatic changes of geographical characteristics than the Yellow River. Before the Yangzi broke through the Three Gorges it nurtured the Sichuan basin, with its ancient name Shu, which was also the center of a mysterious bronze culture, contemporary with the mid-Shang dynasty, known today as the Sanxingdui 三星堆 culture. Following the current, in the middle reaches, early agricultural societies such as Daxi 大溪 (c. 4400–3300 BCE) and Qujialing 屈家嶺 (c. 2500–2400 BCE) became prosperous, while in the lower reaches, the Hemudu 河姆渡 and Liangch良渚 cultures flourished during the fifth millennium BCE.[14]

In general, the major crop of North China, irrigated by the Yellow River system, was millet, while the major crop of the area irrigated by the Yangzi River was rice, at least from the late Neolithic period. In between the two river systems was an area where rice and millet cultivations overlapped, as

[12] *Shiji* (Henceforth *SJ*) 6: 277.
[13] Boltz (1999: 82); Loewe and Shaughnessy (1999: 82).
[14] Chang (1986).

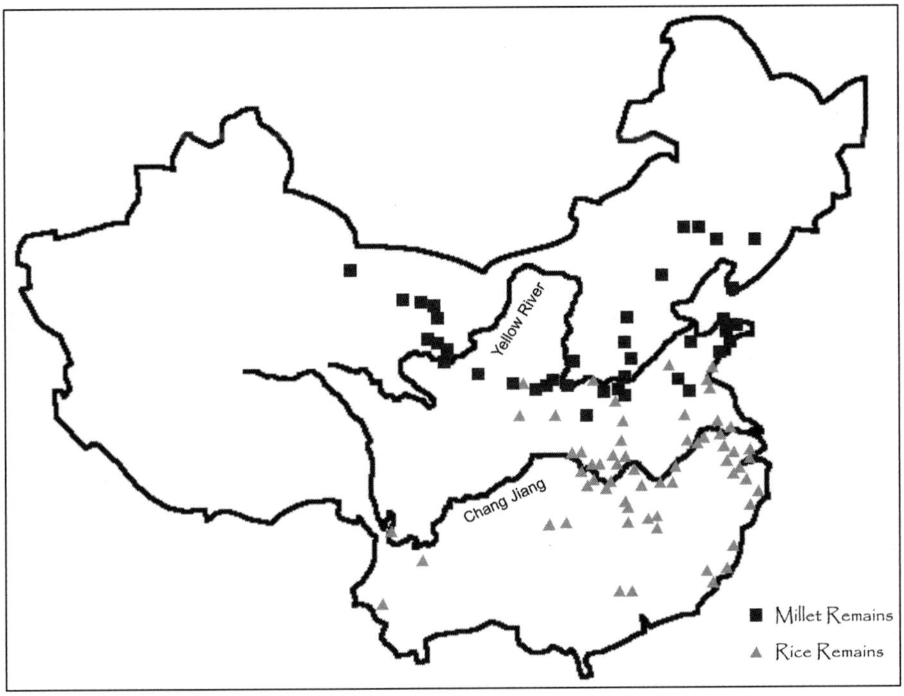

1. The distribution of rice and millet remains in the rice and millet blended zone in the Neolithic Age. After Fang Xiuqi 方修琦, Zhang wenbo 章文波, Zhang lansheng 張蘭生, "Quanxinshi nuanqi woguo tudi liyong de geju jiqi yiyi 全新世暖期我國土地利用的格局及其意義," Ziran ziyuan xuebao 自然資源學報 13. 1(1998): 17

the region was a transitional zone from subtropical climate, which was more suitable for rice cultivation, to temperate weather, which was more suitable for millet (Fig. 1).[15] Climatic studies show that between 6000 and 1000 BCE the North China Plain experienced a period of relatively warm weather, during which there were greater numbers of subtropical plants and animals in the area. The onset of cooler climate after 1000 BCE led to a division between the temperate and the subtropical zones that remains to the present day.[16]

Farmers in both areas cultivated a variety of plants for food in addition to the major staples of millet and rice. By the beginning of recorded history, that is, the late Shang dynasty, domesticated animals included pigs, dogs, cattle, and goats and were a major meat source of these people, in addition, of course, to the abundance of game in the forests and fish in the rivers and lakes. In the south, that is, the Yangzi River Valley, buffalo were also domesticated (Fig. 2).

[15] Huang et al. (2012).
[16] Winkler and Wang (1994).

2. Shang bronze tripod with buffalo head. Courtesy of the Institute of History and Philology, Academia Sinica. R001750

SHANG

The earliest literate society in this part of the world, the Shang dynasty, with its last power center at Anyang, Henan Province, succeeded an earlier dynasty, the legendary Xia. Although still unidentified archaeologically, it is generally assumed that the Xia dynasty originated in the west, in Shanxi Province.[17]

The early history of the Shang could be represented only by archaeological discoveries and the information preserved in the transmitted pre-Qin texts and the *Records of the Grand Scribe* of Sima Qian. So far the earliest Shang power center to be identified was the site at Yanshi (偃師), Henan. With a total area of 1.90 million square meters and well-built city wall, palace buildings, ordinary housing area, cemetery, pottery kilns, wells, as well as drainage pipes, the city of Yanshi marked the beginning of a powerful and well-organized state. As it is also close to the pre-Shang (possibly belonging to the legendary Xia dynasty) site of Erlitou 二里頭, which displays many similar material features, a reasonable assumption would be that the Yanshi site was a successor of Erlitou.[18] A little later than Yanshi was the site of Erligang 二里崗 at Zhengzhou 鄭州.

[17] Chang (1980); Loewe and Shaughnessy (1999: 124 ff.); Li Liu (2012: 350 ff.).

[18] Feng Li (2013: 41–65); Wang Zhenzhong (2013: 416–28).

With an increased area of 3.17 million square meters, this city shows improved design and consideration of the living environment.[19]

Later sources mentioned that before choosing Anyang as the last capital, the Shang court had moved a number of times, indicating a certain unstable situation of the regime, either politically or economically. Presumably, as the most powerful and culturally sophisticated state from the multicentered tribal system at the end of the Neolithic period, the Shang had acted as a kind of overlord of a loose confederation of smaller states, known collectively as the "Four Lands" (situ 四土) in the oracle bone inscriptions, which would bring tribute to the Shang court, and which would form a buffer zone surrounding the Shang. Punitive warfare with certain tribes or chiefdoms, notably the Guifang 鬼方 and Tufang 土方, was often mentioned in the oracle bone inscriptions, lending some weight to the assumption that the Shang had a certain power over these tribal states.[20]

During the late Shang period when the capital was at Anyang, more than fifty independent states mentioned in the oracle inscriptions were scattered around the Shang capital, and more than forty small townships were under the rule of the Shang king. One of the largest independent states not mentioned by the oracle bone inscriptions was the early to middle Shang state, perhaps the early capital of the state of Shu (蜀), at Sanxingdui, modern Guanghan, Sichuan Province. The extraordinary bronze objects, including the huge masks, the bronze tree, and the statue, indicate a culture that was powerful, vibrant, and although related, quite different from the Shang culture.

Much about this culture is still covered in a fog of mystery. The fact that this state could have the control of such enormous bronze industry indicates that one should reevaluate the status of the Shang among the contemporary power structures, and view it as one of the main cultural centers, though perhaps better known to later generations because of the use of an effective writing system that allowed the passing down of knowledge and information that privileged the owner of the writings.

It should be clear that, although a dominant political power with sophisticated bronze industry and working bureaucracy, the Shang was not the sole player in the land, and many sizable and independent communities, whether under the cultural influence of the Shang or not, followed their own course of development. One of these states, the Zhou, eventually accumulated enough strength to challenge the leadership of Shang, and was able to replace it.

One conspicuous feature of the Shang in terms of possible communication with the outside world was the funerary pits of chariots and horses. It has been argued that the use of a horse and chariot came from the West, perhaps

19 Chang (1980: 263–83); Loewe and Shaughnessy (1999: 165–68).
20 See Loewe and Shaughnessy (1999: 269–90); Wang Zhenzhong (2013: 466 ff.).

from the Near East through central Asia, since there was no trace of the use of a horse and chariot before early Shang. What can be certain is that the construction of a chariot involves the use of sophisticated bronze components that only the ruling elites who controlled the resources and production of bronze objects – including the ritual vessels and weapons and armor – could have afforded.[21]

BRONZE CULTURE

Ever since the excavation of the royal tombs of Shang at Anyang in the early twentieth century, the Shang bronze culture and oracle bone inscriptions have been at the center of scholarly attention, as these were the most prominent testimony to the achievements of the people who created this culture, and whose imprint on the later development of the Chinese culture was permanent. The royal cemetery at Anyang, with the huge royal tombs, the median tombs of the nobles, and the small tombs of the lesser officials, graphically shows the formation of a well-established complex society.

The bronze vessels found in the tombs and storage areas at Anyang and elsewhere, in various shapes and numbering in the thousands, and now often occupying a central position in museums around the world, testify to a refined ritual practice that at the same time was an expression of religious ideas, political order, economic power, aesthetic articulation, and technological innovation. They are not merely vessels for cooking and for making offerings to deities and ancestors; they are markers of political status, as the size and number of vessels in a burial chamber often correspond with the political status of the deceased. They also imply a well-established chain of resource appropriation and production management, as revealed by the discovery of casting workshops.[22] They are, furthermore, the embodiments of a special kind of aesthetic sentiment with highly refined casting technology, as shown by the ubiquitous and ever-changing *taotie*-animal (饕餮) style designs on the vessels (Fig. 3).[23]

The function of the bronze vessels, besides daily use at banquets and meals, was to contain food offerings at religious rituals. When food was cooked and the aroma rose upward to reach the spirits, the gazing eyes of the *taotie* on the container could have added a sense of intense expectation.[24] Such sensual but mute communication with the spirits, whether ancestral or divine, must have been supplemented by verbal communications such as prayers, songs, or spells.

[21] Shaughnessy (1988).
[22] Chang (1983).
[23] Childs-Johnson (l998).
[24] Sterckx (2011).

3. Bronze vessels with animal style designs. Courtesy of Freer Gallery of Art and Arthur M. Sackler Gallery, Smithsonian Institution, Washington, DC: Purchase-Charles Lang Freer Endowment, F1940.11a–b. Source: Zhongguo qingtongqi quanji bianji weiyuanhui 中國青銅器全集編輯委員會, *Zhongguo Qingtongqi Quanji* 中國青銅器全集, Vol. 3 (Beijing: Wenwu chubanshe, 1997), 132)

Yet what we do have are records of another form of communication with the spirits, the oracle bone inscriptions.

DIVINATION

Being a form of divination, the Shang oracle bone records open a window for us to the spiritual world of the Shang people, albeit that of the ruling elites. This spiritual world, seen through the looking glass of divination, could be severely distorted when we gaze into it. Thus we need to pay extra attention to contextualize the information we gain from the divination records.[25]

Divination exists in many cultures, under the basic assumption that there is a certain connection between worldly phenomena and future events. Through certain skills and knowledge in reading the signs, whether natural or man-made, one was expected to be able to interpret the meanings of these signs

[25] Eno (2009).

and thus discover the divine wills or future events. The divination records of the Shang preserved for us some of the questions, and therefore the concerns, of the Shang people regarding various aspects of their lives. Among the most commonly asked questions were those related to agricultural topics such as rainfall and harvest; warfare with foreign peoples; sacrificial ceremony for deities and ancestors; and even the personal health and well-being of the king or royal family members, concerning matters such as toothache, illness, or childbirth.

Divination could be an ambivalent pursuit. One wishes to know what the future holds, but also fears that the message will be inauspicious. The dilemma between "to divine or not to divine" must have troubled many who felt pressed to learn about the future. Thus the Shang diviners often cast their inquiries more than once, and as both positive and negative queries: Will it rain? Will it not rain? The answers that they received were then carved on the oracle bones after the queries.

Scholars have tried to explain the fact that some of the divination records contained only the questions but not the answers. Could these be a way of communicating with the divine power as a form of supplication rather than divination?[26] It seems that the "powers" to which the Shang diviners posed questions were never directly mentioned. We are thus unsure whether a question such as "Will it rain?" was addressed to the rain god or to another more powerful god who could order rainfall. We are still not certain if even questions such as "Will Di (i.e., the god on high) cause it to rain?" were addressed to Di directly, and not to some intermediate power or messenger, as the question was not addressed in the second person, such as "Will thou cause it to rain?" Thus although the act of divination is based on the assumption that there is a way to have access to the divine will, there might not be sufficient grounds to view the queries as a form of prayer.

The implication of divination may be elaborated further: since there is a connection between certain worldly signs and the future, there had to be an assumption that the future is already determined or prescribed, and, importantly, knowable. The fact that people also offered prayers and sacrifices to the deities implies that they hoped to manipulate the divine will and to change the prescribed future. As the deities could presumably change the fate of the people, knowing the future became important: one should keep the good prognostication, and try to change any inauspicious predictions. This, indeed, was a widely held conception in the ancient world.[27]

What can be certain is that Di was a major deity who could command various natural phenomena such as rain, clouds, drought, and flood, as well as

[26] Keightley (2000).
[27] Raphals (2013).

bestow a harvest and bless the king with land and victory.[28] It seems logical to see the lesser deities as obeying the command of the Di, much as subjects obeying the ruler in a secular court. If there were a pantheon, therefore, Di would be the presiding deity. The royal ancestors were sometimes said to be able to visit with Di, indicating that the Shang people regarded their deceased rulers as possessing a certain divine status and thus becoming objects of cult worship. Besides sacrificial rituals to the deities, ancestral temples and ritual offerings associated with the temples were often mentioned in the oracle bone inscriptions. This two-track ritual system, one for the deities and another for the royal ancestors, was followed by later ruling regimes and formed the basic structure of the Imperial Cult.

FOOD AND DRINK

The intensive care and effort put into the production of ceremonial food offerings can be seen not only in the variety of bronze vessels used in the rituals, but also in the treatises found in later texts such as the *Book of Ceremonies* (*Yili* 儀禮) and the *Book of Rites* (*Liji* 禮記).[29] Here it should be pointed out that we could probably treat the theoretical considerations of food offering of the Shang and Zhou as one continuous tradition. In this tradition, the major components of an august offering would usually include meat and alcoholic beverages, the produce of husbandry and agriculture.[30]

Archaeological findings from the Shang period include the remains of such domesticated animals as cattle, goats, pigs, dogs, horses, and chickens. Wild game includes bear, fox, raccoon, tiger, leopard, elephant, hare, deer, boar, gazelle, buffalo, rhinoceros, monkey, and tapir. There were also various types of fish, turtles, and clams. The appearance of some of these creatures, which cannot be found in later records, indicates a warmer climate in North China during the second millennium BCE.

The staple diet consisted of millet, barley, wheat, sorghum, and rice, plus various fruits and vegetables. Alcoholic drink made of millet was known to the people far earlier than the records found in history indicate; thus only some legendary accounts are able to fill the void.[31] Since grape was not a native plant, grape wine was unknown to China until the Han dynasty. For convenience's sake we use the term wine to refer to all kinds of alcoholic drink made from grain.

One of the major features of daily life was the way people sat and consumed their meals. Until the invention or importation of the idea of a chair

[28] Eno (2009).
[29] Loewe (1993).
[30] See K. C. Chang (1980:142 ff.); Sterckx (2011).
[31] Poo (1999).

into China, possibly with the coming of Buddhism in the years after the fall of the Han dynasty,[32] people sat on the ground, in the posture of either kneeling or squatting, or resembling a winnowing basket. The last posture, according to later sources, was considered rude in public places and could carry apotropaic meaning because of its sexual implication. Depending on the means available, a mat made of various kinds of fabric would serve as a sitting surface between the ground and the body. The vessels containing food would be put on the ground or on a low table. Although knives and spoons were used to help with cutting and scooping, in general food was taken by hand, since chopsticks, though found in late Shang tombs, were not used for eating until the Han dynasty.

As for cooking, ancient texts such as the *Book of Rites* mentioned a host of culinary terms, including various ways to barbeque meats; to use cooking pots to boil, steam, and fry; and to prepare food by marinating and making sauces using salt, wine, sweet (honey and malt) and sour (plum) ingredients, indicating that these people had developed a very mature and complicated food culture. It is true that although the *Book of Rites* dated probably to the Warring States period, the sophisticated way of food preparation contained in the text could have had a long history.[33] This attention to the culinary experience had a rather unusual impact on the development of religion and philosophy. The ancient Chinese authors were very much attracted to the idea of using culinary metaphors to convey all sorts of philosophical and religious ideas. Many of the important discourses on personal cultivation, wise governing, and human–divine interactions were cast in the thinking and vocabularies of culinary art.

For example, meat consumption, by virtue of its importance in the diet of the rich and noble in ritual sacrifices to the spirits, became the object of philosophical speculation. Whether, how, and when to consume meat were subjects of discussion for the ancient Chinese authors. This train of thought has much resonance in the life and teaching of Confucius. It has been argued that in the Confucian tradition, the attitudes toward food and food consumption are reflections of an accomplished gentleman's appreciation of social hierarchy, ritual propriety, and moral integrity.[34] Yet one of the most famous metaphoric uses of culinary art is the story of the Cook Ding told by the Daoist philosopher Zhuangzi (莊子, c. 369–286 BCE). The story relates Cook Ding's superlative skill at dissecting cattle, which stemmed from his thorough understanding of the animal's anatomic structure. By recognizing how the cow's muscles, sinews, and joints intertwined with each other and by perceiving the cavities between them, he was able to pass his cleaver through the cavities and dismantle the entire structure without ever hitting the bones. After nineteen

[32] Kieschnick (2003: 222–48).
[33] Sterckx (2011).
[34] Sterckx (2011: 47).

years, as the story goes, his cleaver was still as sharp as one fresh from the grindstone.[35] Of course, Zhuangzi is not really talking about culinary art, but about the importance of searching and following the Way. Yet the use of this culinary art, in fact the basic art in any kitchen, as a metaphor for the achievement of supreme knowledge, indicates that culinary art occupied a particular position in the theoretical articulation of the author. It also expressed vividly his idea that the most exalted revelation of truth could be found in the most mundane situation. Similarly, Laozi's terse one-liner, "governing a large state is like cooking a small fish," is not about cooking, but about mastering the art of governance. Although one cannot assign a definite explanation to this sentence, it appears that the text does not suggest that cooking a small fish is an easy matter. On the contrary, since to cook a small fish properly takes delicate mingling of various ingredients and controlling the timing and temperature that only an experienced chef could have achieved, governing a large state is no less of a complicated and delicate matter that requires the mastering of the Dao, just like Cook Ding's ability to follow the Dao in his art of dissecting the bull. This love of expressive use of culinary experience was understandably a sign of a prosperous society, in which a whole stratum of social elite was responsible for the nurturing of such a sophisticated taste.

DRESS

Certainly, signs of opulence could be observed not only in delicate food and luxurious food vessels, but also in the style of dress. According to ancient legend, the queen of the Yellow Emperor, Leizu, invented the art of silk weaving. Silk fabrics were found as early as the Neolithic period. By the time of the Shang, silk was widely used by the upper classes, as weaving had become a mature craft. Six kinds of different weaving techniques are found in fragments from the tomb of Fuhao, the queen of Shang King Wuding. In all likelihood, for the common people, a cheaper material would be more practical. The use of flax fiber for weaving was also a long-established practice, and linen would be the main textile that people used to make garments. Although the Shang people also knew how to use wool and other fabrics, these were never the major garment materials. The few available examples of human figures from the Shang period show that the dresses that people wore were either a short dress with a lap from left to right or a join in the middle, plus a short skirt, or a long dress that fell beneath the knee. People usually walked bare-footed, but they were also known to wear shoes made of cloth or leather, sometimes with high soles made of wood to avoid the dampness on the ground.

[35] Watson (1964: 46–47).

LIVING SPACE

A way to avoid dampness, of course, is to build one's residence higher, either on elevated ground or by making the ground higher. Long before the Shang dynasty, people had learned the technique of making pounded earthen platforms for building beds, houses, and palaces. The higher one's social and political status, the higher the ground floor on which one's residence was built. Taking the palace site no. 1 at Erlitou as an example, the entire area measured 108 × 101 meters, had a pounded earth ground base, and the main palace was built on a platform measuring 36 × 25 meters, about 3 meters high. The entire palace compound of the late Shang capital at Anyang was located on a piece of higher ground overlooking the nearby river Huan.

A salient feature of the Shang city was the city wall, a testimony of the conflict and warfare between various political powers. The wall ofYanshi measured 1,700 × 1,200 meters, with seven gates, checkerboard-like roads within the city, and a surrounding moat that protected the city. The city at Zhengzhou has a wall measuring 1,690 × 1,870 meters, with eleven gates, a palace area that occupies 380,000 square meters, and the largest building with a base measuring 65 × 13.5 meters.

The majority of the people, needless to say, lived in much smaller residences. Within the Anyang area, a house with a suite built above ground, about 30 square meters in size, would count as being rather comfortable and perhaps fit for the nobility. Next to this would be a half-underground single-room house measuring about 15 square meters, perhaps occupied by ordinary residents. The smallest houses would be an underground pit that was only large enough for a single person to reside in. No doubt this would be for people on the lowest scale of the social ladder. Conceivably, residences outside of the city in the countryside would be considerably larger, yet without the various support and conveniences that a city could have offered.

ZHOU

According to ancient texts such as the *Book of Poetry*, the Zhou dynasty originated to the west of Shang, in the area of present-day Shaanxi and Shanxi area, and was a subordinate vassal of the Shang. Oracle bones discovered at the site of Zhouyuan, the ancient cultural center of Zhou, indicate a cultural background similar to that of the Shang. The early Zhou rulers, including the kings Wen, Wu, Cheng, Kang, and the legendary chief architect of Zhou ritual system, the Duke of Zhou (Zhougong 周公), were represented by later sources as consciously building a state institution based on ritual (*li* 禮) and music (*yue* 樂). They made a departure from the Shang custom of indulging in the belief in spiritual beings and opted for a more rational understanding of the workings of the world. Most importantly, the concept of the Mandate of Heaven was invented to account for the political transformation. The Mandate was seen as representing the moral principle of the supreme power, Heaven, which would be conferred on the rulers who exhibited high moral standards. According to this concept, in order to gain the Mandate, that is, the legitimacy to rule, the ruler had to act according to this moral principle. Thus any ruler who successfully secured political control of the state could claim that he had gained the Mandate of Heaven, because Heaven would bestow the Mandate only on rulers who were morally worthy of the position. Thus Heaven was seen as having a rational and moral will that distinguished the evil and the good. This concept of the Mandate would thus become the official position for generations of rulers to claim their legitimacy to be on the throne. The replacement of the Shang by the Zhou rulers, therefore, was interpreted by the Zhou as the shifting of the Mandate.[36]

Yet what were the vices of the Shang that caused it to lose the Mandate? Understandably it was the Zhou rulers who supplied the answer. In a chapter entitled "Announcement about Drunkenness" in the *Book of Documents* (*Shangshu* 尚書), the newly established Zhou king attributed the fall of the Shang to their indulgence in wine drinking. It was the excessive consumption of alcohol that eroded morale and corrupted the entire ruling apparatus. Anyone who engaged in wine drinking, thus announced the apprehensive Zhou king, would be arrested and executed. The bad example that the Shang rulers set, though most likely a piece of Zhou political propaganda in support of the shifting of the Mandate, was remembered by later generations as a grim reminder for those in power to be aware of the destructive potential of alcohol. What is significant about the charges against the last Shang ruler is that they had identified a ruler's personal moral character with the legitimacy of his political authority as well as his ability to govern. In other words, a person without virtue would not have the authority or the ability to rule, and vice versa, a person with virtue was commensurate with a person with the authority and ability to rule. This, although comparable to the Platonic philosopher king, is of course not true at all in reality. Yet the myth of virtue as equaling ability and legitimacy persisted henceforth as the enduring legacy of the Zhou political culture.

There is, of course, no use in speculating on whether the charges against the Shang rulers were historically true or not. The bronze objects excavated from the Zhou dynasty tombs contain a considerable number of wine vessels, which demonstrates that wine drinking was not at all prohibited in the Zhou. As demonstrated by various documents, it seems that the Zhou rulers did not and could not really forbid the use of alcoholic drinks either in public or in

[36] See Falkenhausen (2006).

private lives. Thus the prohibition against the consumption of alcoholic drink was no more than lip service, moralistic advice that had no actual effect on the customs of society at large.

To ensure the success of the dynasty, the early Zhou rulers instituted a system of vassalage based on kinship ties. Sons and brothers of the king were given fiefdoms to rule as vassals. This assumption that kinship ties could guarantee strong political alliance, of course, proved only wishful thinking in reality.[37] From the beginning when the system was implemented, as the story has it, powerful brothers of the kings were not satisfied with being subjects of their siblings. Throughout the Zhou, therefore, peace and prosperity existed only when the ruler himself was capable of controlling the vassals. The benefit of support from the vassals grew ever slimmer as time went by, until the situation became uncontrollable under the corrupt King You (c. 795–771 BCE), when the vassals rebelled and overthrew the king and established another, King Ping (reigned 771–720 BCE), as the symbolic head of the state. This ruler moved the capital from Chang'an to Chengzhou (i.e., Luoyang). This move between Chang'an and Luoyang became a pattern of later dynastic transition: the Western Han established its capital at Chang'an, and the Eastern Han moved to Luoyang. The Tang dynasty, after the long confusion following the fall of the Eastern Han, again returned to Chang'an.

The Spring and Autumn period (770–476 BCE), that is, the period from the beginning of the Eastern Zhou when the capital was moved eastward to Luoyang, was a time when powerful vassal states took turns at playing leading roles by claiming their loyalty to the Zhou kings, while developing their own power sphere. At the time, numerous small vassals and independent tribes were scattered among the larger Central Plain states and were collectively known as the Hua/Xia, that is, the cultural descendants of the Xia, Shang, and Zhou dynasties. It was a time when the Hua/Xia people (including the Zhou and their vassals) were engaged in conflicts and rapprochements with foreign tribes and states known as Rong, Yi, Man, and Di, which must have begun long before they were recorded in any written form, such as texts inscribed on the bronze vessels, or the *Zuozhuan* 左傳 (*Commentary of Master Zuo*), a historical commentary to the chronicle of *Chunqiu* 春秋, the *Spring and Autumn Annals*, attributed to the hand of Confucius.

The *Zuozhuan* was the first narrative account of the events of the Eastern Zhou or the Spring and Autumn period. Although certainly a literary representation of what could have happened instead of what really had happened, it was most probably partially based on state archives, in particular that of Lu, Confucius's home state. It shows frequent political activities in the form of war and diplomacy, court intrigues, and marriage alliances, not only between

[37] Feng Li (2008: 235–69).

the states, but also between the states and the non–Central Plain states, the so-called "Rong-Di barbarians." For lack of other extant historical records for this period, the *Zuozhuan* became the major source of information. It was also one of the most favored literary texts in China, as generations of literati read and quoted from it, not only for the elegance of the writing, but also for the moral of the stories.[38]

By the end of the period, most of the smaller states had been obliterated from the map, with only seven strong states left to continue their struggle for political supremacy. This Warring States period (476–221 BCE) saw a rapid change in the development of statecraft, the blooming of intellectual diversity, the progress of agriculture, the expansion of commercial activities, and the advancement of military technology.

This was also a time that a new medium of economic activities was needed to facilitate commercial exchange. Unlike the round coins invented in the Greek world, the earliest "currency" found in the Shang dynasty was made of cowry shells, indicating that sea shells during that time were regarded as something valuable and could serve as the medium of exchange. Subsequent forms of money produced after the Zhou were in the shapes of bronze spades, hoes, and knives, reminiscent of the time when these objects were valuable objects of daily use, and thus served as common media of exchange. Various kinds of money were issued by the states to facilitate the exchange of goods, although, expectedly, the lack of a common system and the knowledge of how currency functioned in an incipient market system made it difficult for the currency to actually become a convenient tool for commerce, not to mention the cumbersome shapes of coins (Fig. 4). It was only after the unification of the empire by the Qin state that a unified currency was issued by the government, so that a common means of exchange could be used by people everywhere. This attempt, however, was short lived, as the Qin regime collapsed after a short lifespan.[39] As we shall see in Chapter 4, the Han government, or, for that matter, all the subsequent dynasties, had to confront a very difficult task of producing a sound currency policy.

CONFUCIAN IDEALS

The key players of this age of reform – if we can use this term – were an emerging social group, the *shi* 士, literally "knight," who originally belonged to the ruling nobility class. During the incessant political turmoil of the Spring and Autumn period when many noble families were brought down, their members became displaced and sought employment among those still

38 Schaberg (2001); Pines (2002).

39 Hsu (1965); Von Glahn (2016: 100–108).

4. A type of money circulated during the Warring States period. Courtesy of the American Numismatic Society. Source: Wang, Yü-Ch'üan, *Early Chinese Coinage* (New York: American Numismatic Society, 1951, Plates 16, 17, 32)

powerful enough to stay in the game. With their knowledge of the affairs of the state, they gradually became, in a sense, advisors to the power holders, i.e., rulers, princes, or nobles of different ranks. They became people with knowledge, "intellectuals" who participated at every level of the government. Confucius, or Kongzi 孔子 (c. 551–476 BCE), was one such example.[40]

Although credited with the founding of "Confucianism" or "Ru-ism," Confucius himself was never aware of this term and was known to his contemporaries as a person with enthusiasm about propagating a set of moral

[40] Schwartz (1985); Mote (1989).

principles derived from the Zhou dynasty ritual system. Confucius himself claimed that he only represented this system of ritual that the Duke of Zhou established without creating anything new, although he did in fact transform the meaning of the ritual system from outward court ceremonies to inward moral principles by teaching his followers through discussions and personal example.

According to the Confucian view, in order for a society to function harmoniously, all sorts of interpersonal relationships should be respectable and amicable. As later developed by Mencius (Mengzi 孟子, c. 372–289), Confucius's spiritual disciple, people should follow a fivefold hierarchical order that defines all possible interpersonal relationships: "filiality between father and son, duty between ruler and subject, distinction between husband and wife, precedence of the old over young, and trust between friends."[41] Except between friends, all the other four relationships are clearly hierarchical, that is, the former dominates the latter. This hierarchical order was explained as not being an outside requirement forced upon people, but rather an inner appreciation that grew out of mutual respect and appreciation. What was the nature of these relationships? From the perspective of emotion and empathy, the interpersonal relationship could be summarized in the concepts of benevolence (*ren* 仁) and forgiveness (*shu* 恕); from a rational perspective, the interpersonal relationship could be summarized in the concepts of loyalty (*zhong* 忠) and justice (*yi* 義). How these concepts were to be implemented in the five relationships without creating contradictions and impediments occupied a central position in the Confucian discourse. For example, Confucius said, "One who is benevolent loves people." Yet this does not mean that one should love everyone with an equal amount of love, because different social relations would define different degrees of love. In comparison with the Christian concept of love, which, ideally, is an equal and undifferentiated love for all humankind, the Confucian love has to be considered in a hierarchical order based on the Five Relations. One could treat one's enemy only with straightforwardness, but not love. In the end, when and if these virtues could be completely immersed and embodied in the Five Relations, society would have become an ideal world.

Since, like Socrates, Confucius, as well as his spiritual disciple Mencius, never put down his thoughts in writing, it is important that one should try to understand the major points of their ideas, and not insist on discovering a systematic philosophical treatise on moral philosophy. The Warring States Confucian thinker Xunzi 荀子 (313–239 BCE) was different, for he did write down his thoughts in a more systematic way. Xunzi discussed in his essays, for example, the origins of ritual and music, and human nature. He believed that human nature was evil by birth, and that only through education could one

41 *Mengzi zhushu* 5B: 3. Translation follows Lau (2003: 116–17) with minor changes.

bend or guide this nature and force it to become good or to desire goodness. This theory is fundamentally opposite to that which Mencius propagated, that human nature was basically good, and there was an inner source of goodness that could be cultivated and expressed to become a positive force to benefit society. Both Xunzi and Mencius argued with a certain degree of persuasion, yet it is also understandable that their theories could generate debates, without producing firm answers, as the problem of human nature remains unsolved to this day.

In general, the Confucian thinkers were interested in developing a moral and political philosophy that could be of practical benefit to society at large, for this was the aim of their humanistic concern. This propensity of interest gravitated into a system of thought that combined personal and social ethics with a political philosophy based on the hierarchy of the Five Relations, which evolved into the fundamental ideology of government that underwent its most important period of growth during the Han dynasty.

THE DAO AND ITS PROPONENTS

In opposition to, or as a kind of critical reflection of, Confucian ideas was the strain of thought later coined as "Daoist," with its leading characters Laozi 老子 and Zhuangzi 莊子. Leaving aside the complex issue of who is earlier than the other,[42] we can characterize the central idea of Daoism as a kind of naturalism. In contrast to the Confucian idea of active social responsibility and belief in the efficacies of moral teachings in achieving an ideal world, and also because they saw the weakness of human nature in its tendency to abuse power and wealth once in hand – along the line of thinking that "power corrupts, absolute power corrupts absolutely" – the Daoist renounced the pursuit of political power and abandoned the cunning maneuvering in the insinuating intrigues of political struggles and opted for a life in tune with nature – simple, quiet, and spiritual, without the pursuit of material gains that went against nature and ultimately caused only anxiety, fear, doubt, and pain in one's mind.

Being a kind of critical thought that was developed in response to the contemporary intellectual environment, which could be described as intellectual warring states that reflecting the political situation of the day, we need to see the Daoist idea of naturalism not only as a way of expressing disagreement with the Confucian ideal of social ethics, but also as an expression of disillusion with the contemporary political scene, in that the naked display of power crushed the livelihood of many ordinary people, mainly because the rulers had an incessant ambition to expand their power. Thus there was an underlying criticism in *Laozi* of the way politics were run by those with grandiose ideas,

[42] See Loewe (1993).

who taught the rulers how to rule, how to educate and mold the people into having a mindset of servitude in order to benefit the power holders. This was perhaps the true meaning behind the remark of Laozi: "Abandoning sainthood, forsaking wisdom, people will then return to the state of benevolence and filiality." That is to say, the Confucian emphasis on following the examples of saints and moral teachings would only produce the opposite effect. Thus, "the better known the laws and edicts, the more thieves and robbers there are."[43] One could therefore observe in Daoist thinking some elements that do not totally abandon this world or are alienated from contemporary society, but, on the contrary, offer a sense of compassion for the lives of the common people and provide a different route to alleviate some of the problems they suffered. This is why during the early Han dynasty Daoist rhetoric was adopted by the rulers, although only briefly, as a means of healing the war-torn society. This Daoist rhetoric, now assuming the name of Huang-lao, i.e., Huangdi (the Yellow Emperor) and Laozi, was actually a blend of Daoist thought of Laozi and Zhuangzi and the Legalist attitude of the late Warring States period, most famously represented by people such as Shang Yang 商鞅 and Han Fei 韓非, about whom we shall have more to say in Chapter 3. Thus, ironically, the Lao-Zhuang Daoism of the pre-Qin era that originally despised secular power turned out to become Huang-lao Daoism of the early Han that served the secular regime.

A brief mention of the philosophy of Mozi should also be made here. A unique visionary with a radical idea of achieving peace in the world by promulgating the principle of universal love, Mozi, or the philosophy that this name represented, was nevertheless the product of his time, the late Warring States period. He accepted most of the Confucian ethics, but criticized the Confucians as prone to excessive ritual paraphernalia and of not being thrifty and prudent enough. His idea of "anti-aggression," also a product of the Warring States period, was related to his "universal love," because love brings peace, and when aggression is curtailed, peace could also be achieved. He also accepted the conventional religious ideas that revered Heaven, gods, and ghosts, and considered these useful to teach the people proper behavior. Mozi's philosophy was prevalent for a time during the late Warring States period, but did not continue in the ensuing chaotic period of the Qin Han transition. Although one cannot pinpoint the reason, it could have to do with the very utilitarian attitude toward "love" and "peace." Mozi's reasoning was focused on the "benefits" one could have to promote "love" and "peace," which might not have a deeper connection with one's compassion and therefore lacking a lasting commitment.

[43] *Laozi*, chapter 57. See Lau (2001: 83).

5. Han dynasty wooden slip roll. Courtesy of the Institute of History and Philology, Academia Sinica, 128.1

By the end of the Warring States period, however, a more or less integrated cultural entity was beginning to emerge from the shadows of war. There were signs that show that people who lived in different parts of the land, whether in Gansu to the far west, Hubei to the south, or Shandong to the east, were adopting similar lifestyles by using the same divination system, observing similar funerary customs, obeying similar laws, and accepting a common dynastic ideology.

This situation indicates that the cultural landscape of China was undergoing a process of assimilation through times of war and peace. To be sure, the cultural differences among various areas, notably the Qin, based in the Wei River basin; the Jin, based in Shanxi; the Qi, based in Shandong; and the Chu, whose territory covered present-day Hubei and Hunan, were still noticeable even in the time of Sima Qian. They nonetheless were kneaded – voluntarily or not – into the same cultural outlook defined largely by the Zhou ritual system and ideology. More effort and time were needed for the states of Wu and Yue, which occupied the present-day lower Yangzi basin, and the Shu, in present-day Sichuan, to be integrated into the larger cultural sphere of the Hua/Xia people.

The complexity of the situation can also be shown by the use of different writing systems, such as the Qin, the Chu, the Shu, and the Central Plain Shang-Zhou system, not to mention the different spoken languages each area used. When the Qin finally unified the entire land, a single writing system was enforced to facilitate communication. Yet there was never an attempt to unify the spoken language until the twentieth century. The adoption of a unified writing script eventually led to the cultural unification of the country, the effect of which can be perceived throughout the following chapters (Fig. 5).

This chapter thus sets the stage for the main acts in the subsequent chapters. For without this basic background such as the land, the historical development of the political regimes, the material condition of living, as well as the fundamental intellectual and religious propensity, many of the subsequent developments in the sphere of daily life, to which we shall pay special attention, would be less easy to imagine. Yet eager as we are to look at history from the bottom up, it would be better to have some idea of the superstructure of the society that we plan to explore. Such a structure, consisting of government organization and legal system, not only set a limit on the imagination and creativity of the elite, but also placed a restraint on the lives of ordinary citizens.

TWO

GOVERNMENT ORGANIZATION AND ELITE IDEOLOGY

When an ancient statesman made the observation that "People are the foundation of the state, when the foundation is secured, the state will be at peace,"[1] it should be understood not naively as a humanitarian respect for the welfare of the "people," but as a hard-nosed assessment of how a state could have existed in the first place. That is to say, without the people, there would be no state to begin with. All the components of a state – the ruler, the bureaucracy, the army, the people, the city, and all the supporting systems that these establishments imply – are built on the premise that there are people who could supply the necessary resources in the form of taxes and services. To make this happen, those who are on the receiving end of the supply chain would have to find a way of reaching the people and extracting their resources. The sources passed down through history in the form of literary texts are usually not too concerned about this very basic level of the realities of daily life. Yet enough evidence, including newly excavated legal and administrative texts from the Qin and early Han periods, has survived to allow us a glimpse of the structure of the society from the bottom up.[2]

1 *Shangshu* 7: 176.
2 Loewe (2006).

THE COUNTY AND LOCAL GOVERNMENT

Most of the peasants who lived in the countryside during the Qin and Han periods would have had little idea of "government" as an abstract concept representing an impersonal power structure. Most of their contact with the authorities above them who controlled their lives would have been with the local magistrate officers, who would have come to demand tax or corvée labor.

Since the Qin dynasty, people in the local communities were organized by the administrative unit of the *li* (里), or hamlet, consisting of a number of families, from more than a dozen to perhaps a hundred. Ideally, ten hamlets would form a *xiang* (鄉), or district, which would be under the leadership of the *sanlao* (三老, literally the "three elders"), usually selected from elders aged fifty or older, whose duty was to educate the people regarding customs and morals. The *sanlao* existed in the pre-Han period as more or less unofficial local leaders because of their seniority and their familiarity with local affairs and traditions. During the Han, the *sanlao* seemed to have evolved from unofficial local elders to occupying a semiofficial position in the local administration, although there is some uncertainty regarding whether they received an official salary and counted as the employees of the local government. Perhaps because of this neither official nor private status, they were tentacles of the government, and served as the mediators between the state and the individual people in the countryside.

Thus in a local district, or *xiang*, the *sanlao*, together with the other officials such as the *youzhi* ("petty official with rank" 有秩), *youjiao* ("chief of police" 游徼), and *sefu* "overseer" 嗇夫), carried out some basic administrative functions that the individual farmers would most likely have to encounter when poll tax and land tax were due, when corvée labor and military service were demanded by the government, or when disputes and banditry needed to be settled. Thus stated the *History of Han*: "The district has *sanlao*, *youzhi*, *sefu*, *youjiao*. *Sanlao* is responsible for moral teaching, *sefu* is in charge of litigation and collecting taxes. *Youjiao* keeps bandits and thieves in check. These are all institutions from the Qin Dynasty."[3]

From an administrative point of view, of course, the very first thing that a local official needed to know and to do was to establish a population register so that the number of households and the people living in the community could be registered for taxation and conscription purposes. Tens of hundreds of such local registers would have been produced every year and submitted to the counties; then the total figures would be submitted to various levels of government above the county level, e.g., the commandery (*jun* 郡), kingdom (*wangguo* 王國), or estate (*yi* 邑), and finally to the central government in the capital.

[3] *HS* 19: 742.

One empire-wide census record for the Western Han at around 1–2 CE has the following figures: total population: 57,671,400; total households: 12,366,470, which gives an average household size at 4.66 persons per household. Another figure dated to 140 CE gives an average household size of 5.1.[4] It would be hard not to imagine that – given the vastness of the country and the fact that imprecise data collection can be caused by, for example, miscalculation, abscondence, distortion, or simple inaccessibility – the reported figures could be quite different from the reality. We can only assume, to the best of our knowledge, and as much as the evidence allows, that the average farmer's family size during the Han dynasty was about five persons per household. Whether this indicates that a small, nuclear family with parents and several children was the norm in Han society might, however, be more complicated than one can assume because three generations of family members living together might not have been rare.

When the number of people comprising the taxable population was accounted for, the local officials could then levy tax on the people. These in general include poll tax, land tax, and property tax. Obviously during the long 400 years of Han rule, there were fluctuations in the tax rates because of many circumstances. In general, one should note that the land tax was based on the production from the land that the farmer either owned or rented from a landlord or the government. The rate, usually calculated on five-year average crop production, could be from one-fifteenth to one-thirtieth, and it was generally paid in kind, with occasional cash payments. The poll tax, on the other hand, was to be paid in cash. An often-mentioned figure is 120 coins per head. Obviously, given the unsteady monetary system and the largely agricultural economy, people in farming communities would have less cash at hand to pay tax; thus they had to endure much uncertainty and hardship trying to make ends meet. Moreover, if one was fortunate enough to have accumulated a certain amount of wealth, there was the property tax. A tax record from the Western border garrison of Juyan during the Eastern Han has the following account about the property of a low-level official:

> Two non-adult slaves: worth 30,000; one adult slave: 20,000; one carriage, worth 10,000; five horses, worth 20,000; two ox-carts, worth 4,000; two oxen, worth 6,000; one house, worth 10,000; farm land, five *qing* (頃), worth 50,000. Total property worth: 150,000.[5]

This record shows a rather well-off person's property value, which, of course, exceeded that of the ordinary farmer, for it was usual for a farming family of five to work on 100 *mou* (畝) (= 1 *qing* 頃) of farm land.[6]

4 See different calculations in Bielenstein (1947); Hsu (1982); Loewe (2006: 48).

5 Xie, Li and Zhu (1987: 69).

6 Usually, 100 *mou* = 1 *qing* = 6,666 2⁄3 square meters, or 11.39 English acres. See Weights and Measures at the front of the book.

In addition to taxes, the average farming family had to face another demand from the government, i.e., conscript labor, including corvée and military service. Just like taxes, conscription was known to the people long before the establishment of the empire, and men of knowledge had realized the severe consequences of such measures in the lives of the common people. The Confucian thinker Mencius once mentioned that "there is taxation levied in cloth, in grain, and in labor. A gentleman employs one to the full while relaxing the other two. If two are employed to the full, there would be death from starvation amongst the people, and if all three are so employed, father will be separated from son."[7] During the Han, when a young man reached adulthood – defined variously as being twenty to twenty-three years of age – he would have to serve one month per year as conscript labor until the age of fifty-six. He also had to serve in the army as a soldier for at least two years, depending on the time and place where he served.

In 192 BCE, for example, during the reign of Emperor Hui (195–188 BCE), a massive mobilization of 146,000 male and female conscript laborers within a 600 *li* radius of the capital Chang'an was called for thirty days to build the city wall of Chang'an. The same task was repeated two years later, with a conscript number of 145,000.[8] One can hardly imagine the logistic reality of this massive and mostly nightmarish deployment of laborers, because they had to provide themselves not only with food and sustenance, but also with a place to rest and sleep. The conditions on the roads and at the work camps would likely have been very harsh, to say the least. Note here that both male and female laborers were called for; presumably the work was extraordinarily large in scale.

Apparently, the vexing issue of conscript labor did not subside for as long as the policy persisted. In 81 BCE, Emperor Zhao called for a court debate on government policy owing to the increasing difficulties the government was facing on all fronts, in particular the policies on the government monopoly of the sale of salt and on the iron foundries. The record of this most extraordinary debate was collected as the *Debate on Salt and Iron* (*Yeantie lun* 鹽鐵論), which we will have other chances to discuss. The participants included the more practically minded and "legalistically" inclined government officials on one side, and the more idealistic Confucian scholars on the other. While debating the policy regarding economic measures, a sympathetic scholar described the distress of the common people when facing conscript labor: "The parents were in sorrow, and the wife was in lamentation. Hearts were filled with grief and discontent; the thought of separation hurts so deep as into the bone marrow."[9] Apparently the dangers and hardship involved in serving under the conscript labor system were far more severe than just one month's or one year's

7 *Mengzi* 29: 999–1001. Translation follows Lau (2003: 321).

8 *HS* 2: 89–90.

9 *Yantie lun* 9: 520.

separation; it could mean life and death. The description was not refuted by the officials, although they proposed different measures to resolve the problem.

When tax assessment reports from each village were assembled at the county office, the county magistrate and his staff would be busy preparing for the annual report to the central government, usually in the tenth month of every year. Above the counties were the commanderies, ruled by a governor. Parallel to the commanderies were a number of kingdoms and estates that were bestowed by the emperor on the descendants of those who had helped to build the empire, and those royal relatives, princes, and princesses who were remote from the capital enjoyed their lives in a small fief, and, willingly or otherwise, were involved in court politics. These kingdoms and estates were also managed by teams of officials who would collect their own taxes and also report to the central government. According to the *History of Han*, during the Western Han, at around 1–2 CE, there were 1,587 county-level units, including counties, kingdoms, estates, and marches (*dao* 道, the area where the minority people dwelt) in the entire empire.[10] The figures are, of course, only an indication of the general situation, and not to be taken as an exact account. A rough estimation of the number of officials of all ranks in the Western Han gives about 100,000 at the commandery level and below, and about 3,000 in the capital city of Chang'an.[11] Most of them were supported by the taxes collected from the countryside.

THE COMMANDERY

At the commandery level, the administration was under the charge of the governor (*taishou* 太守), with the assistance of an assistant minister (*cheng* 丞); a chief secretary (*zhubu* 主簿); an investigator (*duyou* 督郵) who was responsible for inspecting the affairs of the counties; and various bureaus (*cao* 曹) dealing with matters regarding personnel, taxes, population census, storage, coinage, law enforcement, litigation, etc. A group of texts found in a tomb dating from the reign of Emperor Cheng contains a copy of the annual report of the Donghai Commandery (東海郡), which allows us to have a first-hand view of the organization of the local government.[12] The document, entitled "Collected Records" (*jibu* 集簿), is an account of the administrative units and number of staff of the entire Commandery, which amounted to a total of 2,203. The record also contains the annual statistics of households (266,290), population (1,397,343), and cultivated land (512,092,085 *mou* 畝), presumably forming part of what the central government would have collected from the entire country as bases for taxation. In addition, in the tomb were found various documents

[10] The figure was calculated by using the records in *HS* 19: 742.
[11] Loewe (2006: 113).
[12] Lianyungang bowuguan (1997).

such as records of personnel movements and promotions, sick leave, death notices, transportation of money, etc. Most impressive is a list of weaponry, which listed various weapons and military equipment such as armor, chariots, and spare parts – a total of 23,268,487 items. For example, the list mentioned some special weapons used in chariots: 11,181 cross-bows; 34,265 cross-bow arrows, 2,650 shields, and 2,377 spears. As for weapons used by foot soldiers, the list mentioned 526,526 cross-bows, 11,424,159 cross-bow quarrels, 77,521 bows, 1,198,805 arrows, 99,901 swords, to name only a few items. It gives us a vivid idea of the military capability of the Commandery should all these weapons be deployed in battle. It also implies that military action was the duty of the governor. Indeed, incidences were recorded in which the soldiers and armory of a commandery were deployed by the central government in fighting battles of various sorts.[13] Although only an isolated example, these documents nevertheless give us a realistic view of the organization of the local government.

The tomb owner, by the name of Shi Rao (師饒), was a scribe of the bureau of merits (*gongcao shi* 功曹史), with an annual salary of only 100 *shi* (1 *shi* 石 = 31 kg) of grain. Thus, he was not a high-level official, compared to his superior the governor, whose salary was 2,000 *shi*, twenty times Shi Rao's income. He was buried with his wife in a tomb of modest size, measuring 4.20× 2.70 meters, typical of the Western Han tombs of lower-status officials.[14] He nevertheless was an important person in the administration, probably in charge of all the reports that the Commandery had to produce and send to the central government. Very interestingly, among the inscribed tablets are a number of "greeting cards" – some inquired about his health when he was sick – that he received from various officials, ranging from governors to marquises. The fact that these documents were buried with him was probably intended to suggest his important position despite his rank. It also shows that the social interactions of the day were not strictly following the administrative hierarchical order but a crisscross of different social status and family backgrounds.

CENTRAL GOVERNMENT

As can be imagined, the business of the commandery office would be many times smaller than that of the central government. The location of the central government was in the capital city of Chang'an for the Western Han and in Luoyang 洛陽 for the Eastern Han. The city of Chang'an, near the present-day city of Xi'an, was constructed and modeled after the Qin dynasty capital

[13] *HS* 10: 319; 24: 1173; 95: 3843.

[14] The average tomb size for double burials in the Western Han that contains one coffin and one casket was 5.14 × 3.20 meters according to one calculation, thus slightly larger than this tomb. See Poo (2008: 119).

of Xianyang 咸陽 which was burned down during the wars that caused the downfall of the Qin regime (see Chapter 5). With the physical structure of the Qin government gone, its institutional structure nevertheless was largely adopted by the newly established Han regime, because there were some undeniable merits in the Qin institution as the first attempt to rule the entire land with a certain degree of logic and practical efficiency. The founder of the Han dynasty, Liu Bang 劉邦, was not a man of much education. He was a police head (*tingzhang* 亭長) from the County of Pei 沛 at the end of the Qin dynasty when rebellious forces began to rise against the regime. Thus, when he found himself presiding over this vast country after several years of hard-fought civil war, he had to rely on the support of experienced officials who had served in the previous regime and were familiar with the Qin system. One such person was Shusun Tong (叔孫通), who served at the Qin court and later became the first to hold the title Erudite (*boshi* 博士), the so-to-speak most learned person at court. According to Sima Qian, when Liu Bang first gathered his supporters to celebrate the victory and proclaim him the emperor, he disregarded the tedious court rituals of the Qin and opted for simpler versions. Thus, his subjects drank wine at court and argued and clamored about their merits – they even slashed at the pillars in the hall with their swords.[15] Liu Bang was made to realize that one could conquer the world on horseback, but could not rule the world on horseback.[16] He therefore asked Shusun Tong to construct a set of court rituals based on the practice of the previous regimes. After several months' study, the new rituals were proposed and implemented. When all the officials were lined up each according to their proper ranks before the court, and each was given the precise order and manner to toast the emperor in turn, all was quiet and solemn. Liu Bang was heard saying: "Today I finally learned how prestigious being an emperor could be!"[17]

The court ritual, to be sure, was only a small part of the structure of the entire ruling apparatus and it could not have been set up without following and adopting that of the Qin, which, in turn, was the culmination of the experience of government gained by earlier regimes since the Zhou and by the subsequent states of the Spring and Autumn and the Warring States period.

Given the vicissitudes and reorganizations that any long-lasting institution is likely to experience, the central government of the Han was ideally composed of the offices of the "Three Excellencies" and the "Nine Ministers" (*jiuqing* 九卿). The three excellencies were the chancellor (*chengxiang* 丞相), the imperial counselor (*yushi dafu* 御史大夫), and the supreme commander (*taiwei* 太尉). The chancellor was in charge of all affairs of the state, being the most powerful person below the emperor. The counselor was the second person in

15 *SJ* 99: 2722.
16 *HS* 43: 2113.
17 *SJ* 99: 2724.

charge of affairs, and was often seen as the assistant or deputy of the chancellor. The commander was in charge of the military affairs of the state, although the actual title for this post sometimes changed during the Han period. Thus, between the three excellencies the civil and military affairs of the state were taken care of. The practical operation of the government then fell on the offices of the ministers. These could also be divided into two categories: those in charge of palace affairs and those in charge of state affairs.

The notable offices of the first category included the superintendent of ceremonials (*fengchang* 奉常 or *taichang* 太常) who was in charge of court ceremonies, including those relating to the imperial ancestral shrines, and many ceremonial functions relating to the imperial family. The director of the palace gentlemen (*langzhong ling* 郎中令) was in charge of palace security; his duty partly overlapped with that of the superintendent of the guards (*weiwei* 衛尉), who controlled the imperial guards stationed at the palace. The superintendent of the imperial clan (*zongzheng* 宗正) handled the affairs relating to the imperial family members, including their safekeeping, welfare, legal problems, and adjusting their status within the kinship system in relation to the reigning emperor. Thus, they could be involved in some difficult cases that concerned problematic imperial relatives. As for the expenditure of the palace, it was the responsibility of the lesser treasury and its superintendent (*shaofu* 少府), who would make sure that special taxation and supplies were delivered to the palace.

As for state affairs, finance and law enforcement were probably the most important offices. The superintendent of agriculture (*dasinong* 大司農) was the equal of the finance minister, who was responsible for the proper operation of the economy of the state, including the collection of taxes, the distribution and balancing of the supply of goods, and the control of commodity prices. Legal matters, on the other hand, were the responsibility of the superintendent of trials (*tingwei* 廷尉), who presided over the litigation of criminal cases, including the difficult ones sent to the capital by provincial offices, and who enforced the implementation of law throughout the land. A specialized office, that of the superintendent of state visits (*dahonglu* 大鴻臚), was responsible for "foreign affairs," that is, contact and negotiations with the peoples outside of the Han jurisdiction, and also for the visits of provincial officers to the capital on official duty – in a sense "foreign affairs" in relation to the Han court. An official who served both the palace and the state military affairs was the superintendent of transport (*taipu* 太僕), who was in charge of the supply of horses and carriages for both the palace and the army.

Needless to say, there could be various subordinate offices under each ministry, depending on the complexity of the affairs handled by the office, and some of the subordinate offices gained more power in the course of time. As can be imagined, people who had the opportunity to get easy access to the inner court, including access to the emperor and the imperial family, would have the potential to manipulate the affairs of the state or the palace. The secretariat (*shangshu* 尚書) under the charge of the office of the lesser treasury, for example, because of its duty of handling documents to and from the emperor and its proximity to the court, in time played an important role in court politics. There is thus a parallel situation between the secretariat in the central government and the secretary of the bureau of merits in the office of the commandery. In the Tang dynasty, several hundred years later, the secretariat became the leading office in the government, similar to that of the prime minister. The fact that such offices could arise in the government indicated that although there was a more or less rational design of various departments responsible for specific duties, the wielding of real power on a day-to-day basis still depended heavily on the factor of personal access to the power center, that is, to the emperor, or, in the case of the secretary of the bureau of merits, to the governor.

Such was the government framework within which the people of the Han Empire organized their lives. When we understand the duties of even the highest offices in the government, we can see their connection with the daily lives of the people they ruled. The chain of command began with the emperor, through the three excellencies and the nine ministers and the various departments under their charge, to the governor of the commandery, who in turn received the reports from his subordinate officers, much like the emperor receiving reports from his ministers, and finally to the county magistrate, whose power was able to penetrate into the villages and individual households. The most important issues for the operation of this system, again, were those related to the daily lives of the common people, i.e., taxation in all its forms, social security, and the enforcement of law. These were practical issues, yet the measures taken to deal with them were inevitably based on a distinct ideological foundation.

IDEOLOGICAL FOUNDATION OF THE STATE

The art of governing, to be sure, was not the invention of the Han. The political philosophy – or ideology – that the Han regime relied on had been gradually forged during the preimperial times, and could be traced to the early Zhou dynasty, if not beyond. The fact that the Zhou dynasty lasted 800 years, according to the traditional reckoning, implies that a certain wisdom of statecraft must have been forged along the way. Part of that wisdom, perhaps mixed with the idealizations and imaginations of the subsequent intellectuals, was preserved and passed down as the *Rites of Zhou* (*Zhouli* 周禮), which is generally considered as having been compiled during the Warring States period, but that was discovered and reconstituted only during the early Han period.[18]

[18] Loewe (1993).

In fact this text was not about ritual or ceremony, for which there was another text, the *Book of Ceremonies* (*Yili* 儀禮), the bulk of which was probably also compiled during the Warring States period. Rather, the *Rites of Zhou* was a blueprint for an ideal government structure, with every department and its duties and number of staff set out. The actual duties of various offices described in the *Rites of Zhou*, or at least the greater part of them, could, however, have been derived from practical experience, such as that of the offices in charge of state ceremonies, legal and military affairs, taxation, law enforcement, etc., which any political entity would have to manage to ensure its survival. The *Book of Ceremonies*, on the other hand, is a text that prescribes all kinds of rituals and ceremonies that people (mainly the ruling elites) should follow on different occasions, such as marriages, funerals, adulthood initiation rites, even drinking parties, etc., often in precise step-by-step instructions. Needless to say, this text also represents an ideal reconstruction and embellishment of ceremonies that might have existed in society at various times and places, with the aim of expounding a certain value system that later, together with the *Rites of Zhou*, was branded "Confucian."[19]

It behooves us to explain why Confucius is associated with these texts. Confucius, as mentioned in Chapter 1, regarded human beings as social animals; thus all the ethics and morality he propagated were considerations of interpersonal relationships. In these relationships, Confucius recognized and expounded certain core values, such as benevolence (*ren*), propriety (*li*), righteousness (*yi*), forgiveness (*shu*), and loyalty (*zhong*). These values were regarded by Confucius as closely related to various fundamental and functional values that were necessary if a society, or a government, was to survive and prosper. Because Confucius belonged to the class of social elites who were familiar with the operation of state affairs, including the proper organization of rituals and government offices, and the conduct of the officers, it might not be far-fetched to assume that this was the reason why his ideas would be associated with the *Rites of Zhou* and the *Book of Ceremonies*. The *Rites of Zhou* laid out a plan for government organization based on the recognition that the state operates on a hierarchical order not only to carry out mundane work such as taxation and law, but also to teach the people the proper way to conduct themselves and to forge harmonious interpersonal relationships through the example set by the officers. The *Book of Ceremonies* gave specific instructions regarding the proper procedures for conducting all kinds of rituals with the aim of propagating the hierarchical social order based on the Five Relations that was embodied in the rituals. It is not easy to determine how much Confucius's ideas were inspired or influenced by what he had learned from the institutions before him, or how much of his ideas were absorbed and incorporated into the composition

[19] Nylan (2001).

of these texts. In their present forms, in any case, the two texts are inseparably intertwined with the later development of the Confucian school of thought, and with good reason. For example, if we read chapter 10 of the *Analects*, the core text of Confucian teaching that recorded the sayings of and anecdotes about Confucius, we see how Confucius and his disciples actually carried out his ideas through his own personal performance in difference social situations:

> When talking to people in the village, he [i.e., Confucius] was like one with few words, while at the court and ancestral temple of the ruler, he talked freely yet with caution. When he entered the gate of the palace, he bent down as if he could not pass through the gate. He would not stand in the middle of the gateway, nor would he step over the threshold to enter. When he passed by the place where the ruler usually stood, he was very alert, walking tiptoe, and lowering his voice. While at home he had certain choice of proper dress, and he would not eat food not properly cut and prepared. He would not talk while eating, and he would not chat while in bed.[20]

All these, even though hardly an eyewitness account, resonate in spirit with what we find in the *Book of Ceremonies*, that is, using ritual acts to distinguish or to embody the social hierarchy between people of different status.

On the other hand, plenty of evidence in the *Analects* testifies to the fact that Confucius was very concerned about how a government should be run, with proper rituals and persons of upright moral integrity who promoted benevolence and righteousness. Once someone asked Confucius: "Why would you not join the government?" Confucius answered: "The *Book [of Zhou]* says about filial piety thus: with filial piety one should be filial toward brothers, it is like managing a government. Thus to rule [a family] is also a kind of governing. What is the need to go into [real] politics?"[21] Here Confucius was probably using the opportunity to say that family values or filial piety should be the principle in governing a state, which is in tune with his idea that only a virtuous person could be a good ruler. The teaching of Confucius stresses the connection between personal moral integrity and the benevolent rule of the government, with the aim of promoting the ultimate goal of humanity, that is, the realization of a world of peace, as described in the chapter on "The Promulgation of Ritual" (*Li Yun*) that is found in the *Book of Rites*.[22] The idea of a sovereign as a man of virtue began to surface in the discussions of the court officials during the uncertain time before the accession of Emperor Wen:

> The King of Dai [i.e., Emperor Wen] is the eldest son of Emperor Gaozu, known as being benevolent, filial, and generous. The king mother née Bo

[20] *Lunyu* 19: 635–64.
[21] *Lunyu* 4: 121.
[22] *Liji* 21: 1–4.

> is from a good family. Moreover it is proper to choose the eldest son of the former Emperor, and it is felicitous that he is known to the world as a person of benevolence and filiality.[23]

These attributes of the emperor hint at two of the most essential Confucian values, benevolence and filiality; the former refers to treating others with compassion and love, therefore being exemplary of interpersonal relationships, while the latter refers to the love of parents and siblings, therefore being exemplary of family ethics. By being known to the world as possessing such qualities, the emperor would become the model that the people, especially the officials in the government, should accordingly emulate.

Confronted with such a description of the emperor, a question imposes itself upon us: How should one assess such qualities in a person, particularly if the person were an emperor? Shall we accept the description of the *Records of the Grand Scribe* on its face value? Could we find evidence to support the claim that Emperor Wen indeed lived up to his reputation? Moreover, what would be the practical application of benevolence and mundane justice? Some insight could be gained by looking at a story about Zhang Shizhi (張釋之), a superintendent of trials (*tingwei* 廷尉) during the reign of Emperor Wen. He was known as a fair-minded person and several times refuted the opinion of the emperor concerning a harsher sentence. For example,

> One time Emperor Wen had gone out on an excursion and was passing over the middle of the three bridges that span the Wei River, when a man suddenly ran out from under the bridge, startling the horses in the emperor's party. The emperor ordered his outriders to seize the man and hand him over to Zhang Shizhi, the superintendent of trials. When Zhang Shizhi questioned him, the man replied, "I came from the district around here and I was on my way to the capital when I heard the order to clear the road for the emperor, so I hid under the bridge. After a long while I supposed that the emperor had already passed over, so I came out. Then I saw the carriages and horsemen and I started to run, that was all."
>
> Zhang Shizhi sent a report to the emperor stating that the man was guilty of having violated the order to clear the roads and should be fined. "But this man actually startled my horses!" the emperor objected in a rage. "Fortunately my horses are very docile and even-natured, but if it had been any other horses, they might very well have upset the carriage and injured me! And yet you propose to let the fellow off with nothing but a fine?"
>
> "The law must be upheld by the Son of Heaven and by everyone in the empire alike," replied Zhang Shizhi, "and that is the penalty the law prescribes. If I were to impose a heavier penalty in special cases, then the people would cease to have any faith in the laws. If at the time the incident

[23] *SJ* 10: 413.

> occurred Your Majesty had ordered the man executed on the spot, then that would have been the end of the affair. But now the case has already been referred to me and, as superintendent of trials, it is my responsibility to see that everyone in the empire is treated with absolute fairness. Should I once deviate from that standard of fairness, then the entire legal system of the empire would lose its impartiality and the people would be at a loss to know how to conduct themselves. May I ask Your Majesty to consider these consequences?" After a long time the emperor replied, "The sentence which you propose is quite appropriate."[24]

Thus it seems that although on the surface Zhang Shizhi could be seen as a law-abiding legalist who cared only about strict implementation of the law, even those involving the emperor, the fact that he could somehow bend the emperor's wish and save the accused person from a horrible demise could actually be seen as a more benevolent act that fits the Confucian ideal. Emperor Wen, on the other hand, although known as a person of compassion, actually could not match Zhang Shizhi's sensibility when it came to dealing with real people in real life. This is an example that shows how the Confucian ideas could have penetrated into the thoughts of some officials and affected their conduct of daily affairs, and how the true spirit of forgiveness (*shu*) and righteousness (*yi*) was not necessarily expressed with empty claims. Of course we do not consider that such examples bear any statistical significance. What is worth noticing, however, is that it is possible to trace the ideological background to the daily working of government business. It also reminds us that, whatever the claims were – regarding benevolence, filiality, righteousness, propriety, for example – the reality of life might not operate according to a simple formula, and that moral claims, be they Confucian or otherwise, should be examined against the reality of the day-to-day workings to see whether they had achieved the desired result.

THE LEGALIST APPROACH TO GOVERNMENT

The case of Zhang Shizhi, then, is an interesting example with which to introduce the idea of the "Legalist." It was during the late Warring States period that, because of the fierce competition between the powerful states, rulers began to seek ways to reform the government and to enhance both military and economic power. Emerging from such an environment were a number of political philosophers who promoted the idea of an efficient governance based on the strict application of law, centralized economic policy, and strong military power – they were later generally identified as the "Legalists." One of the most famous advocates of such philosophy was Shang Yang 商鞅

[24] *SJ* 102: 2754–55.

(c. 385–338 BCE), who was the main architect of the reform of the state of Qin, and whose reform, 100 years after his death, finally helped the Qin to conquer all the other states and to unify the entire land. Thus, his ideas were obviously very effective in creating an efficient government.

As a student of various schools of thought that concerned the issues of law and military strategy, Shang Yang gained the trust of Duke Xiao of Qin (361–338 BCE) and began his career as a reformer at around 359 BCE. With a series of reforms that encouraged farmers to farm the land, and that established the household registration and liability system (i.e., mutual reporting among the households) down to every household in the country, Shang Yang's policy was to ensure that nothing illegal was left unreported in the countryside because the people obeyed the law for fear of being reported by their neighbors. Because of the stern measures and fair execution of the law, the state of Qin experienced a rapid enhancement in both its military power and economic prosperity.

In the process of the reform, Shang Yang implemented harsh regulations to put down the old aristocracy and to compel the population to perform difficult tasks, which in the end made him unpopular. He finally lost the trust of the new ruler Duke Huiwen (c. 354–311 BCE) and was charged with treason, arrested while trying to escape, ironically because of his own strict law to prohibit people from hiding fugitives, and was executed. The central idea of his philosophy, despite having a certain truth about how to run a government efficiently, was nevertheless based on a rather crude understanding of mass psychology. In his view, and obviously from an elitist stand, the "people" cared most about having a secure life, even at the expense of losing their freedom of expression. In the following paragraph, which allegedly was Shang Yang's writing, he explained his idea of human nature and how the state should utilize it to achieve this goal.

> A weak people means a strong state and a strong state means a weak people. Therefore, a country, which has the right way, is concerned with weakening the people. If they are simple they become strong, and if they are licentious they become weak. Being weak, they are law-abiding; being licentious, they let their ambition go too far; being weak, they are serviceable, but if they let their ambition go too far, they will become strong."[25]

As with many other early Chinese authors, Shang Yang's argument was based on his assumptions about human nature and simplistic logic. One could even say that his words are not a logical argument but wishful thinking, even if there is a certain truth in his observations, which are relevant even today. On the other hand, although his death was perhaps an ironic comment on his own

[25] *Shangjun shu* 76; see Duyvendak (1929).

enterprise, many of his policies such as household registration, noble degrees based on military merits, the tax system, and administrative units of central and provincial governments, were passed down and became the foundation of the institutions of the Qin-Han Empire.

Unlike Shang Yang, whose ideas were at least put into practice, the last and most sophisticated "Legalist" philosopher Han Fei (韓非, c. 281–234 BCE) was not so lucky. Han was actually a student of the Confucian thinker Xunzi. What he inherited from Xunzi, however, was not the Confucian ideas of benevolence and compassion, but the idea that human beings are by nature evil. His idea of realpolitik, therefore, was based on a calculation of how to utilize this evil nature to achieve the maximum control of the state under the rule of one person, the sovereign. The affairs of the state, according to him, should be built on rational and impartial law and order, which in turn should be based on human nature's tendency toward self-interest. The gist of this political order, however, was the absolute power of the sovereign. The sovereign uses the law to establish public order, uses the practical tactics to manipulate various factions in the government, and uses his overwhelming power to force the submission of his subjects. Modern scholars had compared his ideas with those of the Italian political philosopher Niccolò Machiavelli (1469–1527), with some justification. Needless to say, Han Fei's idea was very attractive to the rulers of his time, and King Zheng, later the First Emperor of Qin, recruited him and prepared to use him as an advisor. Unfortunately, Han Fei's friend and schoolmate, but also archrival, the prime minister Li Si (李斯), became jealous and had Han murdered in prison. Han Fei's work was nonetheless preserved and widely studied by generations of literati, Confucian or otherwise, as part of their knowledge base.

Throughout the Han dynasty, the prevailing concerns of the government were issues of law, taxes, measures to control commodity prices, and balancing the circulation of goods. These were issues directly affecting the livelihood of the people that also concerned Shang Yang and other Legalists. On numerous occasions during the Han period the emperor would issue edicts to implement various measures to relieve certain problems, either natural disasters or human misdeeds that were seriously hurting the people. Wei Xiang the Chancellor (67–58 BCE), for example, once recommended that the throne should pay attention to the supply of food for the people in times of difficulty, because this would be an ideal policy for a Confucian ruler.[26]

Yet what is more benevolent? A fair execution of law? Or the special and favorable weighing of the cases based on the power holders' goodwill? Such was the inherent problem facing the Confucian and the Legalist approaches of governing by law. The special favor may be seen as the showing of Confucian

[26] *HS* 74: 3137–38.

compassion, yet the fair execution of law could also be a kind of compassion to save the people from harm caused by distortions and manipulations by powerful people. One can make a case that the Han government employed measures of Legalist ideology to alleviate practical problems for the people, so that the Confucian claim to care for the people could be achieved. In this way, the elite ideologies, whether Confucian or Legalist, could have made a certain difference regarding government policy. The most famous debate at court between the officials who were utilitarian and legally minded and the scholars who were more conservative and under the influence of Confucian ideas, held during the time of Emperor Zhao, known as the Debate on Salt and Iron, was a clear demonstration of the dilemma faced by those who were instrumental in formulating the policies of the Han government.

THE RECRUITMENT OF GOVERNMENT OFFICIALS

How, then, did the officials get into the government in the first place? In the early years of the dynasty, members of the imperial family and the most distinguished generals were given positions such as kings and marquises. The bulk of the offices in the central government were occupied by family members and descendants of the veterans of the war that overthrew the Qin. For the greater part of the Western Han, perhaps because of the expediency of making money for the government, certain offices could be bought, although it was people with power already who could afford to pay the money and purchase the office for their own kinsfolk. This was apparently not a wise manner of recruitment, with Dong Zhongshu (董仲舒c. 179–104 BCE) voicing criticism against it in his famous treatise presented to Emperor Wu. Another way of recruiting was through the recommendation of high officials to sponsor offices for their brothers or sons. According to a fragment of Han law, "Officials ranked at two thousand bushels and above, who have been in charge of affairs for fully three years, are allowed to stand surety for a brother of the same father, or for a son (and to have him appointed as) Gentleman."[27] This, again, was not a fair means of recruitment, and it was abolished by Emperor Ai in 7 BCE.

On the other hand, the selection of talents from people without a high-status family background had been a policy of the pre-Qin states, and it was made into a normal channel for the recruitment of government officials for the Qin and Han dynasties.[28] Specific orders to select talents to serve in the government had already begun in the reign of Emperor Gaozu, and became a regular institution for the recruitment of officials during the reign of Emperor Wu. At the recommendation of Dong Zhongshu, Emperor Wu ordered that

[27] Hulsewé (1990; esp. 209–10).
[28] Loewe (2006: 71–85).

every commandery and kingdom in the country should elect one filial and upright (*lian* 廉) person annually to be sent to the capital to serve as court attendant (*lang* 郎), and then train for further employment there. To be sure, they had to pass further examinations before they could be assigned formal offices. A rough estimate indicates that during the Western Han, around 200 such elected persons were recommended annually to the central government.[29]

The bulk of the low-level officials or clerks, however, were people who learned their skills and knowledge in the law and regulations through apprenticeship at the local government offices, a practice traced back to the Qin dynasty. They were people who were familiar with the numerous government regulations and laws and were able to draw up documents regarding investigations and lawsuits as well as various routine reports and records that were necessary for the government to function properly. These clerical personnel, moreover, were recruited from people of wide social backgrounds, thus opening up opportunities for talents from nonaristocratic backgrounds to enter into the government apparatus.

The recruitment of low-level staff from the general population can be exemplified by a statute discovered among the legal documents found in the early Western Han tomb of Zhangjiashan, in present-day Hubei Province. This is a statute with the title "Scribe Statute" (*shilu* 史律):

> Sons of scribes and diviners, when they are seventeen years of age, are to [commence] study. When the student scribes, diviners, and invocators have studied for three years, the study mentors are to present them to [the Director of] the Grand Scribes, [the Director of] the Grand Diviners, or [the Director of] the Grand Invocators; the student scribes in commanderies are to be presented to their respective Commandery Governor. In every case, at the appointed time of the first day of the eighth month, test them. Test the student scribes on the *Fifteen Wooden-Prism Bundles* [book]. When [a student scribe] is capable of reciting and writing out 5,000 graphs or more [from the book], then he may become a scribe. Furthermore, test them on the eight forms [of written graphs]. The commandery sends an evaluation [of the examinations from the commandery exam] on the eight forms to [the Director of] the Grand Scribes. [The Director of] the Grand Scribes reads out loud the evaluation [of the two examinations] and selects the best individual [from the central-government examination and from each commandery examination] and makes him a Scribe Director in his (viz., the Capital Area's or each commandery's) counties. For one who is of unacceptably poor quality: do not make him a scribe. Once each three years, combine the evaluations [of the examinations]. Take the best individual and make him an Accessory Scribe in the Imperial Secretariat. Test the student diviners. When [a student diviner] is capable of reciting and writing 3,000 words more from the *Scribe's*

29 Yan (1952: 122).

> *Book* and chanting 3,000 words or more from the *Diviner's Book* and, in divining, makes one or more accurate divinations out of six tries, then he may become a diviner ... Test the student invocators on the *Invocator's Fourteen Wooden Prism* [book]. When a student invocator is capable of chanting 7,000 words or more [from the book], then he may become an invocator and perform a one-month tour of periodic service every five months.[30]

More detailed stipulations about the employment length, transfer, and retirement age for these positions were also made in the statute; thus we can see the typical career of low-level scribes, from training, testing, to allocation of office, in the Han bureaucracy.

During the transition from Qin to Han, because the governing apparatus at the central government was in disarray, the daily operation of various local governments basically continued the Qin practice. After the period of recuperation in the reigns of emperors Wen and Jing, when political instability, i.e., the rebellion of the seven kingdoms, was resolved and the economic situation improved, a new measure of establishing a government learning center and the position of the Erudite was reopened during the reign of Emperor Wu. Although all through his reign, Emperor Wu did not employ any Confucian scholar to work in the central government, with the exception of Gongsun Hong(公孫弘 c. 200–121 BCE), and later Dong Zhongshu, his promotion of Confucianism was more in name than in reality. It was not until the reign of Emperor Cheng that Classical learning became closely associated with holding an official position. Thus began the long tradition of studying for offices in Chinese history.

It should be pointed out, however, that the Confucian learning in the early Han was not a systematic "school of thought" that had its core texts and commonly accepted tenets. Rather, each of the "Canons" (經 *jing*) was painstakingly recollected and reconstructed by various scholars who, after surviving the turmoil of the changing of the dynasties, were scattered across the countryside, most notably in the former Qi (齊) and Lu(魯) areas, where Confucian learning had deep roots. There was no standard edition of any of the canons; the *Book of Changes* (*Yijing* 易經), the *Book of History* (*Shujing* 書經), the *Book of Poetry* (*Shijing* 詩經), the *Book of Rites* (*Liji* 禮記), and the *Spring and Autumn Annals* (*Chunqiu* 春秋) each had their own history of transmission that is often difficult to retrace.[31]

The phenomenon of the development of the Confucian (*Ru* 儒) Canon in the Han raises a very interesting question for us: What was the motivation for people who promoted the Confucian classics? What, for example,

30 Zhangjiashan (2006: 80–81). Translation follows Barbieri-Low and Yates (2015: 1093–97).

31 Nylan (2001: 14–15).

made it attractive for the emperors of the Western Han (Wu, Zhao, Yuan, Ai, etc.) to study the *Book of Poetry*? The fact that the Han government found it useful to set up the Office of Erudite as part of the government apparatus as early as the time of Emperor Wen indicates that the learning of the Confucian classics was considered to be part of the governing strategy. The recruitment of persons with filial and upright character to serve in the government, moreover, demonstrates that the imperial emphasis on Confucian virtues as prerequisites for official position was transmitted to the entire country. If other offices dealt with the practical measures of taxation and military affairs, the Erudites and their students would be the suppliers of the ideological foundation of the government, which was also the legitimation of the imperial rulership. The claim, of course, needs to be built on a commonly agreed source, a moral source that first defines the cosmological order, and then the ethical order, according to the Confucian interpretation, which also conformed to the cosmological order, and finally the political order in which the emperor claims that he was the culmination of the ethical order, namely, the holder of the Mandate of Heaven. Thus, political authority is identified with moral integrity and ethical propriety, backed up by cosmology.

The ups and downs of the use or acceptance of various classics, the argument and confrontation of the various interpretations of the texts during the Han, are, in a nutshell, the manifestation of the process of competition between different intellectual traditions for obtaining influence in the government. Because influence meant having real official positions and power, not to mention economic gains, the competition was in essence not much different from the ideological contests between the Republicans and Democrats in modern US politics: all parties considered that their policies were better for "the people." Meanwhile, of course, the interpretations of the meaning of the canonical texts were not merely academic arguments – they had their practical implications in government policies. Nowhere was this competition demonstrated more clearly than during the famous Debate on Salt and Iron, to which we will turn in the following chapters.

THREE

SOCIAL STRUCTURE AND LAW

The preceding two chapters have outlined two kinds of structures that affected the lives of the people in ancient China. The first is the geographic and climatic condition of the land in which people lived. The second is the bureaucratic and ideological environment, whether they lived in a village, a town, or a city. These structures prescribed their outward framework of existence. No less important, however, are the internal systems that guided the life and behavior of these people. These are the social institutions, including family relations and kinship systems, or social groupings formed by a number of defining features such as locality or profession, and, of course, law – the means by which the government is able to control the people so long as it is efficient and strong enough to execute the law and maintain social stability.

We shall first briefly introduce the process of evolution of the society from a clan-based organization, to a nonclan, bureaucracy-based organization. During this process, the hereditary nobility and its kin gradually lost their position during the social and political transition from the Eastern Zhou through the Warring States period. Instead, formerly landless common people had the chance of being absorbed into the newly formed state organization and gained a higher status through their talent and service to the state.[1] By the Han period, although the government was run by a group of educated elite, this was not a

[1] Hsu (1965).

self-contained caste, and social mobility was possible through various channels, including education.

For the majority of the population, the obvious stratification of society was between the rulers and the ruled, the provided and the providers. The ruled and the providers were farmers and craftsmen, who were the basic productive force of society, and whose lives are least known to us. Merchants, on the other hand, were an emerging social class that benefitted from the unified country, safer transportation, and more regulated monetary system. The poor reputation that the merchants acquired as profit seekers, however, often put them at a disadvantage with the prevailing ideologies, whether Confucianism or Daoism. As the lives of the farmers and merchants are subjects of separate chapters, here we concentrate only on their position in the overall social structure and their relative positions in regard to each other.

As a result of the evolution of the nature of society from "clan based" to "state/bureaucratic based," and as the state itself had then become a vast country that previous political regimes lacked the experience to handle, the rule by a common set of regulations, or law, became imperative for the country to remain a unified and functional entity. Recent archaeological finds have provided abundant sources for us to understand how this system of rule by law actually operated at a local and daily level. Detailed regulations regarding many aspects of agricultural and commercial activities can be found in these new materials, not to mention bureaucratic day-to-day operations. Thus by utilizing these new materials, this chapter aims to provide a framework of law and regulations, within which the social groups operated and interacted with each other. Before we discuss the situation in the Han dynasty, however, a brief view of the pre-Han background is in order.

THE SOCIAL STRUCTURE OF THE SHANG AND ZHOU

To imagine the reality of daily life in the Shang and Zhou periods involves a basic problem: What kind of evidence could be used to allow us to begin such imagination? And what aspects of daily life could possibly be recovered?

The oracle bone inscriptions provide us with information mainly concerning activities in the imperial household, e.g., war, religious sacrifice, marriage, childbirth, and illness. All these were mentioned in the context of divination; that is, we are told about these activities because the diviner wished to discover the auspiciousness of the subjects in question, but the sources do not mention the details of the subjects themselves. The social structure revealed in the oracle bone inscriptions was a clan-based kinship system, wherein the patriarchal blood relation determined the hierarchy of social status. Within the imperial family, polygamy was practiced, and marriage alliance with other clans of a comparable standing was the common practice of the day. Sifting through the oracle bone inscriptions we find mention of various elements of marriage customs: proposal of marriage, engagement, taking in wives, and marrying off daughters, all of which needed to be confirmed through divination. We can also see that social units below the imperial house were clan-based elite groups led by members of the imperial house and nonimperial noblemen whose status was conferred by the king and who were able to rule a certain area as a kind of vassal in relation to the king, and who would provide military as well as economic services in times of need.[2]

Besides the ruling elite, Shang society largely consisted of the common farmers who might also have served as soldiers in times of war. Yet we have little information about most of them. Did they follow similar religious and material modes of life as those of the imperial house and their leaders? Did they have different kinship systems and marriage customs? It is reasonable to assume that the anonymous common people – the silent majority – basically conformed to or accepted a system that was modeled on the elite social structure. Hence, there must have been some degree of agreement or consensus among different strata of society regarding the basic tenets of morality and customs to enable the ruling elite to claim the right of interpretation or to act as holders of tradition. Burial customs of the Shang period, in fact, point to a common religious culture, which could support the foregoing argument.[3] However, we should not presume more than what evidence allows. Apart from the commoners, from whom soldiers and craftsmen were recruited, there existed a social group of slaves, mostly prisoners of war or criminals, who were mentioned in the oracle bone inscriptions, and whose presence was demonstrated by being sacrificed at funerals and religious ceremonies. Again, very little is known of their role in the daily life of the Shang.[4]

The Zhou dynasty, as mentioned in Chapter 1, tried to consolidate its political control by establishing a system of vassalage based on kinship relations. The most prominent feature of this system was the major lineage and minor lineage structure, which was simply an extension of the kinship structure in a patriarchal line of descent. Thus the sons of the patriarch of the major lineage would be given land and form the minor lineage, who in turn would be the major lineage in relation to their own descendants. The original design was to use the minor lineages of the imperial house – who were now vassal states – to protect their major lineage. This institution was called *fengjian* 封建 – usually translated in modern English as "feudalism," though somewhat incorrectly. Whereas in Medieval European feudalism, a vassal was also given land and people by the lord, there was not necessarily a blood relationship between the two. The Zhou institution of *fengjian*, on the other hand, was based on blood relations. This

2 Keightley (1978, 2000); Chang (1980).

3 Poo (1998: 23–29; 2008: 39–44).

4 Keightley (2012).

institution thus formed a web of self-contained power structure. The society, therefore, was dominated by rulers and powerful families whose members controlled the state machine, leaving the commoners to serve their masters.

On the whole, the social composition at large did not seem to have undergone any major change during the Shang–Zhou transition. The inscriptions on the ritual bronze vessels, for example, often provide information about the relationship between the maker of the vessels and the persons for whom the vessels were made. Certain kinship relations such as the subordinate position of the wife versus the husband could be gleaned from the inscriptions, though these basically concern the elites. However, the wife of the lineage leader was required to be on the podium of religious sacrifices together with her husband – admittedly in a secondary role. She therefore commanded respect from members of the sublineage, and could exercise a certain authority as the leader of the lineage, when her husband was absent or deceased.

The *Book of Poetry*, as another example, describes many aspects of the life and feelings of the elite of Zhou and its various vassal kingdoms, even social customs and farm life. The social components, as seen in the poems, consist mainly of the ruling elite, but also include the larger population of the realm: soldiers, farmers, servants, and retinues of the noble families. The vast majority of the common people lived in the countryside and worked as farmers. These farmers were attached to the land that they worked, and their produce was taken mainly to supply the needs of the landowners, the aristocrats. A poem in the *Book of Poetry* describes the seasonal activities in a manor, the difficult life of the farmers, their services to the noble household, and their humble wish to toast their lord at the year's end celebration of the harvest.[5]

We should, of course, not take for granted these sentiments, joyous and grateful though they seem, as a direct representation of the feelings of the common farmers. The poems in the *Book of Poetry* were supposedly collected by court officials and compiled for the use of the elites. During the Spring and Autumn period, the poems became the medium of communication during diplomatic conversations or friendly gatherings. This was suggested by Confucius's famous line: "If you do not study the Poems, you would not know how to speak."[6] It was like quoting a line from the Bible or a verse from Shakespeare, a necessary refinement for a cultured gentleman. In our case, the poet expressed some sympathetic understanding of the life of the farmers, and the fact that such a theme was expressed at all indicates a certain revelation of the disparity between the life of the farmers and that of the nobility.

[5] *Maoshi* 8a: 388–92.
[6] *Lunyu* 33: 1168–69.

On the other hand, there was evidence indicating the beginning of skepticism regarding the establishment, the traditional way of life, and the belief system. One striking example was a poem about human sacrifice during the funeral of Duke Miu of Qin (秦繆公, 659–621 BCE). According to the *Records of the Grand Scribe*, 177 people were sacrificed to accompany Duke Miu into the netherworld, including three prominent young members of the nobility.[7] Apparently this incident created serious controversy at the time, so that it was remembered and mentioned in a poem.[8]

Whoever composed the poem, the sentiment was clear: human sacrifice at the funeral of the rulers became a cause for protest; tradition and custom were called into question. Even if this protest was not meant to discredit the idea of human sacrifice, it at least expressed a critical reflection of and brooding discontent with what was taken for granted by the rulers, that there was some justice that ranked above the personal wish of the sovereigns.

After the beginning of the Warring States period (c. 476–221 BCE), the ruling families that perpetuated from the Zhou through the Spring and Autumn period began to disintegrate drastically because of the incessant warfare that destroyed the old regimes. The king of Zhou became merely a nominal figure who had only ritual significance and ruled a small area, and the former strong feudal lords now began to call themselves "kings," competing with each other for land and wealth. These new rulers realized that only by recruiting talents from a wider pool could the state find able administrators to manage the affairs of an increasingly complicated government. Thus the privileged position of the old aristocratic families was challenged and broken to make room for talented people without a family background. This means that the social structure gradually changed from lineage/blood based, to merit based, as commoners were able to rise to high positions, and being a blood descendant of a famous family might not be very helpful.

The rulers of the states no longer seriously cared about the lineage of the talents that they recruited. High-ranking officials and people who gained favor with the rulers and were given a large amount of land and wealth could be from any state so long as their talents were deemed useful. The ordinary officials and lower level bureaucrats, moreover, were often made up of a new kind of social group, the *shi*-gentlemen (士).

The *shi*-gentlemen were mostly members of the old aristocratic families who had lost their old status but because of their personal talents had found employment with the state or the ruler. As a result, an increasing number of "freelance" men of talent became regular visitors at the courts of the various rulers and in the households of ministers and high officials, seeking

[7] *SJ* 5: 173.
[8] *Maoshi* 6: 373.

employment. Many of the powerful lords of the Warring States would harbor a large number of *shi*-gentlemen, sometimes hundreds and thousands, as a sort of talent pool that could be utilized in times of need. This somewhat resonates with the Roman custom of "clients" at the houses of nobles.

The majority of the farmers were probably given (or assigned) land by the state, in return for taxes and corvée labor. Since it was a time of turmoil and rapid change, the situation might vary from one state to another. In general, we may note that at least some of the farmers were given land by the state, for whatever reason: reward for military service, or as a favor from the lords. Their labor provided the essential wealth of the state – food and produce, and the supply of soldiers in times of war.

By the time of the unification of the country by the Qin, therefore, society at large was composed of a ruling sovereign with a bureaucracy that was designed mainly to manage the extracting of taxes from the people and the supply of goods and soldiers to the state. The majority of the common people were small farmers with their own land, and it was the major task of the state bureaucracy to have an account of the number of the people and the size of their land so as to serve as the basis for taxation. A common trend among the Warring States, therefore, was the development of a population census system that had a record of the households in the state, and the number of male members of the household. This trend converged after the unification by Qin, as witnessed by such official documents as the legal texts found in a Qin tomb at Shuihudi 睡虎地, Hubei Province.[9]

HAN SOCIAL STRUCTURE

The establishment of the Han dynasty was a major break from the past in terms of the social background of the ruling house. Emperor Liu Bang and his entourage were people without a noble or prominent family background, which was quite different from his competitors, who were mostly descendants of the royal houses or prominent families of the Warring States. With few human resources to rely on, Liu Bang reverted to the Zhou system and established his relatives and the military leaders who helped to secure his regime as vassal kings. The hopes that these kings would help consolidate the regime were dashed, as troubles between the emperor and his siblings continued to surface, which finally culminated in the rebellion of seven kingdoms during the reign of Emperor Jing (156–141 BCE).[10] When the fight was over and order gradually restored, it was decided that the power and land of the kingdoms should be kept as small as possible, with administration controlled by

[9] Hulsewé (1985, 1986).

[10] Twitchett and Loewe (1986: 139–44).

the central government to avoid further confrontation. Thus the autonomy and prestige of the kingdoms were considerably reduced and their status became somewhat equivalent to that of a commandery or a county. By the time of the mid-Western Han, society was composed of the imperial house at the top of the pyramid, with the help of a bureaucracy that was responsible for the daily operation of the various levels of government. These bureaucrats were from all levels of society, as people of humble descent could rise up the ladder and work together with people of a prominent family background. In this respect, the social composition could be seen as rather heterogenic in the government.

As for the vast majority of people, most of them were small farmers who worked a piece of land. Professional craftsmen and merchants were fewer in comparison. Most of the families were probably the type of small nuclear family with a couple and their parents (usually the husband's) and children. Since the size of a family could change as the children grew up, got married, and established their own households. But depending on the social status and the financial situation, there might be times when there was a large extended family with married brothers living together with their parents and children.

One institution that had a certain impact on the social fabric was the system of the "rank" (*jue* 爵) invented by the Qin.[11] Originally the Qin devised a twenty-rank system as an incentive and to reward soldiers who fought gallantly and cut off heads of enemies in battles. The accumulation of ranks could allow the acquisition of certain benefits for the rank holder, such as obtaining an official position, enjoying the privilege of gaining more estate property, and exemption from corvée, or from being sold as a slave. Theoretically, a soldier who beheaded many enemies and collected a sufficient number of ranks could rise to the highest level, the twentieth rank, and become a "marquis." There was no doubt that such a system had a certain effect on the success of Qin, as the traditional aristocratic values loomed large behind this system, and common people (males) were able to ascend to a higher social status by climbing up the ranks ladder.

When the Han took over the Qin regime, this rank system was still in place. However, since there was considerably less warfare during the first seventy years, the earning of a rank through battles gradually became unrealistic. On the other hand, the government began to reward commoners with ranks on various occasions, to celebrate certain events and show the emperor's compassion toward his people. In time, however, the rank gradually lost its practical value and became an empty honorific title. By and large, therefore, the common people of Han, whether or not they had managed to collect certain ranks, were basically equal in terms of social status.

[11] Loewe (2006: 135 ff.).

On the other hand, we should also look at the social groupings that had developed over the years, based on family background, marriage alliances, and intellectual affiliation. Given the household and population statistics, and compared with the estimated number of officials in the country during the time of Emperor Yuan (48–33 BCE), it would be no exaggeration to say that the society was ruled by a small number of "bureaucrats." Whatever their family backgrounds might have been, once they were recruited into the government, they became privileged persons who might have more opportunities to have access to the social ladder and further their family fortune.

Besides these lower-middle echelon bureaucrats, in terms of social grouping, we can delineate several categories. The first is the imperial family and its relatives. As the Western Han emperors tended to marry the daughters of common families, the social origin of the imperial relatives was relatively broad, while in the Eastern Han, owing to the growing influence of Confucian ethics, emphasis on a comparable family background led to marriage choices favoring families with a similar social standing; thus the empresses were mostly chosen from prominent families. The growing power of the in-laws of imperial families became an important political force during the Eastern Han, and often caused disastrous conflicts at the court and contributed to the eventual downfall of the dynasty.

Below the imperial family, high officials were also making connections through marriage alliances with each other, and with local magnates who had gained wealth and fame through various means. In the Eastern Han, this growing power of prominent local clans also became an important social and political force and had a great impact on the fortune of the Han dynasty. In addition, an unusual group of players was the eunuchs and their relatives. Owing to their privileged position in the inner court, they were able to have the ear of the imperial family, thus gaining the opportunity to manipulate court politics. The Eastern Han politics was particularly affected with the influence and control of the eunuchs, and they were seen as comparable to the imperial in-laws in terms of eroding the health of the state.

Finally, a self-conscious group of Confucian scholar-officials, linked by their shared ideology, often banded together to try to "correct the wrongs" caused by the imperial in-laws and the prominent local magnates. Their efforts were often weak in comparison with the other two groups who held the real power and thus were able to persecute them easily. The interplay of these groups of people tended to take up a great many of the pages of the traditional written histories, as they were seen as being those who had the greatest impact on the political fate of the Han dynasty. In terms of their influence on the daily lives of the masses, in additional to the practical measures of social and economic policies as well as decisions of warfare that they might have helped to formulate in one way or another, their legacy was a permanent imprint on the collective memory of the people, a memory transmitted through literary texts and historical accounts passed down through the ages, first among the intellectuals, then trickling down through the literary elites, and finally arriving at the common people with anecdotes and legends about a distant past. Our interest, however, would be the practical measures that people experienced, including the laws that people had to abide by.

LAW AND SOCIAL LIFE

The rule of law was an invisible net that was cast over society. By virtue of the power of the state, people were obliged to follow the law in conducting their daily affairs. Despite the claim that the early Han regime, especially during the reigns of Emperors Wen and Jing, followed the policy of "letting the people rest" and abided by the "do nothing" philosophy of Huang-Lao黃老, i.e., the Daoist-Naturalist philosophy developed during the Warring States period represented by the teachings of Laozi, fused with certain practical political strategies derived from the Legalist philosophy but presented in the name of the Yellow Emperor,[12] the day-to-day operation of every level of government basically was conducted according to the laws and regulations that the Qin government had instituted. Recent archaeological discovery of Qin and early Han dynasty legal texts amply testify to this situation.[13] The household registration system that we shall discuss in the text that follows is one example of the embodiment of law in social life.

THE DEVELOPMENT OF HOUSEHOLD REGISTRATION

The *Records of the Grand Scribe* has a story about a miracle that involved King Yuan of the State of Song, dated to 530 BCE. In the story, King Yuan dreamt of a turtle that asked for his help because it was caught by the fisherman. When the king ordered to seek for the fisherman, the local magistrate simply ordered the officers to view the household register and map, and found that there were fifty-five fishing families by the water, and easily located the one who caught the turtle.[14] What interests us here is the matter-of-fact reference to the record of local fishermen's households. It seems that people, or at least the author, took it for granted that if one needed to find a person, one could simply refer to the local household registration at the county district office. We do not have to believe that such a detailed record already existed in the mid-sixth century BCE in the state of Song, but we may have less reason to reject the idea that when the story was written down by the author of this chapter of *Records of*

12 Yates (1997: 10–19).
13 Barbieri-Low and Yates (2015).
14 *SJ* 128: 3229–30.

the Grand Scribe, presumably in the first century BCE, similar household registration systems must have been a common practice, so that the author could use it to give an authentic flavor to the story. It is interesting to speculate how this system came about, and how it affected people's lives. What kind of a governing mindset was there behind such a system? And what could it tell us about the society as a place where people passed their days from generation to generation? These are fascinating questions that we need to address.

In fact, the household registration system probably began to be formulated as early as the early Spring and Autumn period, although solid evidence came only from the mid-Warring States period.[15] The rationale behind such measures was for the state to have a better control of the number of the people in a given state, and the area of farm land under cultivation, so as to establish a basis for taxation and military service. Given the practical physical conditions of this ancient society, that is, a lack of proper roads and means of transportation that made access to many places difficult, such an effort could not have been all-encompassing and thus required the constant attention of the government. An ambitious government, therefore, would most likely have to develop a way of managing its people and the cultivation of land in terms of numbers. Such a measure was the beginning of a bureaucratic system that was further developed during the Qin and Han Empires. Archaeological discovery of around 360,000 wooden slips, dated to the end of the Qin Empire, that belonged to the archive of county office of Qianling County (modern town of Liye 里耶), located at the remote mountain area of western Hunan Province, are extraordinary evidence of the extent of the bureaucratic work at a small county office.

HOUSEHOLD REGISTRATION AND FREEDOM OF MOVEMENT

After the overthrown of the Qin and establishment of the Han, many households were broken up, and properties and people were lost during the turmoil. In the year 201 BCE (6th year of Han), Emperor Liu Bang passed by the county of Quni 曲逆. He climbed up the city wall and saw that the houses in the city were quite large. He exclaimed: "What a magnificent county! I have travelled the country, only Luoyang and this city have the right to be mentioned [as great cities]." He then asked, "How many households does Quni have?" The answer: "During the time of the First Emperor of Qin there were more than 30,000 households. Later when war was widespread, many people escaped and tried to hide. At that time, there were about 5,000 households."[16] The situation continued for some years, as the *Shiji* records in the 12th year of Han (195 BCE), "the population in some of the large cities is dwindling,

[15] Yang Jiping (2007: 5); Yin (2012: 68–69).
[16] *SJ* 56: 2058.

and only about two or three out of ten households can be accounted for."[17] To account for the loss of the population, there could be several possible factors. First is the loss of population due to the casualties of war. Yet another factor was probably the destruction of cities and communities and the subsequent dispersion of the population. More importantly, however, should be the fact that people "escaped" from the control of the previous dynasty, the Qin, and were "hidden" in the countryside, thus freeing themselves from the obligations of taxes and corvée labor. Among these, there were imaginably a considerable proportion of slaves who took the opportunity to escape from their masters and regain their freedom. Thus even in the Qin period when the empire was still in power, laws regarding these "runaway people" were already part of the legal system, as the example below indicates. We must imagine that the early Han period was still a time when the road system was primitive and travel between one place and another involved considerable difficulty; thus it was not easy for the newly established government to exert effective control over the vast area outside of the larger cities and townships.[18]

In response to the situation, and acting as an incentive to secure the population as a basis for taxation, the Han government implemented a policy that allowed people without household registration to reregister and become legal residents and to be given land to cultivate according to their rank. This meant that, for example, a former slave who had run away from his or her master before the establishment of the Han could then become a free person in the new dynasty as long as he or she registered with the government office and obtained a new legal status. However, this chaotic situation must have made it difficult for some unfortunate people to start a new life. Early Han legal documents found at Zhangjiashan provide us with some vivid examples about the fate of some runaway slaves.[19]

According to one record, in the state of Chu, just before the conquest of Qin in 223 BCE, a female slave named Mei, who was approximately thirteen years old, escaped from her master, whose name was Dian. Twenty some years later, after the Han dynasty was established in 202 BCE, she did not manage to register at the county office, and was caught by Dian, who registered her as a slave. Then in the year 201 BCE Dian sold Mei to a person named Chuan for 16,000 coins. One month later, Mei escaped again, and, at a point of time unspecified in the document, was caught again by Chuan. Mei disputed her case and insisted that she was a free person and should not be treated as a slave. Finally in 196 BCE, when Mei was already forty years old, Chuan took the case to the Jiangling county magistrate. The county court official came to the

[17] *HS* 16: 527.

[18] See Wang Zijin (1994: 59–61).

[19] For the following account, See Zhangjiashan (2006: 92); Barbieri-Low and Yates (2015: 1184–91).

suggested verdict: either that Mei should be considered as a slave, receive the punishment of *ching* (黥 tattooed on the face), and be returned to Chuan, or that she should be set free as a commoner. Since the record does not show the final verdict, we do not know the end of this extraordinary story and the fate of Mei. But similar cases indicate that it was indeed possible that once a person underwent independent registration as a free commoner in the new dynasty, his or her former status as a slave could be considered as eliminated.[20] In the case of Mei, even if she did not register, it was also possible that she could be considered free, as one of the suggested verdicts in the document indicated.

While slaves were bound to the master's household, ordinary people's freedom of movement was also an issue that the state was very concerned about. One could not move one's household from one place to another without reporting to the appropriate officials and undergoing proper registration. During the Qin and early Han periods, and presumably in later periods too, household registration had to be carried out by the local officials every year and recorded in duplicate copies; one copy was to be sent to the county office, and the other was kept at the district office. One statute from Zhangjiashan stipulates that officers who failed to carry out the registration properly would be punished with heavy fines, which was an indication of the serious determination of the government to have a tight control over the population in every district.[21] An interesting example regarding the movement of households was found on a slip from the corpus of Qin legal texts found at Liye 里耶, dated the twenty-sixth year of the First Emperor of Qin (221 BCE):

> [Recto] In the 26th year, 5th month, 20th day (*gengzi*) [of king Zheng, 221 BCE], Zhun of Qiling District [of Qianling County] humbly reports: Jia, the Bailiff of Du District, stated: "He of Zhu Ward, … and 17 households who had moved to Du District, they all did not transfer registrations concerning their ages." The ordinance states: "[If you] Move, report." We have now investigated the records of He and those who moved, and thereby give notice to the Du District: Qiling District does not possess the relevant records, and thus is not able to confirm the age of these people … We ask [the Probationary Assistant of Qiangling County] to order the Du District to inquire about the age of He and others. End of Report.[22]

Here we see a realistic picture of the daily operation of county and district offices: officers and clerks busying themselves with the copying, dispatching, and receiving of documents between offices, and in the midst of these, an office was unable to produce records that were supposed to be there. It is interesting to speculate whether this was due to negligence or to mismanagement.

20 Zhangjiashan (2006: 94–95); Barbieri-Low and Yates (2015: 1216–21).
21 Zhangjiashan (2006: 54); Li and Zhao (2011: 471).
22 Li and Zhao (2011: 61–62).

It might simply have been because there was no record to begin with. As for the seventeen households that moved to a new district, the fact that none of them had the necessary documents for household registration makes one suspect that there might be some hidden motives behind their move. As noted earlier, when a person changed his or her residence, it was necessary to report to the local office to change the household registration, and failing to do so ran the risk of incurring fines. We do not know whether these seventeen households were really people from Qiling District, or another place, or simply people who somehow evaded household registration, which should not be surprising considering the time was exactly the final year of the Qin conquest of the entire country, and one year after Qin had conquered the State of Chu, where the Qianling County was located. The whole incident reveals the general situation regarding the freedom, or lack thereof, of people to move about in the state.

When people needed to travel for reasons beyond agricultural activities, there were various regulations to be followed, especially regarding the passing of certain mountain passes and river ports. These were not necessarily state borders, but controlled passages from one area to the next. The Hangu Pass, for example, controlled the passage from the Central Plain area to the Wei River basin, the area where the capital Chang'an was located. Passing through these passes would necessitate having the proper documents, especially if the person carried precious golden and metal objects or horses. A detailed record of these had to be preserved each time when a passage was made. Of course people who were involved in such traveling were mostly not farmers, but rather merchants or persons connected to the government in various capacities. The tight control of the passes indicates a state policy that considered the movement of people and wealth within and beyond the state borders a serious matter that needed to be addressed. It was suggested that the basic purpose of these internal passes was for the control of the newly established vassal kingdoms in the empire and thus the security of the area surrounding the capital; it could also be understood as a means of maintaining social stability by monitoring the possible movements of rebellious local forces and bandits.[23]

For people who lived in a farming village, the village gate acted as a border, and passing through the gate was also regulated by a designated officer who carried the key to the gate and closed the gate according to the rules. When the gate was closed for whatever reason, one could travel through the gate only with the proper documents. Of course, in emergency situations such as flooding, fire, or pursuing thieves, free passage would be granted. An extremely severe measure was the stipulation that people in the village should take note of the movements of their neighbors so as to detect if they had carried out a

[23] Lai (2012: 365–408).

burglary or run away from the village.[24] Whether or not this could be practically implemented, the mentality behind the law was a hard fact indicating that the will of the state to control had extended to the daily lives of the ordinary farmers.

In general, the household registration system must have had a rather wide-ranging impact and become ingrained in the social life of the Han people, so much so that only one generation after the establishment of the Han rule, people began to imagine a netherworld with a similar registration system. That is to say, when a person died, he or she needed to present a document to the underworld bureaucracy to announce his or her arrival and make a registration as a newly arrived resident. The registration consisted of not only the name and age of the deceased, but also the property that he or she had brought with him or her in the form of funerary equipment. For example, a tomb inventory dated to 177 BCE has the following statement: "In the fourth year[of Emperor Wen], the ninth month, day of *xinhai* 辛亥, the Bailiff of Five (*wu-fu* 五夫) of Ping-li hamlet, Zhang Yan dares to tell the Lord of the Underground: the garments and objects of Yan, each are dispatched according to the laws and ordinances."[25] Another funerary text is addressed to the "Assistant Magistrate of the Underground": "On the thirteenth year [168 BCE], the fifth month, day of *gengchen* 庚辰, the Assistant Magistrate of Jiangling dares to tell the Assistant Magistrate of the Underground that the Bailiff of Five of Shiyang, by the name of Sui Shaoyan, and the slave Liang and others, a total of twenty-eight persons, ... and four riding-horses, can be used to serve. (I) hereby dare to report to the Lord."[26] The language and terminology used in such funerary texts was no different from the official documents that people employed for ordinary bureaucratic records. Over time, this imagined underworld was to look very much similar to the world of the living, in particular with respect to its bureaucratic nature. The aspects most frequently touched on in these texts are certain functions of the underground bureaucracy such as the collection of taxes, the conscription of corvée, and the businesses of the underground local officials such as reporting about the coming of new residents, that is, the newly dead.[27]

CONTROL OF PROPERTY

The state control of the property of the common people was also amply demonstrated by the statutes that governed the farm land, the most important

[24] Zhangjiashan (2006: 51).
[25] Poo (1998: 168).
[26] Poo (1998: 168); Zhang and Bai (2006: 285).
[27] Poo (1998: 168).

asset of the farmers. Thus stated one statute in the legal documents found at Zhangjiashan:

> As for the ordinary people's household registers of their homesteads and grounds, the detailed age registers, the land registers indicating neighboring field, the unified registers of agricultural fields, and the registers of their agricultural field taxes, carefully make copies and forward these up to the County Court, and in every case, contain them in a bamboo chest or a wooden coffer, bound shut with cords, and seal [the chest or coffer] using the seal of the Magistrate, the Assistant Magistrate, or the Bailiff of the Office. Place them by themselves as a document archive and seal the door of the archive … For those who do not obey the statutes, fine four *liang* of gold each."[28]

Obviously all these records were required for the purpose of taxation. The measures taken to protect the records indicate that they were regarded as most important official documents. The legal texts so far found in Qin and early Han have amply demonstrated that numerous laws and ordinances were promulgated so that the state had control not only of the population numbers and their land, houses, and properties, but also of the transmission of the properties and various economic or commercial activities, as well as different obligations to the state, such as public labor or military service.

Take, for example, the issue of family property within a household. It is the nature of a family that children grow up, their parents' age, and family property is divided among the children. According to a statute found at Zhangjiashan, when a parent wishes to make a will to bequeath his property, including farmland, house, slaves, and other valuables, the district bailiff (*xiangbu sefu* 鄉部嗇夫) should personally attend the announcement, make a record of the will that is to be divided into three parts, and register it on the household registration at the district office. Later, when and if disputes arise, the record should be presented as evidence for any allegation. If no record is presented, there will be no case. When a child obtains a share of the land and property according to the will and yet lacks household registration, the child should be allowed to register, in the eighth month of the year. If the bailiff makes it difficult for people and does not make a will for the applicant, he shall be fined one *liang* of gold.[29] This example makes it clear that the power of the state, as represented by the bailiff or other local officials, was the final arbiter and authority of family affairs, especially regarding issues of property.

For other activities concerning family property, such as the division among family members, selling or buying land and houses, as well as marriage and

[28] Zhangjiashan (2006: 54), "Statutes on Households." Translation follows Barbieri-Low and Yates (2015: 799).

[29] Zhangjiashan (2006: 54); Barbieri-Low and Yates (2015: 801).

divorce, the government was also the overseeing authority, as no transaction could take place without the approval of the government office.

The reason all these legal aspects of the family property could be monitored by the state was that there was the household registration and annual report, with the names and ages of the members and a listing of the family properties, including immovable estates, houses, and all movable valuables. The state, through the local offices such as the county bailiff, had therefore gained the ability to "know how rich or poor the people were, and tax them accordingly."[30]

MARRIAGE, FAMILY, AND GENDER RELATIONS

When marriage was entered into between people of comparable social status, e.g., when both the husband and the wife were commoners, the laws that regulated marriage basically had to do with issues concerning family disputes of property, adultery, and divorce. It was true that in the patriarchal system, the wife did not enjoy equal rights with the husband, and this is clearly represented by the conditions for divorce. Although so far direct evidence has not yet been discovered, the tradition preserved in the Confucian canons and the historical records indicates that the "seven criteria for divorcing a wife (*qichu* 七出)," i.e., lack of filial pieties toward the parents, not producing an heir, adultery, jealousy, severe sickness, gossiping, and stealing, were more or less the social norm during the Han period, and actual examples can also be found.[31] We can see that these causes include major types of problems that were most likely to occur in a family. However, despite these and some other rather prejudiced causes for a husband to divorce a wife, a wife could also file for divorce under certain conditions, such as the husband displaying wanton behavior, being seriously ill, or mired in poverty. They were allowed to ask for a divorce, and could remarry at a later date. This means that the Han law did not forbid these initiatives from the wife, and thus they were legal acts.[32] As for adultery, statutes found at Zhangjiashan indicate that it was a capital offense for the act to occur between siblings, and if it was not, the punishment for both parties was hard labor as a wall-builder for men and rice-pounder for women.[33]

A special phenomenon worth noticing was the fact that, according to the Zhangjiashan legal text, a man (free person) was forbidden to marry a woman who ran away from her husband or, if she was a slave, from her master. Once found guilty, no matter whether the man knew about the premarital status of the woman or not, the punishment was "tattooing-face" and enslavement as

30 *HHS* 28: 3625.
31 Ch'ü (1972: 37–42).
32 Liu (1980: 24); Peng (2010: 195–97).
33 Zhangjiashan (2006: 34); Barbieri-Low and Yates (2015: 617).

civil slave laborer for all parties involved: the man, the woman, and the matchmaker.[34] The fact that such a situation, that is, women with a previous "history" who tried to find a new life in a new society, was a reason for the state to stipulate laws to deal with it accordingly indicates that the issue of "escaped personnel" was a serious problem at the time. Apparently those who ran away from their masters included both men and women. Thus a special category, the "Statutes of Abscondance (*wanglu* 亡律)," was stipulated in the early Han legal system represented by the Zhangjiashan legal documents.[35] The phenomenon must already have been a very common problem even during the Qin period, so much so that the divination texts such as the *Daybook* would often mention whether a date was auspicious for capturing a runaway slave or wife.[36]

One curious statute states that "When an ordinary person [woman] is made the wife of a slave and has a child, the child is given to the slave's master. When a female slave engages in illicit intercourse, or becomes the wife of a slave of another family, and has a child, the child is given to the master of the slave woman. In every case, [the child] is made a male or female slave."[37] Apparently social status distinction is at work here, as a man of lower status – a slave – should suffer the death penalty if he tries to marry his superior – i.e., women who belong to the social status of his master. Or if the male slave is to marry a freedman, his child would still be a slave, which means that the status of the male slave could lower the status of the freedman so that their child becomes a slave and not a freedman. On the other hand, we also notice that "[w]hen a male slave engages in illicit intercourse with a [woman who is a] freedman, and there is a child [from the union], the child is made a freedman."[38] Here since the male slave did not formally marry the [female] freedman, their child could inherit the mother's status and be a freedman. Thus whether there is a formal marriage makes an important legal difference regarding the status of the children. Nevertheless, the fact that it was possible that a woman of freedman status could marry a male slave indicates that even with difference of social status, women could choose to marry below their status and be permitted to do so, which is a sign of a certain autonomy that women possessed. Since it is a reasonable assumption that the laws were not promulgated without practical need, these various seemingly rare cases may actually not have been very uncommon at the time.

In general, it has been observed that, as time passed, the gender relationship between husband and wife became even more unequal, that is, women

34 Zhangjiashan (2006: 31, 92, 94).

35 See Barbieri-Low and Yates (2015: 574–87).

36 For the *Daybook*, see Poo (1998, chapter 4); Harper and Kalinowski (2017).

37 Zhangjiashan (2006: 34); Barbieri-Low and Yates (2015: 617).

38 Zhangjiashan (2006: 34); Barbieri-Low and Yates (2015: 617). For "freedman," see Barbieri-Low and Yates (2015: 609–12). Also see Yates (2014) on the status of slaves in the Qin-Han transition.

faced more restrictions in their marriage. In the Western Han, a famous scholar and high official, and the fourteenth generation grandson of Confucius, Kong Guang (孔光 c. 65–5 BCE), once made the comment that "the way of husband and wife is such that when there is a mutually agreed obligation, they might be joined; when there is no mutually agreed obligation, then they should be divorced."[39] This statement sounds quite liberal in that the obligation between husband and wife was mutual and equal. Yet this might only have been Kong Guang's personal opinion. Some years later, the famous Eastern Han female scholar Ban Zhao (班昭 c. 45–117 CE) made a very different statement in her *Commandments for Women* (*nüjie* 女誡): "The husband has the obligation to marry again [if his wife is deceased], the wife has no right to marry again [if her husband died]. Therefore the husband is heaven [to the wife]. One could not escape from heaven, likewise the husband could not be divorced."[40] Here we see a change from Kong Guang's more liberal mutual consent to Ban Zhao's one-sided emphasis on the rights of the husband. Of course Ban Zhao's words could also have represented her own opinion, yet the fact that the *Commandments for Women* later became the epitome of a thoroughly Confucianized ideological statement of female submission in marriage and family relationship indicates the changing of intellectual atmosphere from a more relaxed Western Han to a more restricted and rigid Eastern Han. Such a change affected not only gender relations but also social ethics.[41] The rise of Confucian learning among the ruling elite was no doubt one of the causes that led to this change. Certainly, Ban Zhao herself was from a scholarly family; her father Ban Biao and her brother Ban Gu were all great scholars, the latter being the author of the *History of Han*, to which she also contributed; and she herself enjoyed the privilege of being a favorite literary talent at Emperor He's court, even to the extent of becoming the teacher and advisor of the empress and imperial concubines. This did not seem to have encouraged her to develop a more assertive attitude toward uplifting women's status vis-à-vis that of men. One can only say that she seemed to have been totally convinced by the Confucian ethics that she received from her education.[42] Numerous examples can be found demonstrating the ever more rigid social ethics and gender relations, resulting in the overwhelming moral dogma emphasizing the utmost important distinction between the sexes in every social and familial context. On the other hand, we should also be aware of the possibility that such an impression of a rigid distinction between the sexes only represented the Ru-scholars, who, by promoting Confucian virtues, could gain for themselves a passage to fame and power.

[39] *HS* 81: 3355.
[40] *HHS* 84: 2790.
[41] Raphals (1998: 239).
[42] For Ban Zhao, see Swann (1932).

AGRICULTURAL LAWS

As the majority of the population were farmers, it was not surprising that a government would take an active role in promoting agricultural production for the obvious reason of increasing the wealth and power of the state. It was less common, especially among ancient societies, for a government to institute laws to guide farming activities. There was, for example, a "Statutes of Agriculture" that existed at least from the Qin period and continued in the Han, which set out to regulate how farmers and local officials alike should act in various matters related to agricultural production. One outstanding statute says:

> When there is timely rain and the ears of grain begin to shoot, [the overseer] should report in writing about the size of the area that received rain and shooting grain, plus the size of the area that had been developed but not planted. When it rained after the shooting of the plant, there should also be reports of the amount of rain and the area of the fields which received rain. When droughts, storms, flooding, locusts, or other types of pestilence attack and damage the plants, the size of the damaged area should also be reported. For nearby counties, the report should be delivered by an express messenger. For distant counties, the report should be delivered via a post station, and should arrive before the end of the Eighth Month.[43]

No matter how idealistic this may sound, such meticulous attention being paid not just to the end result of production but also to the process of farming activities demonstrates a rather sophisticated, if not obsessive, type of management strategy. Presumably, information about the rainfall, whether it was timely, and the range of pestilence damage were all important for an accurate assessment of the productivity of the fields. On the other hand, the maintenance of the fields was also a concern, and detailed regulations concerning how to construct the field division banks and the repairs of country roads, bridges, and dikes were also instituted by law and entrusted to the care of the village bailiff and local officials.[44]

Students of early China have long been familiar with the "Monthly Ordinances (*yueling* 月令)" preserved in the *Master Lü's Spring and Autumn Annals* (*Lüshi chunqiu* 吕氏春秋), a collection of essays edited by Lü Buwei 吕不韋, the prime minister and advisor of the First Emperor of Qin. According to the Monthly Ordinances, which can also be found in the *Book of Rites* and *Huainanzi* (淮南子), there were fixed duties to be carried out every month of the year according to the movement of the heavenly bodies and the

[43] Shuihudi (1990: 19). Translation slightly different from Hulsewé (1985: 21).
[44] Zhangjiashan (2006: 42).

corresponding weather patterns, and among these were agricultural activities. This was understood to be an ideal construction of correct actions for various sectors (agricultural, military, and bureaucratic) of society according to the theories of *yinyang* and Five Phases that had been circulating in the intellectual world since the Warring States period. However, a fragmented version found in both the Qin and the early Han versions of the "Statutes of Agriculture" demonstrates that the seemingly ideal construction could have actually been implemented in the Qin and Han society. Thus says the Qin text:

> In the second month of spring one should not venture to cut timber in the forests or block water courses. Except in the months of summer one should not venture to burn weeds to make ashes, to collect [indigo], young animals, eggs or fledglings. One should not poison fish or tortoises or arrange pitfalls and nets. By the seventh month these prohibitions are lifted. Only when someone has unfortunately died and one fells wood for the inner and outer coffins, this is not done according to the seasons. In settlements close to corrals and other forbidden parks, in the season of young animals one should not venture to take dogs to go hunting. When dogs of the common people enter forbidden parks without pursuing and catching animals, one should not venture to kill them; those which pursue as well as catch animals are to be killed. Dogs killed by the wardens are to be completely handed over to the authorities; of those that are killed in other forbidden parks the flesh may be eaten, but the skin is to be handed over.[45]

A vivid description of the various daily activities of people in the countryside, the statute quoted here is aimed at controlling not only agricultural production, but also the use of other land resources. Although a reading of the "Monthly Ordinances" in the *Lüshi chunqiu* and *Book of Rites* seems to suggest that it was a philosophical treatise that fused the theories of *yinyang* and Five Phases with other cosmological ideas, when it is seen in the context of the "Statutes of Agriculture," it reveals itself as a thoroughly rational and meticulous law of agricultural management. In addition, copy of an imperial edict issued in the year 5 CE found at the western border garrison of Dunhuang contains similar ordinances,[46] which implies that the "Monthly Ordinances," or at least a partial and practical version of it, was instituted and followed during the Han dynasty.

[45] Shuihudi (1990: 20). Translation follows Hulsewé (1985: 22). For similar texts, see Zhangjiashan (2006: 42–43).

[46] Li and Zhao (2011:186–209).

ACTIVITIES OUTSIDE OF THE FARMING CONTEXT

Outside the immediate circle of individual household and farming community, there were various laws that regulated an economic and social entity that was larger than the farm villages, laws that regulate the movement of goods and means of exchange, for example. It was during the Warring States period that commercial activities began to push for social change, from the more or less self-sufficient agricultural economy toward, albeit gradually, to a society wherein exchange of manufactured goods not produced by a local farming community became normal or even indispensable. Laws that regulated the use of copper coins, for example, were stipulated to ensure the stable transaction of commercial activities. The prevailing problem with the use of copper money was manifold. Conceivably, given the level of technology in minting coins, and the difficulty in maintaining consistent quality, there were bound to be numerous cases in which disputes would rise about the quality and authenticity of coins. Thus even in the Qin period, it was stipulated in the "Statutes on Finance" that the government office should accept good as well as bad coins, and that common people should use the coins to do business without distinguishing the qualities of the coins.[47] Although the state reserved the right to mint coins, it was apparently not necessarily observed by people in the wider countryside. As the technology of minting was primitive and presumably not difficult to learn, the attraction of making a great deal of money by making counterfeit coins with inexpensive metals was always there. The situation must have been quite serious during the early years of Han when the economy was in disarray and social order was being restored only slowly. According to the Zhangjiashan text, those who were caught producing counterfeit money could be sentenced to capital punishment. There were also laws, though not including capital punishment, against melting coins to make tools rather than using them as a means of exchange, which indicates that, besides the scarcity of copper, the value of coins was not stable, and the use of money in commercial activities not yet a firmly established custom.[48]

Besides minting coins, the manufacturing of salt and iron, two essential materials for the livelihood of any community, as another example, were such important and lucrative industries that the government was also trying to take control, to avoid the fluctuation of prices and supply driven by profit-seeking merchants, and less extensive profit fell into the hands of the private sector. The Qin government initiated state monopoly of the production and sale of salt and iron, but it was abandoned by the early Han. Laws found at Zhangjiashan were quite lenient toward people who produced salt and mined iron and other

47 Shuihudi (1990: 35); Barbieri-Low and Yates (2015: 911–27).

48 Zhangjiashan (2006: 35).

metals privately. The tax for salt was one-sixth, and iron was one-fifth, of the market value of the material.[49] By the mid-Western Han, during the reign of Emperor Wu, the need to supplement the government treasury and to cover the cost of incessant warfare with the Xiongnu, the nomadic empire that was the archenemy of the sedentary Han, however, gave rise to the policy of a government monopoly of the production of salt and iron, which, although implemented from 119 BCE, was constantly at the center of policy debate at court. The court debate on salt and iron at the time of Emperor Zhao (81 BCE) was the culmination of the debate between the pro-government monopoly party and the anti-monopoly party. The pro-monopoly side won in the end as the state control of salt and iron continued for another hundred years. It was only from the Eastern Han that government agencies began to assume the role of inspection and tax collection, while the right to produce salt and iron was returned to the private sector.

Besides salt and iron, of course, the state was also concerned with issues that bore economic implications. A number of laws that regulated commercial activities, though the records we have are certainly incomplete, could demonstrate just how meticulous the governmental supervision could be in the daily lives of those who wished to do some small business:

> For a case of trading or selling cloth whose breadth is not a full two *chi*-feet and two *cun* (c. 50 cm):[50] confiscate it. For one who is able to arrest or denounce [a person engaged in such trade]: give it (viz., the cloth) to him. For fine or rough cloth made from kudzu, plain white-silk banners, deep-purple selvage, vermillion silk strips, woven woolen fabric, fine, white ramie cloth, crepe silk, and bamboo-fiber cloth, no dot apply this statute.
>
> Marketplace traders hiding and not self-reporting [their liability for the market] tax: hold them liable for the tax that they have hidden as illicit profit and consider them to be robbers. Confiscate for the government what they have traded or sold, as well as the cash [they are using for] trade, and remove their market stalls from them. For the Chief of the Market Lane and the persons in the group of five who do not denounce them: fine one *jin* (approx. 248 g) of gold each. For the Bailiff [of the Office] and the official in charge who do not catch them: fine two *liang* (approx. 31 g) of gold each.[51]

Such statutes reveal how much and how detailed the government wanted to control people's economic activities, and how much pressure the law also put on the different levels of officials in charge of the market. Obviously here we

[49] Zhangjiashan (2006: 68); Barbieri-Low and Yates (2015: 927–29).

[50] During the Western Han, one *chi*-foot equals 23.1 centimeters. Two *chi* and two *cun* equals about 50.8 centimeters. See Loewe (1967: 161).

[51] Zhangjiashan (2006: 44–45); translation in Barbieri-Low and Yates (2015: 723).

are dealing with a sales tax that ordinary farmers probably would not have to pay, unless they tried to sell their agricultural byproducts, possibly all sorts of cloth and other artifacts, at the local market.

One of the most common problems in a community would be the need to sustain social security and protect the livelihood of the people. This is where the state was able to demonstrate its power and legitimacy by providing the people with protection. As witnessed by the Zhangjiashan legal texts, laws dealing with the apprehending and convicting of criminals were promulgated, with often very detailed specification of particular crimes or wrongdoings. There were statutes that detailed the punishment for criminal cases such as armed rebellion and killing of officials, robbery, killing or injuring common people, or cases involving theft in many different situations. One prominent feature shared by these statutes was the principle of collateral responsibility. That is to say, in any situation of criminal cases, people who were voluntarily or involuntarily involved and knew about the cases bore responsibility to report the case. Failing to report could result in particularly harsh punishment. At a time when communication was not easy and the state surveillance or policing would not have been comprehensive, this principle of collateral responsibility was probably an effective means to deter wrongdoing. It was, of course, also a means to an end that could be abused in other areas. The principle of *zu* (族), i.e., execution of entire extended clan members, usually reserved for treason, was just one extreme form of punishment for people who dared not observe such collateral responsibility that, from our modern viewpoint, was certainly prone to being misused in persecuting the innocent and creating great injustice.

THE IMPACT OF LAW ON DAILY LIFE

All the laws discussed in the preceding text and certainly many more we have not explored formed a net that was cast over the lives of people and regulated their behavior. The detailed stipulations of some of the laws reveal the severe legal mentality behind the construction of the laws, which in turn indicate the degree to which people's lives were subject to the scrutiny of the state. The meticulously constructed legal documents we see in the foregoing are the product of a broad bureaucratic and legal mentality that was the crystallization of a long development of political discourses over the ways to organize and to control the people, in order to achieve a more efficient and powerful state.

To demonstrate how deeply the lives of the people were affected by the legal system, we only need to look at the funerary texts found in the tombs of both the Western and Eastern Han periods. As we shall discuss in Chapter 10, a netherworld that imitated the world of the living, at least in those aspects of a bureaucratic system, had been conceived in people's minds as early as the early Western Han. Funerary texts from the reign of Emperor Wen already talked about a netherworld that had a household registration system and a large netherworld bureaucracy managed by a host of officials of different ranks. Although such a netherworld bureaucracy should be seen as the creation of the collective imagination, it strongly demonstrates that this collective imagination had already been deeply affected by the worldly bureaucracy that people had to live with daily, so much so that they could not imagine a world after death without the existence of a ubiquitous bureaucracy. One of the most commonly used phrases in the exorcistic texts often found in the Eastern Han tombs (and the subsequent eras, in Daoist texts in particular) is "Quickly, quickly, [carry out the order] according to the laws and statutes" (*jiji ru lüling* 急急如律令), which was actually adopted from official documents. Thus these texts were imagined as having the same legal effects as earthly laws that would command the immediate action of the underworld officials.

FOUR

COUNTRY LIFE

The backbone of Han society, like that of most premodern societies, was the farmer, whose work provided the basis for the sustenance of society.[1] Without a smooth operation from production to consumption, from the field in the countryside to the household in the city, society would have fallen into disarray. Most of the rulers, or their administrators, therefore, took the farmers' contribution to society seriously. For example, the emperors would symbolically perform the spring rite of ploughing of the land to give an auspicious start to the year of agricultural work.[2] Yet, of course, the Han agricultural system was built on more than a millennium of previous development that combined the knowledge of weather patterns, soil composition, farming tools, irrigation systems, and, importantly, the nature of plants. When all this knowledge could be put to use, and given a reasonable state policy regarding taxation, a comfortable life could be envisaged for the farmer. The reality, of course, was not always ideal, as disasters of all sorts, be they natural or manmade, would often strike farming communities and create havoc. This chapter aims to discuss those factors, benevolent or malicious, that affected the lives of the farmers. That is to say, we will not be talking about the "daily life" of a farmer – what kind of chores he or she did throughout the day, what he or she had for lunch or dinner, or what deities he or she worshipped – but the kind of factors

1 Hsu (1980).
2 *HS* 4: 117.

that formed his or her life patterns, conditioned his or her life experience, and eventually nurtured and informed his or her outlook on life.

GEOGRAPHIC CHARACTERISTICS OF AN AGRICULTURAL ECONOMY

Studies on historical climate changes indicate that the period from around 800 BCE to 200 CE was the last period of the warm weather after the Holocene ice age in northern China. The average temperature around the Yellow River basin was 1–2 degrees C higher than it is today. The consequence of this warm weather pattern was that vegetation grew abundantly, and various plants and crops such as rice, bamboo, and many fruit trees, which later were able to grow only in the south, flourished in the Central Plain area, the heartland of Han agriculture. Rainfall was also more frequent then than it is today, which ensured an abundant water supply. Numerous medium-sized rivers, their tributaries, lakes, and ponds were connected by canals, so that irrigation was relatively easy for farming communities (Fig. 6). This favorable climatic background was a major factor influencing the generally prosperous agricultural development during the Han dynasty.

As we have seen in Chapter 1, the entire area covering the Wei River valley where the state of Qin flourished, and the mid-lower Yellow River valley, or the Central Plain, was, from the Neolithic period, the cradle of agricultural activity, where some of the most important crops that nourished numerous generations were cultivated. Crops mentioned in the classic texts, in particular the *Book of Poetry*, *Master Lü's Spring and Autumn Annals*, and the *Rites of Zhou*, include millet, sorghum, barley, flax, soybean, wheat, and rice. These major crops were supplemented by a number of vegetables, melons, and other fruit that farmers in the Han and later eras continued to cultivate.

To the far east, where the Yellow River met the ocean, was the power base of the old Kingdom of Qi and modern Shandong, known for its abundant resources from the ocean, e.g., salt and seafood. People also engaged in sericulture, and growing hemp for cloth-making, both intended for commercial markets and domestic consumption.

In the northwestern part of the empire, the present-day provinces of Gansu, Shaanxi, Inner Mongolia, and northwest Shanxi and northern Hebei, the ecological environment was more suitable for a pastoral economy, and husbandry was the most important economic activity. Horses, cattle, and sheep/goats were the main livestock for the people who lived in an area that had close contact with the nomadic people in the vast steppes stretching from Mongolia to inner Asia.

According to the *Records of the Grand Scribe*, early in the Han dynasty, one certainly enterprising Qiao Yao, following the imperial policy of opening the border region, took the opportunity to accumulate in his possession "a

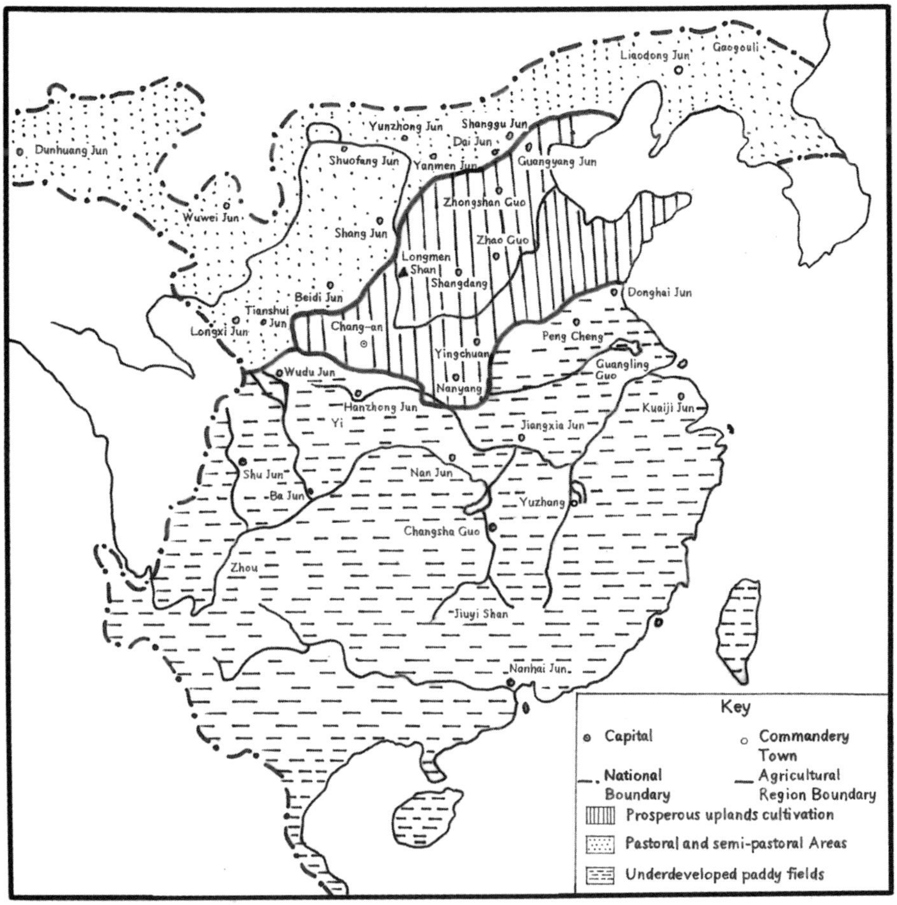

6. Cultivation area in the Former Han dynasty. After Yan Wanying 閻萬英, "Xihan Shiqi Woguo de Nongye Quyu Gaimao 西漢時期我國的農業區域概," *Nongye kaogu* 農業考古 2(1981): 31

thousand horses, double that number of cattle, ten thousand sheep, and tens of thousands of bushels of grain."[3] Regardless of the accuracy of the numbers offered in the source, Qiao Yao's case was certainly not an isolated one. The enrichment in the borderland was thus one of the important factors that contributed to the establishment of a strong military defense, against the nomadic peoples such as Xiongnu匈奴, who used to roam freely in an area where the border was not a meaningful concept for either side.[4]

This, of course, does not mean that no crops were planted in the borderland. In fact, from the early Western Han, the policy of emigration was carried out, as large numbers of people were transported to the northwestern frontier to set up colonies. This was both to solve the problem of refugees fleeing natural

3 *SJ* 129: 3280.
4 Barfield (1989); Di Cosmo (2002).

disasters and also to secure the border defense line by increasing the population and supplies. Whether the numbers given in our sources, such as "seven hundred thousand" in the north[5] and "six hundred thousand" at the western border,[6] were accurate or not, there should be no doubt that the policy greatly changed the natural as well as the human landscape of northwestern China.

As can be imagined, in the northwestern borderland, where the soil was dry and the rainfall was limited, the lives of the farmers could be very difficult. A number of records from the fortress of Dunhuang indicate that dry and cold weather made agricultural activities very difficult, so that the local government needed to take certain measures to help the people. An executive order issued in the name of the deputy governor of Dunhuang and dated 37 BCE bears the following words:

> Yuan, the Senior Secretary of Dunhuang used his private seal to execute the official business of the Governor, and the Assistant to the Governor dared to announce to the officials and soldiers and the three command posts of the Southern Fortress, the county, and the Commandery Storage, commanding that: "The land of Dunhuang and Jiuquan 酒泉 is cold and there is no rainfall, which kills [the crops] in the fields before they ripen. Now let the wheat with thick husks, that can be used as food, be loaned [to the solders]..."[7]

The command referred to the cold and dry weather in a matter-of-fact way, which did not mention any specific severe drought. Thus we can assume such relief measures were probably often issued by the government, even without the seal of a governor.

For the area to the south of the Yellow River, in general the mid-lower Yangtze River valley, the location of the states of Chu, Wu, and Yue [modern Anhui, Jiangsu, southern Henan, Zhejiang, Sichuan, Hubei, Hunan, Guangdong], the terrain was mostly flat and dotted with hills, waterways, lakes, and swamps. Here, the cultivation of rice was an ancient tradition, and people relied on fishing much more than on husbandry, in comparison with the Central Plain area. This vast area was sparsely populated in the Han period, and life was relatively easy, since food sources were plentiful. According to the only two records of population census of the Han period, one in the year 2 CE, another in the year 140 CE, the population of the area south of the Yangtze River increased from about 6.3 million to 10.88 million. The percentage of the population of this area, in relation to the entire population of the Han Empire, increased from 10.94 percent to 22.72 percent.[8] Even if the recorded numbers need to be read with caution, a notable increase of population in this area can be confirmed.

5 *HS* 4a: 1162.
6 *HS* 4a: 1173.
7 Hu and Zhang (2001: 71).
8 Liang (2008: 52).

This, in turn, indicates a corresponding increase in agricultural productivity, so that the increased population could be supported. In the Commandery of Danyang 丹陽 (roughly present-day Southern Jiangsu / Northern Zhejiang / Eastern Anhui Provinces) for example, 50,000 refugees were settled in the Commandery over three years, from 30 to 32 CE, which indicates that the local food supply was sufficient, even in the face of this sudden increase in population.[9] Of course, this one example might not be representative of the entire country, and time and again imperial edicts announced various measures to provide relief for people who were struck by famines due to drought or flood; yet the fact that the government was able to open storages and distribute grain to the needy indicates a healthy reserve of agricultural production. In times of need, areas such as Danyang were able to provide surplus grain to those places where famine had struck.

AGRICULTURAL CYCLE

In order for a traditional agricultural society to operate smoothly, there has to be a rhythm that follows the changing seasons to ensure crops can be planted and harvested at the proper time, so that other supplementary activities can be organized around the major farm duties. Recognizing that farmers in different environments would have planned their activities somewhat differently, it suffices here to give a general description of the livelihood of the farmers at an estate in the Central Plain area in the Eastern Han period. This is the *Monthly Ordinances of the Four [types of] People* by Cui Shi (c. 103–170 CE),[10] a famous scholar-official who had some hands-on experience in managing his estate, but was also known for his critical view of contemporary politics. In this work he listed various activities that should be carried out during the course of the year, beginning with the First Month. Unlike the Roman author Columella (c. 4–70 CE), who wrote an extremely detailed account of agricultural technology that could be matched only by the work of Jia Sixie (c. mid-sixth century CE), the *Essential Techniques for the Common People* (*Qimin yaoshu*),[11] Cui Shi did not write a technical handbook, but an outline of all the important activities pertaining to a farm estate, including the dates to perform various sacrificial rituals for deities and ancestors; the education of youngsters; the proper date for a wedding; weaving; household maintenance; mending farm equipment; repairing irrigation canals; and even the production of various preservatives, sauces, and alcoholic beverages for consumption in the household. These were organized around the main agricultural activities of the farm: planting crops, sowing seeds for various vegetables at the appropriate

[9] *HHS* 21:756.
[10] Shi (1965).
[11] Shi (1957).

time, planting and transplanting trees, and, not least of all, the production of silk. Through this account, we are given a holistic picture of the livelihood of the farmers, that is, the agricultural production per se was only one part of a complicated juggling of various tasks throughout the year in a manor in order to have a sustainable existence.[12] Of course, being an intellectual, Cui Shi was heavily influenced by the prevailing ideology of the *yin–yang* theory. Thus his account of the activities was often accompanied with explanations based on the *yin–yang* theory. For example,

> [In the Fifth month]..., the *yang* and the *yin* forces are contending [for dominance], and the energy of the blood is dissipated. During the five days before and after the summer solstice [the husband and the wife should] sleep separately. The *yin* force enters [the body] and becomes blocked in the stomach, which is then unable to digest oily foods; [hence, for] ten days prior until ten days after the summer solstice, one should eat fewer rich flavors and spices and not have many fatty, rich meals ...[13]

Thus his work is not a technical handbook, but an "ordinance" from a supervisor, an instruction for actions, informed by knowledge of the seasonal characteristics of various plants and crops that incorporated theories of *yin* and *yang*. Here we can refer to the precedent of Cui's work, i.e., the *Monthly Ordinances* mentioned in Chapter 3. The *Monthly Ordinances*, preserved in the *Lüshi chunqiu*, *Huainanzi*, and the *Liji*, which mainly concerns the activities of the imperial court, the various rituals and dress codes that had to be followed according to the corresponding Five Phases, and theoretical stipulations of agricultural as well as political activities according to the *yin* and *yang* theories, could be viewed as a more grandiose version of Cui's work. Or, to put it another way, Cui's work could be seen as the popularized version of the *Monthly Ordinances*, which could be appropriately called *Monthly Ordinances for the Imperial Government*, as opposed to *Monthly Ordinances for the Four [types of] People*.[14]

FARMING TECHNOLOGY

The procurement of efficient farming tools was of paramount importance for the development of agriculture. From the Warring States period onward, farmers began to use iron hoes and ploughs pulled by oxen to till the soil, and the practice continued into the Han period. In central Henan, for example, a number of iron tool workshops dated to the Han period had been found in recent archaeological excavations, and iron farming tools of various kinds,

[12] Ebrey (1974).
[13] Hsu (1980: 222).
[14] Hsu (1980: 61–62).

7. Agricultural activities (lower); iron workshop, ritual performance, spectators (upper). Courtesy of the Institute of History and Philology, Academia Sinica. T683.2 (28180)

including ploughs, hoes, shovels, axes, and picks, were discovered, indicating a rather sophisticated farming technology. Chemical analyses of the tools show that a number of them were made of steel, which indicates the existence of high-temperature furnaces that could weld iron into steel by releasing the carbon content in the iron.[15]

> The use of cattle-drawn ploughs in the field for clearing, turning the soil, and making trenches, was another important technology that was greatly developed in the Han period. In northern China, where the land was flat, larger ploughs pulled by two oxen were common, whereas in the southern rice paddies, smaller ploughs and one cow were more common due the smaller scale of the fields. Painted or molded bricks from Han tombs often display farming scenes that show the use of ploughs in the field, either with one cow, or two (Fig. 7).[16]

This is corroborated by a recent archaeological discovery of the remains of a farming community in Henan, with independent farmhouses surrounded by fields large enough and suitable for a cattle-drawn plough (Figs. 9 and 10).[17] Archaeologists suggested that the community was completely engulfed by a flood dated around 11 CE. The buildings and layout of the farmhouses and the fields have been preserved in great detail, which gives us a rare example of a Han dynasty farming community. However, it may not be a typical farm, since the farmhouses are single-household houses surrounded by fields, rather than being grouped together and forming a sort of village (Fig. 8).[18]

SOIL TECHNOLOGY

Since very early times, farmers must have discovered that in different areas, the soil quality varies, and that it is important to try to adjust their farming

[15] Li and Chen (1995). For farming technology in general, see Needham (2004, Vol. 6).
[16] Hsu (1980: 114–17).
[17] Liu (2006).
[18] Cheng (2008).

8. Agricultural activities: A molded brick with scene of a farmhouse, a two-story teahouse, and a small single hut standing on four pillars in a pond filled with plants. After Zhongguo huaxiangshi quanji bianji weiyuanhui, *Zhongguo Huaxiangshi Quanji*, Vol. 7, 40

strategies, either by choosing crops suitable for the kind of soil, or by changing the soil quality so as to increase productivity.

One of the chapters in the *Book of History* (*Shujing*), the oldest historical documents passed down as one of the *Five Classics*, namely the "Tributes of Yu" (Yu gong), describes the resources of the land, including agricultural products and soil quality. The soil of various regions was described as white, black, red, green, or simply "muddy." It seems that the entire chapter of the "Tributes of Yu" was compiled with the purpose of assessing the resources of the country, so as to form the basis of taxation, and to have an idea of what various regions of the country could offer to the court as tributes. The mentioning of soil quality, in such a "map of state resources," indicates a bureaucratic mind that was quite familiar with agricultural matters. This knowledge and interest in the technology and management of agriculture was one of the salient features of intellectual discourses in pre-Qin China, from the Confucian thinker Mencius, to the book of *Guanzi* 管子, to the syncretistic *Lüshi chunqiu*, and finally to the Han agronomics such as Zhao Guo (趙過 fl. second century BCE) and Fan Shengzhi (氾勝之 fl. first century BCE).[19]

[19] *HS* 30: 1742–43; Shi (1956).

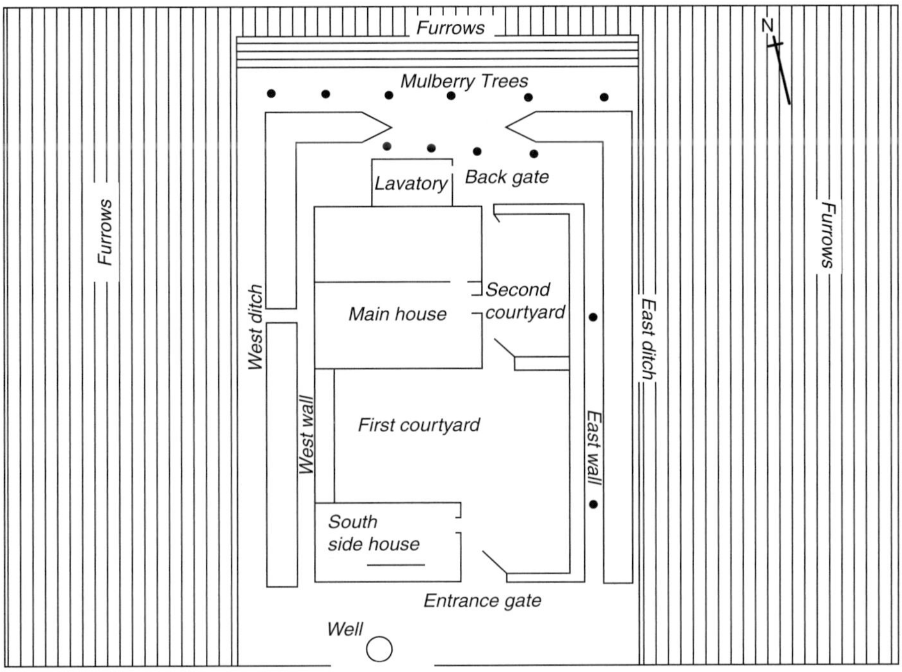

9. Plan of a farmhouse, site of Neihuang Sanyangzhuang. A rare archaeological find of a Han dynasty farm in Henan Province. The plan shows the general layout of a farmhouse surrounded by fields. Courtesy of Zhonghua Shuju. Source: Liu Haiwang 劉海旺, "Shouci faxian de Handai nongye luli yizhi: Zhongguo Henan Neihuang Sanyangzhuang Handai juluo yizhi chushi 首次發現的漢代農業閭里遺址——中國河南內黃三楊莊漢代聚落遺址初識," In *Kaogu Fajue yu Lishi Fuyuan* 考古發掘與歷史復原, eds., Chen Xingcan 陳星燦 and Mi Gaila 米蓋拉 (Beijing 北京: Zhonghua shuju 中華書局, 2006), 74

As we shall see later, Mencius was probably the first intellectual to address the issue of agricultural management and make recommendations to a sovereign as part of his advice about governing the state. He did not mention the soil in particular, yet he emphasized the importance of sustainability by employing mixed agricultural activities.

The book of *Guanzi*, a collection of diverse writings by a number of anonymous writers over a long period of time, with treatises on political and economic affairs with a "legalist" or "realist" inclination, includes a treatise on the soil and agricultural production. It provides a detailed analysis of the various types of soils in the country, and offers explanations about the factors that influenced the quality of the soil, such as the availability of water and the texture of the soil, and discusses the crops that were best suited for the various types of soil.[20] While there are doubts about the date and authorship of *Guanzi*, in general it is dated to the pre-Qin era, somewhat later than Mencius.[21]

20 *Guanzi* 19: 1072–73.
21 Rickett (1985: 3 ff.).

10. Model of a plough drawn by a water buffalo found in a tomb in Gansu shows a bull pulling a wooden plough with an iron sheath on the tip of wooden blade. Objects such this indicate that farming was an important part of the local economy. Courtesy of Gansu Provincial Museum. Source: Zhang Mingchuan 張明川 ed., *Zhongguo Handai Mudiao Yishu* 中國漢代木雕藝術 (Shenyang 沈陽: Liaoning meishu chubanshe 遼寧美術出版社, 2003), 43

A further development of the discourse on soil-related farming technology is represented by a number of chapters in *Lüshi chunqiu*, dated 239 BCE. In these chapters, we find discussions about how to cultivate the fields appropriately, how to distinguish between different qualities of the soil, and how to choose the right timing for planting crops appropriate for the seasons. The author asks a series of questions that summarize the perennial concerns or anxieties of a farmer:

> Lord Ji says: Can you turn the lowly pit into a hill? Can you conceal the poor quality [of the earth] and mitigate it with dampness? Can you make my field flat and the ditch filled with soil? Can you keep the soil moist and be at ease? Can you prevent weeds from growing rampant? Can you make your field experience nothing but mild wind? Can you make the stalk grow many sections and become strong? Can you make the ear of grain large, firm, and even? Can you make the millet grow round with thin husks? Can you make rice so nutritious that people grow strong by eating it? What if you cannot?[22]

[22] *Lüshi chunqiu* 26: 687–90.

The author then proceeds to give answers to these questions by offering his advice about the principles of farming. Although quite a large portion of the essay involved philosophical expositions of the ways of nature and the importance of maintaining a harmonious relationship with nature, the author also suggests ways in which to improve the productivity of the field by careful weeding and spacing out the plants and ploughing carefully. Such a proactive attitude and practical measures could be seen as a step forward from the more passive acceptance of the quality of the soil as described in the *Guanzi*. Although we cannot know whether the methods in the essays in *Guanzi* and *Lüshi chunqiu* were actually practiced by farmers, the fact that these essays were apparently the result of a long accumulation of experience and knowledge in farming technology indicates that there was a tradition of soil management, most likely passed down from an earlier period.

During the Western Han, a major improvement in farming technology was the invention of the alternate planting method by Zhao Guo, who was appointed by Emperor Wu as Commissioner for Grain Supply in 87 BCE. The method was simply to divide a field into three furrows, and each furrow was planted with a different crop every year, so that the nutrients in the soil could be replenished each year because each plant would absorb and return different nutrients to the soil. This method was very successful in northern China, and was adopted by the farmers of later generations.[23]

Another agro-technologist, Fan Shengzhi, further improved on farming methods by increasing the utilization of land in rugged terrain and inventing the fallow field method so that the fertility of the soil would not be depleted by continuous cultivation. He also mentioned various ways to improve the quality of the soil, including techniques to keep moisture in the soil by shallow ploughing and the use of human and animal manure and organic fertilizers such as burnt ashes and cut grass.[24]

IRRIGATION

In addition to soil technology, irrigation was another fundamental farming infrastructure on which any successful agricultural enterprise would have to depend. Just as the legend of King Yu's flood control was built around the channeling of the flood water into the ocean, canals and drainage systems were part of the technology that accompanied flood control, which was also the basis of irrigation for the farming community. Already in the third century BCE before the unification of the country, the Qin government had constructed the famous Dujiangyan (都江堰) irrigation system near Chengdu,

[23] *HS* 4a: 1138; Hsu (1980: 109–28); Needham (2004, Vol. 6: 168).

[24] Shi (1956).

11. Dujiangyan irrigation system in 2007. The protruding sand bank in the middle of the river was the original artificial division that diverted the river water to a branch canal. Photograph by Mu-Chou Poo

which still functions to this day, and the 300-kilometer-long Zheng Guo Qu (鄭國渠) near Xianyang 襄陽 (Fig. 11).

The success of these irrigation systems was part of the reason for the accumulation of wealth and power of the state of Qin. Emperor Wu of Han further initiated several irrigation projects near the mid to lower sections of the Yellow River that benefitted numerous farming communities. It should be noticed that such kinds of large-scale irrigation systems were basically government-initiated projects that ordinary farmers could not have organized. However, they (and the convicts) supplied the labor force needed for these projects.

The implementation of better farming technology and irrigation systems allowed the agricultural production of the Han to increase dramatically. However, there were still many areas that the government-initiated systems could not reach directly and thus people had to construct their own. Although the received historical texts did not mention the details of the operation of these local systems, we are fortunate to have the archaeological evidence to supply the relevant information. In many Han tombs, clay models of farm fields and ponds have been found among the funerary objects. The ponds or small reservoirs shown in the models were connected with the fields to provide water for the crops. In addition, judging from the miniature figurines of various kinds of fish, shrimp, clams, ducks, and aquatic plants in the

12. Hunting, weaving, brewing, cooking. After Zhongguo huaxiangshi quanji bianji weiyuanhui ed., *Zhongguo Huaxiangshi Quanji*, Vol. 7, 38

ponds, we can deduce that farmers then must have raised them as supplemental food sources, some perhaps even for commercial purposes. Wells were also a common source of water supply for the fields and household use, as actual specimens have often been found at archaeological sites (Fig. 12).

NATURAL DISASTERS: DROUGHTS AND FLOODS

The idyllic countryside, or, when countryside was viewed as idyllic, was a reflection of the mentality of the writer who described it so. For the farmers who actually lived and worked in the countryside, there were many things they needed to set their mind to before they could have the leisure, if possible at all, to enjoy the scenery.

Despite the development of agricultural technology, the forces of nature posed the greatest threat to farmers. The devastation caused by flood, drought, and the often accompanying pestilence of locust attacks caught the attention of the historians who wrote the *Records of the Grand Scribe*, the *History of Han*, and the *History of Later Han*. Drought and floods were from the earliest time the most severe natural disasters a farming community encountered. As we have discussed in Chapter 1, the flood legend associated with King Yu was to become one of the most enduring collective memories that were connected with the political legitimacy of a regime. When the waters were under control, the regime could claim its rule as being benevolent and legitimate. Thus the recording of floods as well as droughts that often went together with floods became part of the routine items to be noted in the annals of each emperor. The records of whether these natural disasters were handled with success, however, differed from one emperor to another.

According to one study, over the 400 years of the Han dynasty, there were altogether 346 records of natural disasters, including flood (71), drought (48), locusts (42), earthquakes (7), plagues (18), wind (21), incessant rain (15), hail (20), famine (23), and frost/snow (31).[25] According to another calculation, there appeared to be at least 60 incidents of attack by locusts.[26] Since the records could be only partial because of the vastness of the country and the imperfect conditions of communication and recording, most of the known occurrences happened in the Yellow River basin. Whereas in the Yangtze River area, although fewer natural disasters were noted by historians, one should not rule out the possibility that similar natural disasters could have happened from time to time.

When talking about historical records of natural disasters, especially during the Han dynasty, we are often impressed by the number of disasters recorded. In the face of such records, the question we could ask is: How far can they be trusted? When it is reported that a certain natural disaster occurred, are we able to ascertain the length and extent of the disaster? There were indeed certain cases in which the extent of the disaster was noted. For example, in the year 104 BCE, in the eighth month, a swarm of locusts flew from the east (i.e., lower Yellow River basin) toward Dunhuang at the western border.[27] Should the record be true, the distance covered by this locust attack would be about 2,000 kilometers. The locusts returned two years later. We are not told of the details of the devastation caused by these disasters. Yet judging from the distance covered by the locusts, the size of the swarm must have been very significant in order for them to be able to sustain such a long journey, and, consequently, to inflict severe damage to the plants and crops along the path. Descriptions such as the following are not uncommon in the records. In the second year of Emperor Ping (1 CE), in the fall, the whole of the country was attacked by locusts:

[25] Huang and Wen (2000).
[26] Guan (2001).
[27] *HS* 6: 200.

> The commanderies and kingdoms suffered from a great drought and locust attacks. The area of Qingzhou was the most affected. People drifted away from their homes and became refugees.[28]

The government relief measures were also noted by the historian:

> [High officials and citizens] 230 in all, donated their estates for the relief of the people, and distributed houses and fields to the poor, according to their numbers. The government also dispatched commissioners to catch the locusts. This means that the local residents were given the chance to earn some money by catching the locusts and handing them in to the commissioners by the bushel load. People whose fortune was less than 20,000 coins and disaster-stricken commanderies with less than 100,000 people shall not be taxed. People who are sick are placed in empty houses and provided with medicine. A household with six deaths shall be given 5000 coins for burial expenses, four/five deaths, 3000 coins and two/three deaths, 2000 coins. Abolish the royal garden and pond at Anding, and establish instead the county of Anming, build official housing in the markets and hamlets and recruit poor people to live there and be given food by the county office. When they come to the settlement, they will be given field and house and implements and be loaned a plough, cattle, seeds, and food. In addition, five hamlets (of the residential area) are to be built in the Capital, Chang'an, and two hundred areas are to be built with houses to settle the poor.[29]

We, of course, would never know whether the high officials really "donated" their estates to aid the poor. Yet there should be no doubt about the general picture, that is, the government was trying to settle the homeless and to distribute land for them to plant crops on, as part of the relief measures. Enough records indicate that whatever the cause of the disasters, the situation could have become dire for the farmers, with their farm destroyed and crops gone.

While natural disasters could have been partially caused by human activity and the improper use of the natural resources such as felling trees and cultivating the mountain slopes without measures to protect soil erosion, in the minds of certain intellectuals, they were meaningful portents that were sent down from heaven as warnings of the wrongdoings of the ruling regime. Precedents of such thought could be found earlier; since the Shang dynasty, natural phenomena were associated with the will of the deities. Yet it was during the Han period that some scholars, such as Dong Zhongshu, the main protagonist of Confucian learning during the time of Emperor Wu, developed the theory of so-called "correlative cosmology," which theorizes about the connection between human moral behavior, especially the behavior of the emperors, with what happens in the natural world. Natural disasters of all

[28] *HS* 12: 353.
[29] *HS* 12: 353.

kinds, in addition to numerous common or uncommon phenomena, could be portents sent down from heaven to warn the sovereigns about their deficiencies. As Dong Zhongshu put it:

> The origins of natural disasters are all due to the malfunctions of the state. When the state begins to do something wrong, Heaven will send disasters to warn the state. When after the warning the state still does not change its ways, then extraordinary events will occur to frighten it; if it is still unafraid, then real disasters will come. It is by this the benevolence of the will of Heaven is shown and not hidden from people.[30]

Another scholar, Gu Yong, expressed a similar opinion: "I heard that the disasters are what the Heaven employs to warn and remonstrate the wrongs of the ruler, just as the wise teachings of the father."[31]

The purpose of such warnings, as many scholars agree, was to coerce those in power to be benevolent and take care of the needs of the people. In a sense, of course, natural disasters need to be relieved by the government. If the relief were successful, the government or the emperor would be credited as being benevolent and virtuous. The warnings of the natural disasters were therefore at the same time signs of the malfunction of the government and opportunities for the government to show its capacity for benevolence. The suggestion that such correlative cosmological thinking was designed to curtail the wantonness of the rulers could prove to be a double-edged sword. Not infrequently, heavenly portents could become excuses for court politics and political persecutions.

AGRICULTURE AND SUBSISTENCE ECONOMY

While noting that agriculture was the main livelihood for the majority of the people in the land, this does not mean that agriculture was the only form of food production. In fact, people had always engaged in various activities that supplemented their agricultural production. In different geographical regions and climatic zones people were able to engage in various activities such as hunting, gathering, and fishing in different seasons in order to gain an extra supply for their daily sustenance, even for profit making.[32] We have seen in Chapter 3 how, in the third century BCE, through the "Statutes of Agriculture," the government tried to regulate people's behavior in extracting natural resources from the mountains, rivers, and parks according to proper seasons. Such meticulous regulation regarding the protection of the natural resources reflects a social reality of the time, that is, people in the countryside

30 *Chunqiu fanlu* 8: 11. For Dong Zhongshu, see Sarah Queen (1996); Loewe (2011).
31 *HS* 85: 3450.
32 Hou (2010).

were heavily exploiting the natural resources in their surroundings and this certainly created concern for the government. One could say that these "Statutes of Agriculture" were environmentally conscious, yet they were certainly not an invention of the Qin government, but had a longer tradition in early China. As mentioned earlier, in the book of Mencius the idea of observing the natural order and protecting the natural resources for sustainable development was outlined when Mencius was trying to persuade the king of Liang to adopt a more sensible way to rule:

> If you do not interfere with the busy seasons in the fields, then there will be more grain than the people can eat; if you do not allow nets with too fine a mesh to be used in large ponds, then there will be more fish and turtles than they can eat; if hatchets and axes are permitted in the forests on the hills only in the proper seasons, then there will be more timber than they can use. When the people have more grain, more fish and turtles than they can eat, and more timber than they can use, then in the support of their parents when alive and to mourn them when they are dead, they will be able to have no regrets over anything left undone. For the people not to have any regrets over anything left undone, whether in the support of their parents when alive or in mourning them when dead is the first step along the Kingly way.[33]

Here a sustainable livelihood of a farmer's family consisted of the wise use of natural resources in the mountains and rivers, in addition to the farming of animals and fowls and planting mulberry trees for sericulture. Thus the farmer's livelihood did not rely merely on the cultivation of the field and the harvest of the grain. A similar realization was reiterated in some of the classical texts such as the work of *Xunzi*, the *Lüshi chunqiu*, the *Book of Rites*, and the *Huainanzi*. Yet it was in the "Statute of the Field" that we can confirm that the idea of environmental protection, though limited to aspects relating to resources procurement, was not an abstract argument amongst the intellectuals, but a practical measure promulgated by the government, which could have a real impact on the daily life of the ordinary farmers in the countryside. This statute continued to be in effect during the Han period, as shown in the "Statutes on Agriculture" found in the Zhangjiashan legal texts dated to 186 BCE, as well as the copy of the Royal Decree of *Monthly Ordinances* found in the Western border fortress of Dunhuang dated to 4 CE.[34]

In sum, agricultural subsistence was a complex combination of various ways of grain producing, hunting, gathering, and fishing. From the viewpoint of the farmers, so long as they could manage to obtain enough resources to provide for their lives, they would be contented. This was, of course, not what the

33 *Mengzi* 2: 55. Translation follows D. C. Lau (2003: 7).

34 Li and He (1990: 51); Hu and Zhang (2001: 192–99); Zhangjiashan (2006: 41); Barbieri-Low and Yates (2015: 692–718).

government or the official-intellectuals had perceived on a larger scale or from a more strategic vantage point. The government was mostly concerned about the collective agricultural production of the entire country, and the prospect of having a surplus of grain, which could be put in storage to prepare for times of bad harvest or natural disasters. As the following section shows, the actual functioning of such grain storages often proved to be crucial in providing relief for a disaster-stricken population.

A stela dated to 174 CE commemorating the life of a certain Geng Xun, governor of Wudu Commandery, mentions that in the year 165 CE, excessive rain damaged the crops in the area; Geng therefore opened the official granary and fed the people. Thousands were thus able to endure the hardship. He further distributed uncultivated fields to 300 families who did not have land, and discharged 280 corrupt officials to reduce government expenditure.[35] These statements were part of the eulogy about the beneficent deeds of Geng Xun during his tenure as governor. The interesting information that we acquire from the text is that the kind of disaster relief measures were quite similar to those recorded in the royal annals in the *History of Han* or *History of Later Han*. Even though we need not take every word at face value, there is no reason for us to doubt the truthfulness of the execution of such relief measures by local authorities in times of need.

FARMERS AND COMMERCIAL ACTIVITIES

Besides production of every kind, commercial activities among the farming communities were certainly part of the whole picture if we wish to understand the lives of the majority of the people in the countryside. Since the Warring States period, with the development of technology and production, commercial activities were seen as being more profitable than agricultural production; thus farmers were often lured away from the field and engaged in trade of all kinds. It is nothing new that "the farmers put the greatest effort into their work, but earned fewer profits than merchants or people with skills."[36] Sima Qian agreed in his *Records of the Grand Scribe*: "If one wished to get rich, farming would fare no better than crafts; crafts would fare no better than commerce; and creating embroidery at home would fare no better than selling items at the market gate. Although one may see this [i.e., engaging in commerce] as a trivial occupation, it is the way that poor people are able to make a living."[37]

To make a profit from trade, one needs to have either capital or merchandise. For ordinary farmers, however, capital, or money, did not come easily. Yet if and when they could find the time and means to produce certain objects

[35] Nagata (1954: 208).
[36] *Shangjun shu* 22: 167.
[37] *SJ* 129: 3274.

that could become merchandise to sell or exchange in the market, a rudimentary commercial activity would not be too difficult to develop. Various tools or food produced in individual households could be sold in local markets in return for money or in exchange for other goods. The Grand General Zhou Bo (?-169 BCE) used to produce silk to make a living, Fan Kuai (c. 242–189 BCE) specialized in slaughtering dogs and selling the meat before he became one of the founding persons of the Han regime, while when Zhai Fangjin (?– 7 BCE) the Prime Minister was young, his mother used to make shoes in order to provide for her family.[38] The selling of firewood, poultry, vegetables, foodstuffs, tools and furniture, cloth, or local specialties such as lacquer wares or bamboo products, therefore, could all be part of the local, small-scale commercial activities that farmers engaged in.

Such kinds of local and small-scale commercial activities, where the farmers could engage in their spare time, of course, would not be able to satisfy the demand of a society when it grew and developed in terms of population and social stratification into various sectors, including a large number of government employees and military personnel whose livelihood depended one way or another on commercial activities. The price of agricultural produce was mostly very low compared with that of other merchandise such as tools or cloth. When these were purchased by big merchants and sold to a market far away from the place of production, the profit could be more than tenfold. Thus it was left to those who had the capital to engage in large-scale commercial activities. As the profit of business was considerably higher than those of agricultural production or manufacturing, it is not surprising that farmers might wish to seek their fortune in the more profitable businesses, given the chance.

Officials and intellectuals of the Han often expressed their dismay at the contemporary social trends, saying that people were "abandoning their fundamental occupation in pursuance of the lesser ones," that is, farmers were giving up their fields and trying to engage in commercial activities. When they did not have their own funds to set up in trade, they were employed by those merchants with means to work in the mines, in the salt fields, or handicraft factories such as lacquer wares or furniture. According to one account, "in former times, rich families that were privileged to own the resources of mountains and seas, engaged in the mining of iron ore and minting coins, and producing salt. Often one family would gather over a thousand workers, mostly people who were homeless."[39] "Former times" probably refers to the early Han period, when it was legal, for a certain period, to mint coins privately. It is not certain if the "homeless" were really people who lost their homes as a result of natural disasters such as flood or drought. The possibility that there might

[38] *HS* 40: 2050.
[39] *Yantie lun* 1:78.

be farmers who abandoned their fields and joined the industrial enterprises should not be ruled out. In the eyes of the bureaucrats, they were the origins of social unrest. In early Eastern Han, the area of Leiyang was known to have iron mines, the people of the Commandery of Tuo often gathered together and minted coins illegally and thus attracted desperate people to act "deviously"– the official terminology for illegal business.[40]

As an incipient monetary economy, the Han monetary system was rather fragile, as the government could not keep a tight control over the casting of coins, both in quality and in quantity, thus affecting the function of the coins as an effective means of commercial exchange and price control.[41] In the early Han era during the reign of Emperor Wen (179–157 BCE), the government once allowed the private sector to mint coins on its own, which ushered in a great rush among the people to join this profitable business. It is to be noted that making coins was not a simple household handicraft, but involved complicated operations such as finding the copper mines, excavating the copper ore, preparing the minting equipment, and supplying the fuel, all of which required a large amount of manpower. Thus, farmers who wished to make their fortune, much like the gold rush in the late nineteenth-century California, were drawn into the business en masse. The result was that many farmers abandoned their fields and joined the minting enterprise. Yet in the end it was the rich and powerful families who possessed the means to start the enterprise profited the most, while the coins minted were of inferior quality that actually did great harm to rather than helping the economy. Even after banning the private minting of coins in Emperor Jing's (156–141 BCE) reign, this lucrative business was never completely wiped out. During the reign of Wang Mang (9–23 CE), for example, because of the changes in the system of coinage, hundreds of thousands of people were engaged in illegal coin-minting.[42]

ARTIFICIAL DISASTERS: FARMERS AND TAXES

For the farmers to abandon their "fundamental occupation," the lure of the profitable business of trade was only one pulling factor. The pushing factor, on the other hand, was the burden of insufferable taxes and corvée conscription. The author of the *History of Han* has the following comment:

> Nowadays in a five-person farmer's household, at least two are doing corvée conscription ... They till in spring and weed in summer, harvest in autumn and store in winter. [They also] cut firewood, repair official buildings, and supply conscript labor. In spring, they cannot hide from

[40] *HHS* 76: 2459.

[41] Swann (1950: 377 ff.); Twitchet and Loewe (1986, Vol. I: 585–90); Barbieri-Low and Yates (2015: 913–19); Von Glahn (2016: 100–108).

[42] Huang (2005).

> the wind and dust, in summer they cannot avoid the scorching heat, in autumn they cannot escape from the damp rain, and in winter they cannot take shelter from the freezing cold. Throughout the four seasons there is no day off, yet still there is the coming and going of friends, paying condolences to the sick and their respects to the deceased, and raising the orphans and the young amongst these all. Even with such diligence and hard work, one still suffers flood and drought, harsh rule and severe taxes. Taxes are collected at random intervals, and orders change from time to time. When a debtor has an item to pawn, it is sold at half-price; when one has nothing to pawn, the interest incurred doubles the value. As a consequence, there are people who sold their house and farm, and even sold their sons and grandsons in order to pay back their debt.[43]

It was said that the Han government reduced the land tax to one-thirtieth, which might be considered as rather low. But in fact in addition to the land tax there were other taxes that caused great suffering to the farmers.[44] There was the poll tax (*suanfu* 算賦), which was levied on people aged fifteen to fifty-six, each person was taxed 120 coins per year. A tax on minors (*koufu* 口賦), that is, youngsters from seven to fourteen, was twenty-three coins per year. There was again the tax for the substitution of yearly military service of three days (*gengfu* 更賦), which amounted to 300 coins. Finally, there was family property tax (*zifu* 訾賦), which was about 1.27 percent. According to one study, an ordinary farming family of five (two parents, one grown son, two minors), with family property worth 100,000 coins, and with 60 mou/acre of land, the annual production of the land was about 90 *shi* 石/bushel, which could be worth 5,400 coins 錢 on average. Yet all the taxes added together, that is, $(120 \times 5) + (23 \times 2) + (300 \times 2) + (100{,}000 \times 1.27\%) = 2{,}276$, the total was about 2/5 of the farm income.[45] At such a rate, even though only a very rough estimation, one could see the heavy burden a farming family had to bear. The family property of 100,000 coins was, of course, a calculation based on the value of the house, and the movable property. In the northwestern border, the price of a chariot was 100,000 coins, which gives us a rough idea of what the "average household property" might have meant. Thus, although nominally the land tax was only one-thirtieth, or one-fifteenth, in fact the total tax due might amount to one-half of the yearly produce. There were many times when family members worked all year on the land, yet their income was hardly sufficient to sustain themselves.

Thus despite the willingness to support agriculture and to improve farming technology and irrigation systems, which indeed had some effect as witnessed by the achievement of Zhao Guo in the reign of Emperor Wu, in general the

43 *HS* 4: 1132.
44 Huang (1984).
45 Huang (2006).

Han government's tax system did not help the ordinary farmers very much, as there were also the forces of the rich and the powerful who gained their wealth through the expansion of land-holdings – legally or illegally – at the expense of the small farmers. When the farmers could not pay the taxes, they had no choice but to sell their land to powerful families and become tenant farmers. When they again were unable to pay rent to their landlord, many abandoned their farms and sought other occupations.

From the viewpoint of an ordinary farmer, therefore, the most important thing for him was to secure enough resources by whatever means that he could. Thus there is no reason why he should not try to engage in a more profitable occupation. The intellectuals and officials witnessed the phenomenon of people abandoning their fundamental occupation. They were concerned about this from a government perspective, since agricultural production was seen as the source of the strength of the regime.

At the end of the Qin dynasty when war was widespread and the government collapsed, there was no way to take account of the land that people held as property. In the early Western Han, the government allowed people to report the size of the land that they had, as a basis for taxation. It is not difficult to see that, given the lack of proper surveying techniques, the measurement of land could not have been too accurate, and that there would have been people, especially the rich and powerful families, who would try to conceal the true size of land that they owned or occupied, whether legally or not, in order to avoid paying taxes. In the Eastern Han, there was a time when Emperor Guangwu (25–57 CE) issued orders to investigate this fraudulent practice and punished the high ranking officials who had conspired with local magnates to conceal the amount of land that they owned. As a consequence, a number of governors and high officials were indicted and executed.[46] However, the entrenched interests of the local magnates were by this time too deep to eradicate, and widespread protests broke out, which rendered the government initiative ineffective. The situation of the growing power of the local magnates eventually became unmanageable, and finally contributed to the downfall of the Han.

[46] *HHS* 1: 66–67.

FIVE

CITIES AND URBAN LIFE

The historian Ban Gu was also a literary talent. He once wrote a *fu*-rhapsody praising the magnificence of the capital city of Chang'an. Let us look at one passage:

> They erected a metal fortress a myriad spans long,
> Dredged the surrounding moat to form a gaping chasm,
> Cleared broad avenues three lanes wide,
> Placed twelve gates for passage in and out,
> Within, the city was pierced by roads and streets,
> With ward gates and portals nearly a thousand.
> In the nine markets they set up bazaars,
> Their wares separated by type, their shop rows distinctly divided.
> There was no room for people to turn their heads,
> Or for chariots to wheel about.
> People crammed into the city, spilled into the suburbs,
> Everywhere streaming into the hundreds of shops.
> Red dust gathered in all directions;
> Smoke blended with the clouds.
> Thus the people being both numerous and rich,
> There was gaiety and pleasure without end.
> The men and women of the capital
> Were the most distinctive of the five regions.
> Men of pleasure compared with dukes and marquises;
> Shop girls were dressed more lavishly than ladies Ji or Jiang.[1]

[1] Knechtges (1982: 103–104).

These refined words portrayed the kind of sophistication, literary as well as material, that cities contributed to the culture of the empire. While regional cities were each in their own right the centers of cultural and economic activities, the capital was the center of the all-important business of the state and the residence of the sovereign. It was the most important place in the entire empire, the center of matters political, economic, educational, military, ritual, and cultural, or simply extravagant, and thus a model for every city to emulate.[2]

THE PHYSICAL LAYOUT OF THE CAPITALS

Whether from the point of view of a modern observer, or that of the people of the early Han dynasty, the founding of Chang'an was an act that, in many respects, defined the nature and function of the operation of the imperial government in Chinese history.[3] The capital began as an expansion of the old Qin dynasty palace of Xingle (lit. Promoting Happiness), located on the southern bank of the Wei River, opposite the Qin capital of Xianyang to the north of the Wei, which was destroyed during the war when various military powers were fighting for supremacy (Fig. 13). When Liu Bang, later Emperor Gaozu of Han, unified the country and contemplated building his capital, he considered the city of Luoyang, the old capital of the Eastern Zhou, a renowned political center of great prestige (Fig. 14). However, he was persuaded by his advisers to build the capital at Chang'an, the seat of power of the Qin Empire.[4] The reasons for the choice were mostly strategic considerations. On the one hand were the rich resources available in the Wei River basin area, on the other hand was the control of the Hangu Pass, the gateway to the eastern part of the country, the middle-lower Yellow River basin, where relatives of the imperial house and the disgruntled remnants of the old regimes still had the potential to cause political instability, which they later did.[5] Having controlled the Hangu Pass, the capital was militarily and economically safe from the threats from the East. However, Chang'an was still subject to threats from the nomadic people such as Xiongnu and Wuhuan from the north and west.

The richness of the area around Chang'an, that is, the Wei River basin, was well known. A famous scholar at the court of Emperor Wu once made the observation about the rich natural resources around the Wei River basin:

> The mountain (to the south of the basin) has jade, gold, silver, copper, iron, sandalwood and all sorts of exotic materials, which supply the needs of the artisans, and upon which numerous people depend. The land is

2 Steinhardt (1990); Nylan and Vankeerberghen (2015).
3 Nylan and Vankeerberghen (2015: 55–74).
4 *SJ* 8: 381; *HS* 1: 58. For translation, see Dubs (1938:108).
5 This was the rebellion of seven kings of the imperial Liu family during Emperor Jing's reign, in 154 BCE.

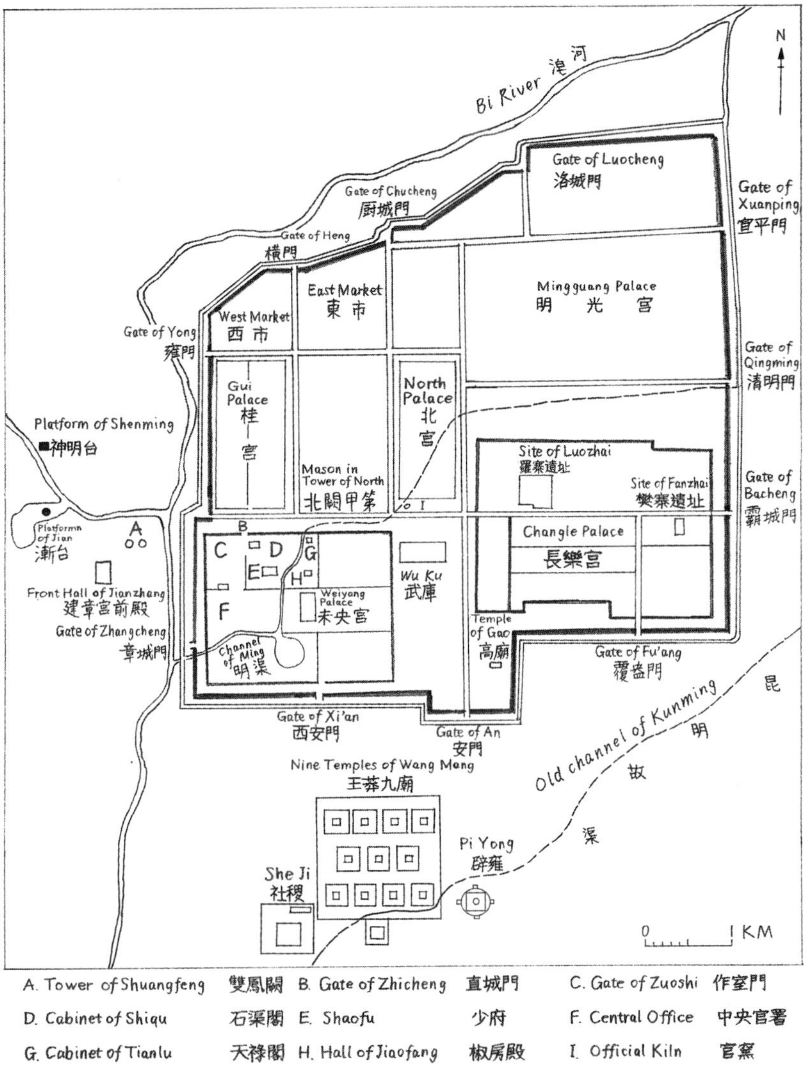

13. Plan of Chang'an. After Zhongguo shehui kexueyuan kaogu yanjiuso 中國社會科學院考古研究所 ed., *Zhoungguo kaoguxue: Qin Han juan* 中國考古學: 秦漢卷 (Beijing 北京: Zhongguo shehui koxue chubanshe 中國社會科學出版社, 2010), 177, 234

abundant with rice, pear, chestnut, mulberry, flax and bamboo; the earth is suitable for growing ginger and taro, and the water teams with frogs and fish, so that poor households can have a plenteous food supply, with no worries about famine and cold weather. Therefore, between the cities of Feng and Hao, the earth was called 'paste,' and worth one ingot of gold per acre.[6]

[6] *HS* 65: 2849.

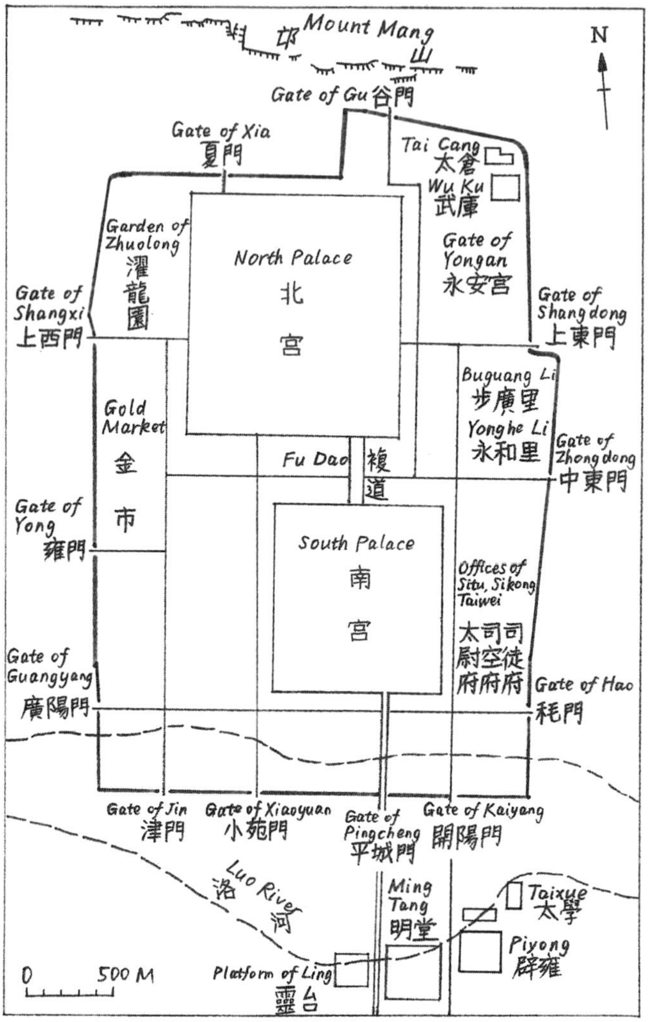

14. Plan of Luoyang. After Zhongguo shehui koxueyuan kaogu yanjiuso 中國社會科學院考古研究所 ed., *Zhounggguo kaoguxue: Qin Han juan* 中國考古學: 秦漢卷 [Beijing 北京: China Social Sciences Press 中國社會科學出版社, 2010), 234

As the capital was built on the site of the Qin palace of Xingle, now renamed as Changle, or Lasting Happiness, the construction proceeded quickly. The decision was made in 202 BCE, and by 200 BCE the capital of Chang'an was ready for the court to move in, with Changle as the temporary imperial palace. The formal imperial palace of Weiyang (Never Ending), a pun to couple with the palace of Changle, was built to the west of Changle, and was finished by 198 BCE. This palace complex was square in shape, with an enclosure wall, 8 meters high, and 2,150–2,250 meters long on each side. Various buildings were constructed within the Weiyang complex, including the Office of Imperial

Expenditure, the imperial residence, the central administrative office, the archive office, and the library. Many famous intellectuals, such as Liu Xiang (77–6 BCE) and Yang Xiong (53–18 BCE), once worked in the library there.

When the Weiyang was first designed and built, Emperor Gaozu was astonished and dismayed about the extravagant and luxurious design of the palace, thinking that it was not appropriate to spend such huge amounts of money to construct the palace when the country was still very much poverty-stricken by the wars that had overthrown the Qin dynasty. The reason given by the main architect to justify the grand design of the capital was that it was necessary for the purpose of stabilizing the country and showing that the dynasty was planning for a long-lasting rule and was expecting great prosperity:

> The Son of Heaven has the four seas [and all within them] for his household. Without great and elegant [buildings], you will not [be able to display] your authority and majesty. We should not, moreover, let it be said that later generations should find anything to be despised.[7]

Liu Bang was duly persuaded. One example showing the elaborate design of the palace was a huge foundation made of pounded earth, 400 × 200 meters, approximately the size of thirteen football fields, the remnant of which is still approximately 3–15 meters above ground.

Of course, like many large-scale projects, the building process was long, as other palaces were constructed one after the other. Besides Changle and Weiyang, there were the Beigong or Northern Palace, the Guigong or the Cassia Palace, and the Mingguang or Bright Light Palace, all to the north of Changle and Weiyang. A very special building was the Armory, built between Changle and Weiyang. Archaeologists found large quantities of weapons from the remains of the building that identified its purpose.[8]

The Chang'an city wall was not finished until 190 BCE during the reign of Emperor Hui.[9] The shape of the city was close to a square, with a 25,700-meter-long city wall surrounding it. The height of the wall was estimated at greater than 10 meters, with a base of 16 meters. A 40–45-meter-wide surrounding moat was constructed outside the city wall for the purpose of defense and drainage. Looking at the map that archaeologists painstakingly reconstructed, we can see that there were twelve gates to the city wall, three on each side.[10] Passing through each gate was a street leading directly into the city, which dissected the city into a number of square or rectangular areas that contained palaces, offices, living quarters, and marketplaces. The longest street measured 5,500 meters, while the shortest was approximately 800 meters; most

[7] *HS* 1: 64. For translation, see Dubs (1938: 181).
[8] Zhongguo shehui kexueyuan kaogu yanjiuso Hancheng gongzuodui (1978).
[9] See Chapter 2; *HS* 1: 49.
[10] See Wang Zhongshu (1982).

of them were approximately 45–55 meters wide. Each street was equipped with two drainage ditches that divided the street surface into three lanes; the central lane measured approximately 20 meters wide and was called the "Speed Way" (*chidao* 馳道) – meaning for horses and carriages to move along – and was exclusively for the use of the emperor. Those who were caught trespassing on the Speed Way suffered severe punishment. Each side lane was approximately 12 meters wide, on which officials and civilians could walk.[11] Drainage ducts made of stone and brick with a width of 1.2–1.6 meters and depth of 1.4 meters were constructed at the bottom of the city wall, which allowed the waste water produced in the city to be drained into the moat. Within the building complexes, clay drainage pipes were used to ensure the sanitation of the area.

It was estimated that the palace area took up approximately 40 percent of the space of the Chang'an city, while the rest of the city was used for various offices, residential quarters, and marketplaces. Between the palaces, if the historical records are to be trusted, there were connecting covered corridors and overpasses; when the emperor and his entourage walked from one place to another they could not be seen by ordinary people.

One of the most important annexes to the city of Chang'an was Shanglin Park, a complex of palaces and parks located to the west of Chang'an.[12] It had been built in the Qin period, but not until 138 BCE, under the order of Emperor Wu, was it expanded so that, when finished, it contained dozens of palaces and mansions and wooded areas with wild animals for hunting. The entire complex occupied a huge area of at least 400 square kilometers, approximately half the size of New York City. The most important architectural feature in Shanglin Park was the Jianzhang Palace. It was connected with the Weiyang Palace by a covered overpass, so that the emperor could travel freely between the two palaces without being seen. The Jianzhang Palace was much larger than the Weiyang, with an enclosure wall measuring more than 10 kilometers, and contained thirty-six luxurious buildings. An artificial lake to the north of the palace symbolized the primordial ocean, with three small islands named Penglai, Fangzhang, and Yingzhou, after the legendary islands in the Eastern Sea that were believed to be the home of the immortals. There was also the large artificial Kunming Lake, occupying a space more than 10 square kilometers, three times the size of Central Park in New York, built for the purpose of training the naval fleet; later, it became a fish pond that supplied fish to the capital.

When the Eastern Han was founded after years of chaotic civil wars, following the demise of the short-lived Xin dynasty (8–23 CE) that usurped

[11] *HS* 45: 2177. Wang Zijin (1994: 33–38).

[12] See Nylan and Vankeerberghen (2015: 99–130).

the Han regime, Emperor Guangwu decided to make Luoyang his capital. The city was located between the Lo River and Mount Mang to the north. As an ancient capital city dating back to the founding years of the Western Zhou dynasty, Luoyang had always maintained considerable importance in terms of its strategic position, and could have been chosen as the capital of Western Han had not Emperor Gaozu been persuaded to move it to Chang'an in the west. The name Western Han and Eastern Han were, therefore, direct references to the respective capital cities. Although not as big as the city of Chang'an, Luoyang was, nonetheless, a magnificent capital, filled with many splendid buildings and populated with imperial relatives, noble families, merchants, ordinary citizens, and foreign emissaries.

The city measured approximately 4,200 meters along the east wall, 2,460 meters along the south wall, 3,700 meters along the west wall, and 2,700 meters along the north wall. Two main palace complexes, the North Palace and the South Palace, occupied the center of the city, with many smaller palace buildings, gardens, and offices located either in the complexes or outside them but within the city wall. A smaller palace, the Yungan Palace, was built to the northeast of the city, with the Granary and Armory nearby.[13]

WARD, STREET, AND RESIDENCE

Although the palaces occupied a large portion of the space, there were still plenty of areas in the capital city for other uses. Besides various government offices, there were the residences that belonged to the kings and noble families, in addition to the officials who worked for the government. However, merchants, minor officials, families of military personnel, scholars from other parts of the country, and ordinary citizens might have had to build their residences outside the city wall if they could not find a living space in the city. In general, the city was divided by the main streets into a number of square or rectangular areas; each area was further divided into smaller units called *li*/ward. Each *li/ward* would have its own enclosure wall, and narrower streets inside the ward would again divide the *li*/ward into smaller units for individual households. One record mentions that there were 160 *li*/wards in the city of Chang'an and, at one point, there were 80,000 households with an estimated city population of 400,000 people.[14]

We will not dwell on how to calculate the population in the city; suffice to say that most of the people would have lived inside the enclosure of the *li* wall, with their house door opening toward the small streets inside the *li*/ward. People had to pass the *li*/ward gate to leave the crowded world inside

[13] Sun Hongfei (2012).
[14] Liu Yunyong (1992: 640–45); Nylan and Vankeerberghen (2015: 175–200).

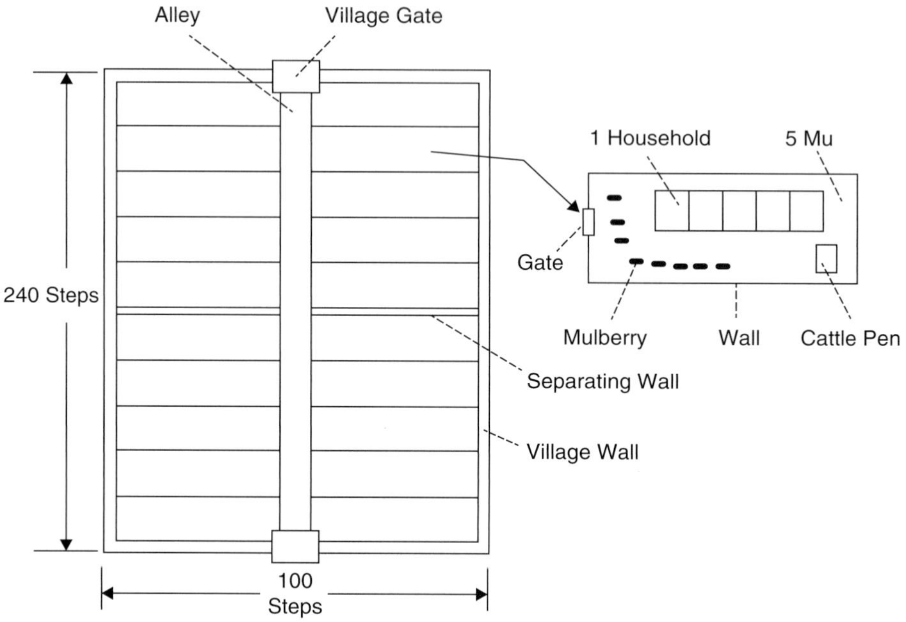

15. Arrangement of the ward. After Koga Noboru 古賀登, Kan Choanjo to Senpaku, ken kyoteiri seido 漢長安城と阡陌・県郷亭里制度 (Tokyo 東京: Yuzankaku 雄山閣, 1980), 294

the *li* and enter the wide open main streets. The law also stipulated that the gate of the *li* should be closed in the night for security reasons. Thus, the movement of people could easily be controlled by the *li* gate. Only some noble families or high-ranking officials could have the gates of their mansions opening through the *li* wall and toward the main street. The gates of those *li*/wards where commoners lived were, in general, not very wide; thus, it was difficult for carriages to go through. This was an indication that people who lived inside the *li*/wards did not have the privilege of using horse-drawn carriages. On the other hand, there were also *li*/wards where the rich families lived, with wider gates that could accommodate carriages. The social distinction between the commoners and the privileged was, therefore, displayed clearly in the design of the *li*/wards (Fig. 15).

As for the residences of the city dwellers, there is no doubt that usually only the privileged kings and nobles, high-ranking officials, and rich merchants lived in well-built mansions, with outer and inner courtyards and with main reception hall, back chambers for the master of the house, side chambers for the servants, kitchen, and storage rooms (Fig. 16). The commoners, minor officials, merchants of all types, and people who were in the service of the rich could only have lived in modest homes that were crammed in small alleys such as the *hutong* 胡同 (alley) that one can still find in the city of Beijing today. We

16. Pottery housing compound decorated with colorful drawings. Western Han. This model house includes buildings and a field enclosed by a wall. The front entrance to the building compound is composed of a gate and a pair of towers. On the two side walls are painted in color three men and three women, being the master and the lady of the house and their four servants. The buildings inside the wall consist of a watch tower, stable, manger, main hall, side chambers, storage tower, kitchen, and toilet. There are also rice paddies and irrigation ditches. Other rice paddy models are found to be independent of the living quarters. Courtesy of Henan Museum. Source: Henan Museum 河南博物院 ed., *Henan chutu handai jianzhu mingqi* 河南出土漢代建築明器 (Zhengzhou 鄭州: Daxiang chubanshe 大象出版社, 2002), 48

are not sure if city dwellers would have raised animals in the house, but clay funerary models show that it was a common custom for a fully functional household to have a pigpen, often built to the side of the house underneath the toilet. It would, of course, have caused some unavoidable hygiene problems for the city if animals were kept in the residences. The disposal of animal waste, not to mention human waste, would be a daily challenge for the residents.[15] Thus, it was significant that there were ditches, at least, along the streets, so that waste water could be drained into the moat outside the city wall, and eventually into the nearby rivers. During the famous case of witchcraft (92 BCE), when fighting broke out in the city of Chang'an between the imperial guards

[15] Xiao Fan (1986).

of Emperor Wu and those who fought for the Crown Prince Wei, the killing was so widespread that the blood of the dead "ran into the ditches."[16]

A city the size of Chang'an or Luoyang, therefore, would be unmanageable without an efficient water supply and drainage system.[17] In this regard, both Chang'an and Luoyang faced the same problem that ancient Rome had, that is, how to provide fresh water for the city. Rome solved this by building aqueducts, and so did Chang'an and Luoyang. In Chang'an, in addition to the use of well water, a special feature of the water supply was a canal that flowed from the Kunming Lake into the city via an aqueduct over the western city wall, into an artificial reservoir to the west of the Weiyang Palace, and from there continued eastward through the city and out through the eastern city wall, eventually into the Wei River. The canal must have played a vital role in the livelihood of the city as a whole, as it brought fresh water from the mountains in the south, and could have disposed of a significant amount of waste from the city.

Such an engineering feat, however, was not the creation of the Han architects, but had already been developed in the previous Qin dynasty. When the palace of the First Emperor of Qin was built at Xianyang, the water from the nearby river Wei was diverted into the imperial park and formed an artificial lake.

The water supply system was even more elaborate in the city of Luoyang. Three main canals carried fresh water into the city from the west and crossed over the entire city and went through the eastern wall, to join either the moat surrounding the city or the waterways further east. Equally important was the drainage system in the city (Fig. 17). Archaeologists found that most of the major buildings, including palaces and official buildings, would have been equipped with drainage pipes and ditches to drain waste water into the ditches alongside the main streets, and finally into the city moat through pipes and ducts beneath the city wall. Although there is no direct evidence, we have to assume that the ground level of the city must have sloped from the west to the east, as did the entire Wei River basin.

THE CITY AS A COMMERCIAL CENTER

Being the seats of the central government of the empire, the cities of Chang'an and Luoyang also functioned as commercial centers, precisely because the richest people in the country would have congregated in the capitals, and they were no doubt the major buyers of all sorts of consumer goods. The city, however, was not a place where one could conduct business anywhere. Since very early times, perhaps in the Western Zhou period, the term *shi*市/

[16] Loewe (1974: 38–44).
[17] Nylan and Vankeerberghen (2015: 99–130).

17. Drainage pipes of Chang'an. Courtesy of Zhongguo shehui koxueyuan kaogu yanjiuso Han Changan cheng gongzuodui 中國社會科學院考古研究所漢長安城工作隊, "Han changan cheng changlogong paishui guandao yizhi fajue jianbao 漢長安城長樂宮排水管道遺址發掘簡報," *Kaogu* 考古 9(2003): 39

market already appeared in documents. No later than the Qin period, the state began to enforce the rule that markets were the only places where commercial activities were allowed to take place. This was, of course, a measure to control transactions and for the purposes of taxation of goods sold. In the Han period, markets were set up by the government at specific locations in the cities throughout the country, and given administrative staff to manage various affairs related to commercial activities such as taxation, price control, and resolution of disputes; the standardization of measures for exchange; and control of criminal activities.[18]

In the city of Chang'an, there were two particularly important markets, located toward the northwestern corner of the city, namely, the Eastern Market and the Western Market. In general, like the structure of the *li*/ward, the markets in the Han cities (including the capital) were surrounded by a wall, with north–south and east–west through streets that divided the market into a number of squares. Of course, the markets in Chang'an were large enough to have two north–south and two east–west main through streets that divided the market area into nine parts. As the through streets ended with the enclosure wall, there were two gates at each side of the wall to allow traffic to pass through (Fig. 18).

The East Market was the main market for all sorts of products where most sales were carried out. These included all kinds of consumer goods such as food, wine, cloth, utensils, tools, medicinal herbs, cattle, poultry, shoes, silk, swords, vegetables, funerary equipment, books, household items, and luxury items such as jewelry and cosmetics. The shops that sold these items were most probably arranged in rows of stalls along the streets.

The West Market was basically the area where manufacturing workshops were located. Among them were pottery kilns, where funerary clay figurines

[18] Zhou Changshan (2001: 180–82).

18. A market scene. A molded brick from the Eastern Han period found in present-day Sichuan shows four street stands, with sellers and customers attending. The market was usually enclosed by surrounding walls with four gates not shown here. Two major streets, one vertical, the other horizontal, divided the market into four areas. A tower – the office of the market mayor – is shown at the right. After Kate Finsterbusch, *Verzeichnis und Motivindex der Han Darstellungen*, Vol. 2 (Wiesbaden: Otto Harrassowitz, 1971), fig. 160

were produced for the imperial tombs, and coin factories, where large quantities of molds for minting the *wuzhu* coins were discovered. According to later records, there were possibly nine markets in and around Chang'an city; six of them were most probably located outside the wall.[19]

In the center of the market at the intersection where the main streets crossed, there was often a watch tower. It was the office of the market management officials where they could oversee the market and keep social order. A common problem for any metropolis as large as Chang'an or Luoyang, inevitably, would be the issue of criminal activity. The enclosure wall of the wards and the marketplace apparently could not prevent thieves finding their way into people's houses and shops. This was recorded in the biography of a certain Zhang Chang who served under Emperor Xuan (91–48 BCE) as the police chief of Chang'an. It was said that "there were numerous thefts in the market of Chang'an, so that the merchants complained about it." Zhang Chang once arrested a few hundred people in one day, and after investigation he found that sometimes a person would have committed more than 100 crimes. They were all duly punished.[20]

Moreover, as a means to control and to tax, for those who wished to conduct business in the market, residence registration was needed; they had to

[19] Zhou Changshan (2001: 172–74).
[20] *HS* 76: 3221.

live in the market and pay due taxes to the government. This was true for all the cities throughout the empire, but at Chang'an, since it was the city of the imperial capital, taxes were collected for the coffers of the imperial household. During the early Han dynasty, in fact, the government followed a policy that was rather unfavorable toward commercial activity. It was reported that merchants were not allowed to wear silk garments or to ride in carriages, and were heavily taxed, in order to humiliate and discourage them. They were also not allowed to enter government service.[21] Moreover, merchants and their family members who had registered in the market were not allowed to own land in the countryside.[22] The rationale behind this law was probably to prevent the merchants from accumulating property with their wealth and becoming great landowners, which was considered as a more secure form of wealth and social prestige. It is, of course, not easy for us to evaluate the effect or the success of such measures. Suffice to say that during the period of peace and restoration from Emperor Gaozu to Emperors Wen and Jing, society in general was prosperous and commercial activity was able to develop and grow; the accumulation of wealth both in the public and private sectors finally allowed Emperor Wu to initiate extravagant expansion, both in terms of imperial palaces and state territories. A famous passage in the *Shiji* vividly captured this dramatic change in the economic situation of the country:

> When the Han dynasty was first established, it was a period that followed the disasters of the Qin as men were drafted in the army and the old and weak were transporting the food. The work was heavy and money was scarce. Even the Son of Heaven could not afford to have the same colored horses for his carriage, generals and ministers were sometimes riding on ox carts, and people had no roof to hide under ... Now several years into the reign of His Majesty (Emperor Wu), the Han rule has lasted for more than seventy years, and there is peace in the country. Unless struck by flood or drought, people in general live in abundance and comfort. The stores of government offices are all full, and the treasuries have surplus. In the capital, money has been accumulated in the hundreds of millions, and the strings that hold the coins are rotten (because of long storage in the treasury) so that they are uncountable. The grain in the imperial granary piles up and spills out in to the open so that it becomes spoiled and inedible.[23]

Since the city was protected by its wall and the market likewise by its own wall, it was relatively safe for the merchants to store their goods there. When the volume of the goods grew along with the development of the economy, there were chances for the merchants to control the prices by stocking up

[21] *HS* 4a: 1153.
[22] *SJ* 30: 1430.
[23] *SJ* 30: 1417–20.

their goods and waiting for better prices to sell. This became an issue for the government, and was heatedly debated during the famous debate on salt and iron at the court of Emperor Zhao (81 BCE). The central issue, to put it simply, was whether the government should be involved in controlling the commercial activities of the merchants and commoners. This was, in fact, an issue that had already emerged during the reign of Emperor Wu when the economy was increasingly prosperous and rich merchants began to have greater influence on commodity prices. Following some shrewd advice, Emperor Wu decided to implement the policy of government control of commodity prices and the monopoly of the production of salt, iron, and liquor, partially to fund his costly military and construction projects.[24] During the debate at the time of Emperor Zhao, strangely familiar to a modern ear, those who were in favor of government control, mainly the officials who were responsible for practical affairs such as taxation and construction, thought that economic equality and stability were important for maintaining the peace of the state; thus, the government should control the prices by doing essentially the same things as the big merchants, i.e., stockpiling goods when prices were low and selling goods when prices were high. The government should also control the important manufacturing industries such as the production of salt, iron, and alcohol, so that big merchants could not make huge profits out of the most basic, important items for people's daily consumption and use. Those who held the liberal view – mainly the Confucian scholars – saw no need for the government to compete with its own people to gain profit, and that seeking profit in general led to corruption and moral degradation. Although the author of the *Debate on Salt and Iron* expressed his personal preference for the Confucians, the government policy largely followed the reasoning of taking control in order to finance public spending and restrain the initiatives of private enterprises. Of course, the reality of the day must have been much more complicated and nuanced. The government control of prices and the implementation of a monopoly on the production of salt, iron, and liquor could never have been achieved without certain mediation from various local agencies – whether official or official with private interests – and thus led to corruption. The Confucian ideal of self-sufficiency and the spirit of compassion and philanthropy, on the other hand, might have been the pretext for expanding the interests of certain local magnates (Fig. 19).[25]

Besides merchants selling consumer goods, there would have been other professionals adding to the hustle and bustle of sophisticated city life, such as medical professionals, fortune tellers, magicians, musicians, and entertainers performing in the markets.

[24] The story is told in *SJ* 30: 1417 ff.

[25] Swann (1950: 13–18).

19. Wine vendor. Molded brick of the Eastern Han period. Two customers stand in front of the shop while the vendor behind the counter attends to them. To the upper right corner are two ram-shaped wine jars. To the lower right is a person pushing a ram-shaped jar of wine away from the shop in a cart. After Zhongguo huaxiangshi quanji bianji weiyuanhui, *Zhongguo Huaxiangshi Quanji*, Vol. 4, 20

The most famous petty vendor in the Western Han was probably the literary genius Sima Xiangru (c. 179–111 BCE).[26] A great literary talent at the time of Emperors Jing and Wu, Sima was from a poor background; he once eloped with the daughter of a rich merchant. The angry father cut off all the support for his daughter, so that Sima and his bride could find no other livelihood but to use what little assets he had to purchase a wine shop in the city of Linqiong and become a wine vendor. Fortunately, this did not last for too long, as the father-in-law's attitude mellowed and he gave a sizable endowment to Sima so that the couple could live comfortably. Thanks to Sima, we have a *fu*-rhapsody that describes the wondrous establishments in the Shanglin Park,

[26] *SJ* 117: 3000.

which, exaggerated as it must have been, is the only elaborate description of a magnificent place seen through the eyes of a contemporary writer, and a lasting source of fascination for later writers.[27]

The most pitiable vendor, if we may suggest a candidate, would be Emperor Ling (156–189) of the late Eastern Han. As the obviously not very flattering historian Fan Yeh (398–445) wrote: "This year (181) the Emperor built a market place in the inner palace, and ordered the maids to sell things, and steal and fight among themselves. The Emperor wore merchant's garments and enjoyed food and drink while watching them play."[28] This short paragraph deserves a special place in the chronicle of the debauchery of the infamous emperors and their entourages.

Besides the markets inside the city, there were some subsidiary buildings and markets outside the city wall, since once the wall was built, any growth of population and construction needed that was not foreseen by the city planners would have had to find an outlet outside the wall. Recent archaeological excavations reveal quite a number of pottery kilns, coin mints, and foundries near the northern wall of Chang'an. One of the largest foundries, identified as the national coin minting office, was located in the remains of Shanglin Park. This mint covered an area of 900,000 square meters, with remains of tools, molds, and kilns for minting coins. The *wuzhu* (five *zhu*/cent) coin, the most widely circulated and influential coin of the Han period, was minted there (Figs. 20 and 21).

During the chaotic years when Wang Mang, the usurper of the Western Han, met his demise, Chang'an experienced serious fighting between Wang Mang's army and rebel soldiers led by Liu Xuan, one of the descendants of the Liu imperial family, briefly controlled Chang'an in 24–25 BCE with the help of a group of not-so-united followers who were more interested in seeking their own fortune than helping Liu Xuan to reestablish the Han regime. The Changle palace was burned during the fighting. Fortunately, other buildings in the palace area and the city in general were intact, and people lived their lives much as usual. The prosperous scene of the city of Chang'an was vividly captured in a passage found in the biography of Liu Xuan:

> Wang Kuang and Zhang Mao (two powerful but corrupt generals) were ravaging the capital area with their abusive power. Those who received offices and nobility titles from them were the rascals, petty merchants, cooks or butchers. They wore embroidered garments and silk slacks, colorful aprons and were clamoring and cursing in the streets. People in Chang'an thus made up a folk rhyme, saying 'He who cooks at the stove

27 *SJ* 117: 3000.

28 *HHS* 8: 346.

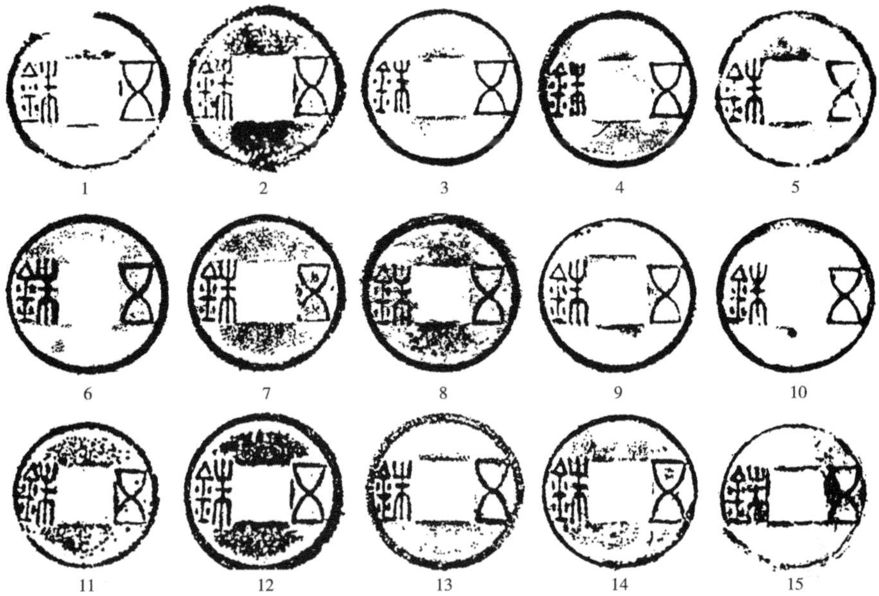

20. *Wuzhu* coin. After Xu Chengtai 徐承泰 and Fanjiang Oumei 范江歐美, "Donghan wuzhuqian de fenqi yanjiu 東漢五銖錢的分期研究, *Wenwu* 文物 10 (2010): 62

21. A coin mold. Courtesy of Zhao Xiaoming 趙曉明, "Shanxi chutu qianfan yanjiu 陝西出土錢範研究," *Shouchang* 收藏 10 (2010): 117

> gets to be a palace guard general; he who sells stewed goat stomach gets to be a cavalry captain; he who sells boiled goat head gets to be a marquis.'[29]

The passage indicates that commercial activities were going on as usual in the city despite the dire military situation, and perhaps in some well-attended food shops. But when Liu Xiu (5 BCE–57 CE) finally secured his position as the new emperor of the Later Han, he decided to move the capital to Luoyang, thus Chang'an city was for several hundred years left in the cold, until the

[29] *HHS* 11: 471.

Western Jin dynasty when it was again the capital, and further down the time line in the Tang dynasty, when Chang'an regained its glory as the capital of the Tang Empire.

In the city of Luoyang there were not only such specialized markets as metal markets, but also many others such as the sheep and horse markets in the area outside the city wall – which makes sense since these required larger spaces. Horses, in particular, were important military assets, and the capital city would be a good place to trade horses for either official or private use. In the Eastern Han, special officials were appointed to take charge of horse trading at the market.[30] Many fine horses were brought by the nomadic traders, the Hu-people as the Han called them. In addition to agricultural produce and handicrafts of all sorts, there were many more different kinds of luxury items, such as embroidery, ivory and pearls, rhinoceros horns and tortoise shells, gold, silver, amber, jade, and incense, many of which were imported from Central Asia or from the Southeast Asia. Some of the workshops were so successful that even the army would purchase military equipment such as swords and shields from them.[31]

There is no record of the capital Chang'an receiving foreign traders in its heyday. Yet other cities, especially those close to the northern border, could have potentially become nodal points of cross-border trade. As represented in a painting found in an Eastern Han tomb at Holinger, a special "Hu-market" was located at the eastern gate, indicating that merchants from the northern Wu-huan tribes were probably trading with Han merchants there. Although the relationship between Han and Wu-huan was not a stable one during the Eastern Han period, the existence of this trade market, nonetheless, indicates that cultural communication could have proceeded with trade relations. During the chaotic time of the early Eastern Han, cross-border trade in the area of Hexi (modern Gansu) was still quite prosperous, and merchants got rich easily.[32] The continuous conflict and reconciliation between the agricultural people and the nomadic tribes was to become a perennial phenomenon along the northwestern borders for a very long time to come.[33]

THE CITY AS AN EDUCATION CENTER

A special market in the city of Chang'an that deserves our attention was the book market. Here, among a few hundred rows of trees, was an open market where scholars met on two days each month, bringing with them the specialties of their hometown, and books and musical instruments, to trade among themselves. It was established toward the end of the Western Han, when Wang

[30] *Dongguan Hanji jiaozhu* 13: 807.
[31] *Quan Shanggu Sandai Qinhan Sanguo Liuchao wen* 46: 724b.
[32] *HHS* 31: 1098.
[33] Yü (1967).

Mang, the usurper of Han, ordered the building of the imperial academy near the Ming Tang (the Bright Hall, the place to worship heaven).[34] In fact, the capital city was also the learning center of the country since the time of Emperor Wu, when the imperial academy was established and the positions of the Erudite of Five Classics were instituted.[35] Many young talents from the regions were first brought in through a recommendation system to study with the Erudite and then given a government office after they passed the examination (see Chapter 2). Their numbers grew with the passing of time, and it was said that by the reign of Emperor Cheng (51–7 BCE) there were 3,000 students from all over the country gathered at the capital to seek entrance to the academy and hoping to find a career in the bureaucracy. There were also local schools at the provincial and county level to train scribes for local government, and to nurture talents for the central government. Thus, one can only assume that such kinds of special people would require specialty shops to supply them with the necessities of their profession.

By Eastern Han, the capital Luoyang was known as having bookshops where knowledge exchange and scholarly debates took place. The independently minded scholar Wang Chong (27–97 CE), according to an account, was from a poor family that could not afford to buy books. He used to browse around the bookshops of Luoyang and read the books on the sale stand. It is said that he could often remember what he read at a glance and, as a consequence, became knowledgeable about many different schools of thought.[36] Another person named Liu Liang was of imperial descent but a poor orphan since early childhood, so he had to sell books in the market to make a living.[37]

Questions remain regarding what kinds of books were on sale in the bookshops. In the early Western Han, the government encouraged people to contribute to the court books that had survived the turmoil after the fall of the Qin, as learned scholars began to teach and study texts that had survived from the pre-Qin era. During the time of Emperor Cheng, for fear of the further loss of books, a large project was launched to collect rare books from all over the country. The project was placed in the charge of Liu Xiang (77–6 BCE); books collected for the imperial library were classified into six categories, including the Confucian Classics, philosophical works, poetry, military works, divinatory works, and medical/technical works. The total count, according to the "Treatise on Bibliography" of the *History of Han* (*Hanshu*), amounted to 596 titles, in 13,269 *juan*/rolls.[38] However, it is only reasonable to assume that plenty of books were circulating and being copied in various cities and old

[34] *Yiwen leiju* Vol. 2, 38: 692.

[35] Nylan (2001).

[36] *HHS* 49: 1629.

[37] *HHS* 80: 2635.

[38] *HS* 30: 1702–81.

learning centers such as the former Qi and Lu states. We can be certain that all of the types of texts that have been excavated by archaeologists in recent years, including copies of various kinds of divinatory books such as the *Daybooks* (*rishu*), classic texts such as the *Book of Poetry*, philosophical works such as *Laozi*, and military works such as *Sunzi* 孫子and *Weiliaozi* 尉繚子, were copies of earlier versions of what have been transmitted to us today. Thus it is not too far-fetched to assume that books of that nature would have been among the books on sale in the bookshops. The phrase that is used to describe the books that the students bought and sold at the book market at Chang'an, "Classics, treatises, books and chronicles (*jing zhuan shu ji* 經傳書記)," to be sure, already hints at the possible kinds of book that one might have found in the bookshops. Considering what would have been the most useful or most in-demand books, we can again surmise that manuals for teaching students to read and write, such as the *Book of Cangjie* (*Cangjie pian* 倉頡篇), and those that were used to teach the students how to become scribes, diviners, and invocators, would have been among the most popular ones. As the "Treatise on Bibliography" mentions, teachers at local schools used the *Book of Cangjie* to teach their students; they divided the book into fifty-five chapters, each consisting of sixty characters.[39] By the time Wang Chong browsed the bookshops in Luoyang, the books that were available must have been quite "academic," so that he could have learned from various schools of thought and built up his knowledge. In summary, the existence of bookshops with a variety of scholarly books on sale surely indicates that the city was supporting a significant number of educated people, thus confirming the claim that it was a center of education.

One should add a note about the physical form of the "book" here. Although paper had been invented by the early Han,[40] it was not in wide use. It was not until the Eastern Han when Cai Lun (蔡倫 63–121 CE) improved the method of paper production that it became widely available. Even after the fall of Eastern Han, most of the writings were done on materials such as bamboo or wooden slips. Silk scrolls such as those found in the tomb of the Marquis Dai at Mawangdui were used only by rich people. Thus, a roll of "book" would normally have been made of slips of bamboo or wood bound together to form a continuous flow of text.[41]

THE CITY AS A MILITARY GARRISON

Being centers of political power, both Chang'an and Luoyang were also places of military importance. The thick walls surrounding the city served as a defense against possible attack. By the time of Emperor Wu, there were imperial guards

[39] *HS*: 1721.
[40] Gansu sheng wenwu kaogu yianjiuso (1989: 9).
[41] Tsien (1962).

who guarded the city gates of Chang'an; the North Army, the most important military force protecting the capital, with its own encampment, was stationed outside the northern wall; foot soldiers were stationed at Shanglin Park and cavalry units, consisting of Hu and Yue riders, were stationed at Changshui.[42] Thus, the capital was well protected.

Inside the city, there was an armory where weapons were stored for emergency use. The armory, built in 199 BCE during the reign of Emperor Gaozu, was rectangular in shape, approximately 880 × 322 meters, with a surrounding wall. Within the walls there were seven large storages, and each was further divided into four rooms. Rows of wooden shelves for the display of weapons, together with specimens of arrowheads and swords were found in the rooms by archaeologists. It was the most important military supply center in the country, although, as we have witnessed from other sources, many commandery capitals would also have had their own armories.

In the famous case of witchcraft (92 BCE), when conflict broke out between the heir apparent Prince Wei and those who were determined to frame him as a traitor by accusing him of performing witchcraft against his own father, Emperor Wu, the prime minister Liu Chuli, who sided with the emperor, was in control of the soldiers in the city and ordered them to search for Prince Wei. The prince, who was then residing in the Changle Palace, had no soldiers at his disposal and so was forced to open the armory next to the Changle Palace and to give weapons to the civilians in the markets to fight for him. When defeated, after tens of thousands died, he fled the city and issued an order to General Ren An, who controlled the North Army, asking for help. Ren An did not act, and, lacking support, Prince Wei ultimately committed suicide. The case, however, was far more complicated than a simple conflict between father and son or of witchcraft. The accusation of witchcraft, as can be imagined, served only as a pretext for a series of persecutions and power struggles among different interest groups.[43]

THE CITY AS A RITUAL CENTER

There is no doubt that the capital city was the political center of the empire, since the emperor resided in the capital and ruled from there. Not only were all the key offices located in the capital, but all the kingdoms in the country had their mansions built in the capital also, and all the regional governments would most probably have had their own guest houses, so that when local officials traveled to the capital to carry out business, such as sending money or transferring criminals, they would have had a place to stay.[44] Many young

[42] *HS* 19a: 737–38.
[43] Loewe (1974, chapter 2); Cai (2014).
[44] Hou (2011).

people from all over the country would also have gathered in the capital to be educated and to seek a career. Criminals were sent to the capital to be imprisoned and eventually executed, if found guilty of a capital offense. The execution would be carried out at the East Market so that ordinary people would be reminded of the authority of the emperor and the terrible fate of someone committing a serious crime. The capital was thus the ritual center of the entire empire, as most of the important religious establishments were built in and around the capital.

As the head of the state with a certain aura of sacredness, the emperor was also the head of the state-sponsored cults or religious establishments. By "religious establishments" we mean various ritual sites that were aimed at worshipping certain deities, or even ancestors, that the emperor or the advisors surrounding him had decided to worship. Logically, these ritual centers should have been established in or near the capital where the emperor resided. But the reality was that the emperors also built many important shrines outside of Chang'an, which later caused considerable debate among the court officials.[45]

When Emperor Gaozu consolidated his rule, he ordered the establishment of the office of ritual incantation and female shamans in the capital of Chang'an. Many local cults were also brought to the capital, not only to demonstrate the grand unity of the empire and how it encompassed the vast land, but perhaps also to consolidate the ritual and divine power at the center. There were the *wu*-shamans from various provinces, who set up many shrines in the palace and performed rituals to worship a large number of deities such as Heaven, Earth, Heavenly Water, the deity of the Inner Chamber, the deity of the Hall, the Five Heavenly Emperors, the Eastern Lord, the Lord in the Clouds, the Controller of Fate, the Earth Shrine of *wu*-shamans, the Mother Goddess of the Stove, and the Nine Heavens.[46] These cults or shrines can be divided roughly into two kinds: those that were made for the purpose of ensuring the health and longevity of the emperor, and thus to enhance his personal welfare, and those that were related to the worship of the cosmic powers, therefore directly or indirectly related to the welfare and prosperity of the empire as a whole.

As the building of Chang'an was a continuous process, most of the religious structures were built after Emperor Wen's reign. Emperor Wu established cult temples for various deities, not only in and around Chang'an but also throughout the entire country. For example, to the north of Chang'an there was the temple of the Five Heavenly Emperors that Emperor Wen had established, while to the south of the city, there was the Bright Hall (*mingtang*) that Emperor Wu built, where rituals related to the worship of the heavenly bodies were held. In Shanglin Park, to the west of the city, there was the shrine of a certain

45 Loewe (1974).
46 Poo (1998: 103–13).

"Sacred Lady" – a woman who died in childbirth – whose spirit manifested herself as an efficacious deity; the shrine enjoyed great fame among the common people as well as members of the imperial families. Emperor Wu also built a number of shrines for various deities all over the country; for example, he established the worship of Heaven at Ganquan Palace some distance west of Chang'an where he often stayed, and the altar for worshipping Heaven on Mount Tai far in the east of the empire. If we follow the description of Sima Qian, and later Ban Gu in his *History of Han*, we are given the impression that all the shrines that were built in and around the capital, as well as those scattered throughout the country, were established more or less haphazardly, owing to suggestions or influences of whoever happened to be close to the emperor and had his ear. It was not until the reign of Emperor Cheng (33–7 BCE) that a formal discussion was carried out at the court among a group of high-ranking officials on the theoretical foundation and the appropriateness of setting up so many shrines. The leading statesman was the prime minister, Kuang Heng, who proposed that, since the emperor was the center of everything in the empire, the most important shrines or temples that were dedicated to the worship of Heaven and Earth should be located in the capital, instead of at Ganquan or Hedong, where the shrines had been located since Emperor Wu's time. Those who were of the opinion that the "old traditions" should be kept were outnumbered by 60 to 8 votes.[47] It was seemingly a "democratic" decision to move the shrines of Heaven and Earth back to the southern and northern suburbs of Chang'an, to be close to the residence of the emperor. As a result, many shrines in the provinces and kingdoms that had been established since Emperor Gaozu's time were also abolished. It is said that out of 683 shrines that were supported by the office of ritual affairs in Chang'an, 475 were abolished by order of Emperor Cheng.[48] However, this "democratic" decision was overturned a year later when Kuang Heng was deposed from office as the result of political struggle; Emperor Cheng reverted his decision and moved the shrines back to their previous locations. Again, immediately after Emperor Cheng died, the empress dowager ordered that Kuang Heng's policy be reinstated, and the shrines were once again moved back to Chang'an. By the time of Emperor Ai (27–1 BCE), the shrines were once again moved back to Ganquan. By the time of Emperor Ping (1 BCE–6CE), on the recommendation of Wang Mang, the shrines were once again moved back to Chang'an. Thus, in a short period of thirty years, the shrines of Heaven and Earth were moved back and forth between Ganquan and Chang'an five times.[49]

All these changes could be seen as the manifestation of various forces at work: the need of the emperors to enhance their claims to divine legitimacy

[47] *HS* 25: 1254–55.
[48] *HS* 25: 1257–58.
[49] *HS* 25: 1265–67.

by worshipping all the cosmic powers as well as local spirits; the advice that was offered by officials to the emperors; the rival factions at court that vied for power; and, finally, the huge financial costs of supporting the sacrifices at all these religious sites. To give a simple example, in the *History of Han*, there was an account of the annual expenditure of the shrines dedicated to the former emperors and empresses during the reign of Emperor Xuan (74–48 BCE): "food offerings: 24,455 times, guards employed: 45,129, cult officials and musicians 12,147, soldiers for raising sacrificial animals not counted."[50] Although there is no independent source to verify this account, we can at least assume that it came from official records. The point is that the figures show there was a significant financial aspect to the religious institutions. The decisions to establish or to abolish certain shrines, therefore, were based on religious or political reasons that were apparent, as well as on financial and personnel factors that were less obvious in our sources.

THE CITY AS A STAGE FOR LUXURY AND PROSPERITY

As centers of political, religious, and economic activities, the capital cities were also centers of information, as people from all over the country came and exchanged not only merchandise, but also all kinds of gossip and rumors.[51] Being a place where the rich and the powerful gathered, the capital became an arena where wealth and opulence were displayed and admired. One particular phenomenon that demonstrates that the capital cities were stages for the display of luxury and prosperity was ladies' fashion. A curious description about Luoyang in the "Treatise on the Five Phases" in the *History of Later Han* recorded:

> During the Yuanjia reign of Emperor Huan, women in the capital displayed 'sorrow eye brow,' 'weeping makeup,' 'falling-off-horse hairdo,' 'bending-waist step,' and 'toothache smile.' The so-called 'sorrow eye brow' was achieved by drawing a thin and curved eye brow; the 'weeping makeup' was achieved by wiping lightly under the eye with dye so that it looked like weeping; the hair brushed to one side was called the 'falling-off-horse hairdo;' the 'bending-waist step' was walking by swaying the body so that the feet were not under the body, and the 'toothache smile' was smiling with a painful and seemingly unhappy look. It started from the household of Generalissimo Liang Ji [?–159 CE], and the entire capital became infatuated, people all over the country were imitating.[52]

All these words sound very much like descriptions of the avant-guard models in a modern fashion show. The intention of the author of the *History of Later Han* was, of course, not to talk about high fashion in the capital, but to try

50 *HS* 73: 3115–16.
51 Lü (2011).
52 *HHS*: 3270–71.

to explain the phenomenon as a kind of omen that foretold the downfall of the Liang family. For two generations, the Liang was the most powerful family in the country, and the extravagant lifestyle and corrupt behavior of its members threatened the regime and finally caused its downfall. The post factum explanation given was: "As the soldiers were about to arrest the Liang family, women were worried and frowned their eye brows in tears; when the officials and soldiers arrested them, they bent the waist of the women so that their hairdo fell to one side; and though they still smiled and talked, there was no more happiness."[53] We can, nevertheless, see this as unintended evidence of the lifestyle in the capital city, that the rich and famous had great impact on the behavior of the general public as the former led the fashion trends.

People of literary talent, however, talked about the city using complicated and exotic expressions to create dazzling mental pictures about the sumptuousness and prosperity that the capitals offered to the world. Writers, such as Jia Yi (200–168 BCE), Ban Gu (32–92 CE), and Zhang Heng (78–139 CE), all wrote about the imperial capitals and their surroundings employing the *fu*-rhapsody style, which was a most extravagant method of displaying the writers' literary skill and imaginative power, as seen in Ban Gu's "Western Capital Rhapsody" quoted at the beginning of this chapter.[54]

Behind the glorious facade that these *fu*-rhapsodies created, however, there was often a sense of criticism or even a moralizing attempt to imply some reservation about the outward prosperity of the cities, and to encourage reflection on the aim and purpose of all the wealth, or what was lacking despite the seemingly prosperous society. If we look at the "Eastern Capital Rhapsody," also written by Ban Gu, we see that he, in fact, was deliberately exaggerating the lavishness of the Western Capital of Chang'an, and making a moral judgment by describing the Eastern Capital of Luoyang in different terms:

> Jianzhang and Sweet Springs,
> Which lodge and minister to divine immortals,
> How can they match the Divine Tower and Luminous Hall,
> Which integrate and harmonize Heaven and Man?
> The Grand Fluid and Kunming,
> The enclosures of birds and beasts,
> How can they compare with the Circular Moat flowing as the sea,
> Replete with the wealth of the Way and Virtue?
> Knight-errantry and excessive extravagance,
> That violate propriety, transgress the rites,
> How can they compare with our uniform conformity to rules and standards,
> Our respectful and reverent attitude, dignified and stately demeanor?[55]

[53] *HHS*: 3271.
[54] Knechtges (1982, Vol. 1: 103–105).
[55] Knechtges (1982, Vol. 1: 173).

Here, Ban Gu explicitly compared the two capitals and derided Chang'an in his comparison with Luoyang in terms of the moral virtue that the latter embodied. This might have been as a way that Ban Gu paid allegiance to the current regime, to divert the reader from the fact that Luoyang was not a match for Chang'an in terms of the grandeur of the buildings and the display of wealth. Yet, the poet implied that the regime should properly promote modesty and propriety, under the influence of Confucianism, which was not yet dominant at the time of Emperor Wu in the Western Han. Another writer, Zhang Heng, also wrote two rhapsodies about the two capitals, with similar moralizing themes. This, of course, might have nothing to do with the actual physical layout of Luoyang, or whether or not Luoyang was, indeed, not built as extravagantly as Chang'an.

The literary works listed in the "Treatise on Bibliography" in the *History of Han*, moreover, provide us with a general idea of what the literati of the time considered fashionable or useful. They talked about being guests of a dignitary, praising the virtue of a scholar, lamenting about disillusioned literati who could not find employment, or musing about the meaning of life and death. Others, with a more playful spirit, would talk about music and swordplay, about scenery and weather, about animals and insects, or about various plants and instruments.[56] All these, in a sense, can be seen as the byproduct of leisurely city life of the educated whose works also contributed to enhance the authority of the ruler (Fig. 22).

CITIES IN THE PROVINCES

Although our discussion of the various aspects of Han cities concentrates on the capitals of Chang'an and Luoyang, as being the most representative, we should not neglect the other cities in the country: many of them were capitals of earlier pre-Qin dynasty states, and were equally prosperous during the long period of peace that the unification under the Han had brought. Many cities destroyed during the wars at the end of the Qin had been rebuilt since the early Han.

It is estimated that there were approximately 1,000 cities after the First Emperor of Qin united the entire country. By the end of the Western Han, as a result of economic prosperity and population growth, there were approximately 1,587 cities of various sizes in the country. The civil wars at the end of Western Han, however, dealt a severe blow to the prosperity of the empire, especially the area of the Wei River basin where Chang'an was located. Many cities were destroyed; people died or drifted away and left their houses abandoned. For the rest of the Han dynasty, the country never fully recovered

[56] *HS* 30: 1752–53.

22. Figures playing music and performing acrobatics. Clay entertainment ensemble with seven musicians who play zither, hand drum, bell, chime, upright drum, and mouth organ; seven performers (dancers and acrobats); and seven members of the audience. Western Han funerary object. Courtesy of Jinan Museum. Source: Zhongguo meishu quanji bianji weiyuanhui 中國美術全集編輯委員會ed., *Zhongguo Meishu Quanji* 中國美術全集, *Diaosu bian* 雕塑編, Vol. 2 (Beijing 北京: Renmin meishu chubanshe 人民美術出版社, 1985), 64–65

from this setback. For example, the county of Changling, where the tomb of Emperor Gaozu was located, originally had 50,000 households in the Western Han. By the time of Eastern Han, there were fewer than 4,000. The total number of cities in the country at this time amounted to approximately 1,000.

The ups and downs of the number of cities no doubt indicated the vicissitudes of the prosperity of the country. The area where most cities were concentrated was the mid-to-lower Yellow River basin, and the Huai River basin, roughly the present-day provinces of Henan, Hebei, and Shandong. It was estimated that approximately 600 cities were scattered throughout this area. The Wei River basin area where the capital Chang'an was located was also a densely populated area, owing to a policy in early Western Han to force a large number of people from the east to settle in this area not only to control some of the rich families but also to provide an agricultural workforce and for the protection of the capital. Some fifty-seven cities were listed at the end of Western Han, as opposed to the twenty-eight listed during the previous dynasty. In contrast, the areas south of the Yangtze River were sparsely populated throughout the Han dynasty, and with far fewer cities mentioned in the historical sources. With the continuous development of the south, however, the population and the number of cities grew from 23.5 percent of the total number of cities in the country in the Western Han to 29.3 percent near the end of the Eastern Han.[57]

Needless to say, there were cities of all sizes, and the salient, common feature among them was the existence of markets where people from the surrounding countryside could go and trade their goods in a safe and controlled environment. The Chinese term for city, *cheng-shi*, in fact, is composed of two characters: the enclosure wall (*cheng*) and the market (*shi*). For the common people, to go to the city could mean a trip to an exciting place where all sorts of novelties could be seen and knowledge about the wider world could be obtained. The growth of the cities, therefore, resulted not only in an increase in economic prosperity, but also in a vibrant intellectual energy that collectively constituted the characteristics of the times.

[57] Zhou Changshan (2001: 21).

SIX

PRODUCTION, CONSUMPTION, AND IDEOLOGICAL CONSTRAINTS

Following the chapters on the livelihood of the farmers and city dwellers, this chapter sets out to explore various aspects of the daily production and consumption of the common people. Abundant materials have been found through archaeological excavations in the categories of clothing, housewares, staple and supplemental foods, furniture, and all sorts of handicrafts that were part of the production of farming communities. However, what was produced in the countryside was often sent to the cities to be consumed by the city dwellers, or to be further processed at the workshops in the cities, forming a web of exchange and reproduction. Thus, we need to move our focus to various industries of the time and discuss what kind of materials people had access to in order to provide for themselves a viable living.

As society developed and became more stratified, and specialized workforces formed distinct communities, there were inevitably uneven distributions of wealth that caused problems for officials and common people alike. Since this volume does not attempt to analyze the details of technology, I will discuss the practical problems that people encountered in their daily lives regarding the use and procurement of various essential materials. By giving an account of these issues and assessing – however provisionally – the income and household expenditure of ordinary farmers, we hope to allow readers to appreciate some of the ideological constraints and practical problems that might have confronted the ordinary people of the time.

WEAVING INDUSTRY

The degree to which many manufacturing industries were sophisticated and flourishing even in the early Han period is reflected by the archaeological findings. The funerary equipment of Lady Dai from Mawangdui tomb no. 1 serves as an example of what the "high-end products" looked like. Silk clothes and embroidery work, totaling more than 140 items, are among the most important finds in the tomb of Lady Dai (Fig. 23).[1] The variety of silk production techniques – gauze, leno, damask, brocade – shown in these examples, plus various dyeing and printing techniques such as exhausting, topping, and mordant dyeing, have opened a whole new perspective in our understanding of the silk weaving industry in early China. The ingenious images and patterns – geometric, floral, animal, etc. – employed in these silk works, besides being representations of wealth and luxury, also embody the specific values – such as youth, longevity, and wealth – held by the elite who commissioned these fabrics. The values, to be sure, may be vulgar – for luxury is often connected with power and wealth and therefore vulgarity, but well suited for noble families such as that of Marquis Dai. These silk fabrics emphatically demonstrate that the weaving industry of this time had reached a very advanced technological stage even when compared to that of the modern period.

Although traditional historical texts such as the *Records of the Grand Scribe* or classics such as the *Book of Ceremonies* often mention many kinds of luxurious fabrics, and that these were considered to be precious commodities, very few samples of these fabrics have survived, and no texts explaining how to produce them have been preserved. There is no doubt, however, that precious silk fabrics were highly valued and used as state gifts by the Han court to the nomadic Xiongnu. During the reign of Emperor Wen, for example, the Han made a peace treaty with the Xiongnu and sent eighty rolls of expensive silk fabrics as a gift.[2] Some of these fabrics were probably produced in the government weaving factories. Government production of these expensive fabrics was obviously aimed at the consumption of the ruling elite, including the noble families.

All these advanced woven products were, of course, based on the foundation of a massive silk industry. During the Han dynasty, the major silk production area was in the former states of Qi齊 and Lu魯, located in what is now Shandong Province. It was an area known as suitable for growing mulberry trees and flax since the early Han.[3] The technology of growing mulberry trees for silk production was of vital importance for the industry, and agriculturalists such as Fan Shengzhi, whom we have met before, paid special attention to the

[1] Kuhn (2012).
[2] *SJ* 110: 2897.
[3] *SJ* 129: 3272.

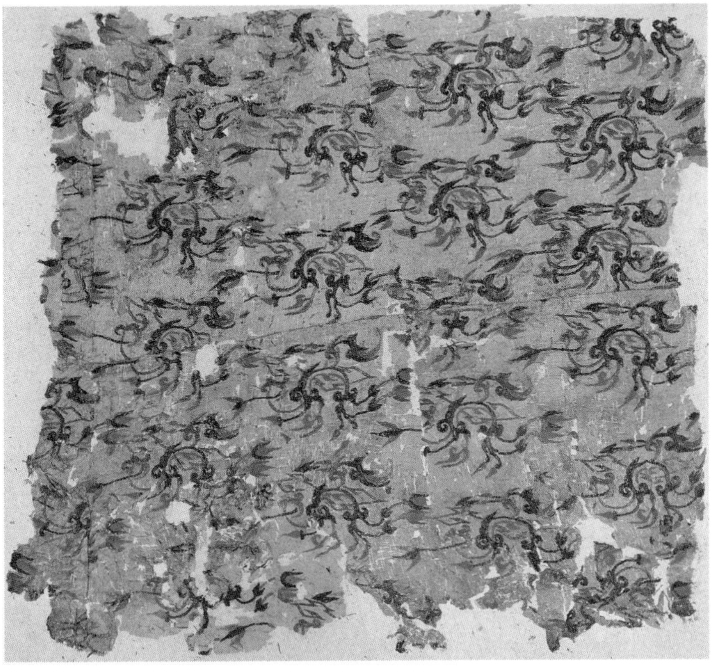

23. Stiff silk embroidered with cornel designs. Courtesy of Hunan Provincial Museum. (Source: Fu Juyou 傅舉有 and Chen Songchang 陳松長 eds., *Mawangdui Hanmu wenwu* 馬王堆漢墓文物 (Changsha 長沙: Hunan chubanshe 湖南出版社, 1992), 94

proper way of planting a short variety of a mulberry tree for the easy picking of the leaves to feed to the silkworms. The planting of mulberry trees and the weaving loom were among the motives represented in tomb decorations in the Shandong area, indicating that the silk industry was an important activity in the daily lives of the people. In fact, throughout the Han dynasty the silk industry was often mentioned together with agriculture in various edicts issued by the emperors as the foundation of the state economy.[4]

Because the government paid special attention to the production and distribution of vital materials such as salt, iron, wine, and silk, it should not be surprising that official factories were set up to produce what the government needed. According to the *History of Han*, there were two government weaving factories in the country, and the most important one was at Linzi, located in the former Qi state. An official in Emperor Wu's reign commented: "In the former times, the official fabric factory of Qi could supply about ten boxes. Now the Qi factory has a few thousand workers, and the yearly cost is about millions."[5] The contrast shows the huge scale of increase in silk production

[4] *HHS* 2: 105.
[5] *HS* 72: 3070.

during Emperor Wu's time, which is also an indication of the general prosperity of the economy.

Of course, official factories could not possibly have dominated the entire silk industry, as weaving was one of the basic household crafts that the farming society had depended on since ancient times. Not only could the ordinary households produce their own fabric, but the rich families could also engage in profit-seeking productions of various capacities. A high-ranking official during the time of Emperor Zhao (86–74 BCE) by the name of Zhang Anshi, for example, was known as "having an estate of ten thousand households, yet he wears only plain clothes, his wife took to weaving by herself, and all the seven hundred household servants were experienced workers. Thus his household production could accumulate goods and sell in the market."[6] What was produced by the private sector, moreover, could be no less expensive or elaborate. A story preserved in a fourth-century work tells that, also during the time of Emperor Zhao, a private silk weaver employed a weaving loom that could produce one piece of fine silk cloth in sixty days, worth 10,000 coins.[7] Apparently, the long period of time needed to produce the fabric pushed up the price considerably. If we look at some of the painted tombs where weaving scenes are depicted, we see that weaving was often part of a more extensive panoramic representation of a rich household, and this could indicate that weaving was an important economic activity in the life of a prosperous family. Silk production, lastly, was also one of the most important items that reached far beyond the borders of China and had a deep impact on the lives of the people along the Silk Road, as far as the Roman Empire.

Despite all the fame and wonders that are associated with the production of silk fabrics, it cannot be denied that for ordinary farmers silk clothing would be a luxury that they could hardly afford. Those who produced the silk fabrics were not those who would wear the silk garments. The common and relatively inexpensive materials for making clothes were hemp (*ma* 麻) and *Kudzu* (*ge* 葛), especially hemp, because it could be grown in most places, except in the northern and western parts of the empire. One who wore hemp clothes, therefore, became a term that referred to a person without official position, that is, a commoner.

LACQUER WARES

Similar to the production of silk fabrics, the production of lacquer wares was also an expensive process that involved heavy investment in skilled craftsmanship and expensive materials. The production of lacquer ware in China can

[6] *HS* 59: 2652.

[7] *Xijing Zaji* 199: 303; Needham (2004, Vol. 5: 203–204).

24. Lacquered tripod with cloud designs. Courtesy of Hunan Provincial Museum. Source: Fu and Chen eds., *Mawangdui Hanmu wenwu*, 51

be traced back to the Neolithic period, but it was not until the early Warring States period that it was commonly made. The Han craftsmen further perfected the technique of production and reached a very high level of sophistication, so that lacquer products became the most valued household items. Some of the best-preserved samples have been found among the funerary objects excavated from the tombs of the nobility, such as from the Mawangdui tomb no. 1 of Lady Dai (Fig. 24).

Because the production of the highly refined lacquer wares involved heavy investment in material and craftsmanship, the Qin and Han governments established official factories, both in the capital and in the provinces, to produce them. On the back or bottom of the wares were often inscribed the location of the factory, the names of the workers who produced the wares, and the names of the officials who were responsible for quality control. One interesting example has the following inscription:

> Year 3 of the reign of Yuanshi (元始), the official workshop of Guanghan Commandery 廣漢郡 made (this) handle-cup, with painted picture and copper nobs, with the capacity of holding 1 *sheng* 升 and 16 *yu* 籥. Molder Chang, painter Li, second painter Jie, copper nobs maker Chang, picture drawer Fang, smoother Ping, cleaner Kuang, the team leader

> Zhong made (this). The Supervisor Yun, Interim Chief of Workshop Yin, assistant Feng, clerk Lin, Scribe Tan in charge.[8]

Such a detailed note of the individuals in charge of the production process suggests that there existed a sort of "production line" that specified the various procedures involved in the production, and that a rather strict "quality control" was implemented. All these indicate the existence of large-scale production, for only this could justify the need for such a division of labor. A similar inscription on a lacquer-ware item indicates that the same production procedure was followed by the official factory at the Shu Commmandery with the exact number of processes, which in turn indicates that the official production of lacquer wares was standardized throughout the country.

The aforementioned lacquer ware was found in tombs located in the present-day Guizhou Province, which means that the ware traveled from Guanghan and Shu, both in the present-day Sichuan Province, for a long distance to reach its last destination. Another item of lacquer ware found in the Mawangdui tomb no. 1, in present-day Changsha city, Hunan Province, also bears the factory mark of Guanghan, thus suggesting that the wares produced at Guanghan were popular all over the country. Since lacquer wares are usually relatively light, it is likely that they could be transported over long distances for greater profit. Lacquer wares in general were often mentioned by Han authors as being quite expensive. An official, Gong Yu, once said to the emperor, "Shu and Guanghan produce painted lacquer wares, their annual expenses are five millions each … I had been in the Eastern Palace (where the empress dowager lives) and saw that the imperial gifts consisted of painted cups and tables with decorations of gold and silver patterns, which should not be given to the subjects to contain food."[9] Gong Yu's opinion was that the painted lacquer wares were expensive and precious, and ones that only the imperial family should have the privilege of using. His words confirm the fact that lacquer wares were actually widely used in society, as long as one had the money to buy them: "Nowadays the rich people use painted lacquer wares and gold colored shoes and jade jars, the less rich use lacquer wares from Yewang, and gold colored lacquer cups from Shu."[10] When the imperial family wanted to show that they encouraged the virtue of modesty, the lacquer wares from Shu and Guanghan Commanderies were among the list of curtailed objects, which again indicates that using lacquer products represented a luxurious lifestyle, and that Shu and Guanghan were the places where expensive lacquer objects were produced.[11]

[8] Guizhousheng Bowuguan (1959).

[9] *HS* 72: 3070.

[10] *Yantie lun* 29: 350.

[11] *HHS* 10: 422; Barbieri-Low (2007: 48).

IRON PRODUCTION

The tremendous importance of iron products in the daily lives of the common people cannot be overemphasized. The farmers could do without silk clothes and without lacquer wares, but they could not do without iron tools for their farm work. The soldiers would need good weapons made of iron with which to fight. Ever since the Warring States period the production of iron was recognized as one of the most important and profitable industries, and the use of iron tools also greatly increased the level of agricultural production.[12] In his *Records of the Grand Scribe* Sima Qian mentioned particularly those people who had accumulated enormous wealth by engaging in iron production, that is, before Emperor Wu implemented the policy of state control. Molds for making farm tools were found bearing the names of private persons, presumably the makers of the iron tools, which suggests the possibility that a private iron workshop was in business. Iron production was apparently so lucrative a business that the Han government finally decided to take control of it, not only to increase the state revenue but also to curtail the growth of local powers, since often the rich local entrepreneurs would work together with the local officials to take control of profitable businesses. The policy initiated by Emperor Wu basically prohibited private iron industries and created a government monopoly, with severe punishment for those who dared to challenge this policy.

According to the *History of Han*, during the second half of the Western Han, there were forty-nine official iron factories in the entire country. The region of Shandong was the most important area, with twelve such factories. At the city of Linzi, for example, archaeologists have discovered an area of 4 million square meters that was the site of a Han period iron factory. Given the actual size of the empire, government control of the iron production could be enforced only to a certain extent, that is, at the mass production level, and it would be impossible and impractical if at the county or village level no iron workshops of any sort existed. For one thing, the repair and remaking of the tools and implements for daily use, whether in the city or on the farm, required that small workshops or factories be available at convenient locations such as in small towns or markets. There must have existed a certain degree of private commercial activities related to the buying and selling of iron tools, and therefore it would be difficult for the government to control these activities entirely. As critics put it, government factories tended to produce only large tools such as plows, while what the common farmers needed the most were the small tools such sickles and hoes. When they could not have access to good-quality tools, agricultural production would be affected. This, confounded with some common problems with any type of government-owned

[12] Wagner (1993).

enterprises, e.g., waste, inefficiency, lower quality, and higher prices, made the program of state monopoly unprofitable and even damaging to the economy of the country as a whole.

Thus the state monopolies on the production of iron and salt, after Emperor Wu passed away, became an issue for many court officials, and the benefits of such a policy were debated at length at court; one such debate was known as the Debate on Salt and Iron. This court debate, held in 81 BCE, only twenty-nine years after Emperor Wu implemented the policy in 110 BCE, was the first and most serious contest between those for and those against the government monopolies on salt, iron, and wine. By the end of the debate, the emperor and the officials made a small concession by eliminating the monopoly on wine, while the production and distribution of salt and iron remained on the monopoly list. Except for a brief suspension during the reign of Emperor Yuan, on the whole the monopoly policy lasted until the end of the Western Han, and it was only in the year 88 CE, in the reign of Emperor He of the Eastern Han, that the monopolies on salt and iron were officially abolished, and private people could again freely engage in the production of salt and iron.

As with the issue of official religious establishments, when the state wished to implement central control of an institution that had certain financial implications, the ensuing debates about the appropriateness of the establishments was always a major bone of contention between factions among the interest groups. A criticism made against the chief architect of the salt and iron monopolies, Sang Hongyang, was that his policies, despite their lofty goal of creating wealth for the state, were also strategies to find jobs for his sons and relatives.[13] In fact, recent studies have shown that while the state monopolies on salt and iron were in operation, high-ranking officials and great merchants always managed to engage in private and profit-seeking enterprises, including those of salt and iron. Such an understanding does make sense, as it dispels the myth about the pure and uninterested motivations of either the Confucian scholars or the Legalist-minded officials.

SALT

The importance of salt cannot be understated, as it is the most basic ingredient that can make food palatable and is essential for health and therefore a fundamental substance for maintaining a healthy population. The production of salt, to which we modern people hardly pay any attention, was a most important industry that could be compared with the production of food, clothes, and iron. The fact that salt and iron were mentioned together as the most important industries in the historical sources indicates that salt was regarded as a

[13] *HS* 66: 2887.

precious commodity, and that the production of salt was a lucrative business. This was true even down to the modern era, when the smuggling of salt from the coastal provinces to inland areas was a serious underground economic activity. This means that the government imposed a heavy tax on the production and selling of salt, which made smuggling a profitable business.

An important aspect of the production of salt is that it can be extracted either from sea water, in which case the production site would probably have to be on or near the coastline, or from salt water wells, if the source of salt was inland, in places such as Sichuan.[14] Records show that in Han China many salt production sites were near the mountains and forests, because the production of salt was through a process of boiling down the salty water, and this required a large quantity of fuel that could be obtained from the nearby forests. This is also the reason why the production of salt was often mentioned together with iron, because both depended on a sufficient amount of fuel to operate. As with the government production of iron, complaints about the state monopoly of salt production also centered on the problems of quality, price, and accessibility. The situation was so grave that Emperor Xuan (74–48 BCE) was once forced to announce that salt was becoming too expensive for the people, and that a price reduction should be implemented throughout the country.[15]

The direct reason for the implementation of the state monopolies on salt and iron production, however, was that Emperor Wu (141–87 BCE) needed the money. After a series of wars against the nomadic Xiongnu people to the northwest, Emperor Wu had seriously exhausted the wealth that had been accumulated during the previous several decades of peace and prosperity. A number of sources confirm this point. For example, at the beginning of the Salt and Iron Debate, the imperial counselor pointed out that the war against the Xiongnu and the need to build defensive fortresses on the border had depleted the government treasury, and that therefore the government wanted to set up monopolies on salt, iron, and wine, and the government agencies needed to regulate the flow of goods to make money and to compensate for the military spending.[16] Even in the Eastern Han period, more than 150 years later, Emperor He was still referring to Emperor Wu's military actions against the Western Xiongnu and the Southern Yue people as being the reason for the state monopolies on salt and iron.[17]

It should be pointed out that the abolition of the government monopolies on the production of salt and iron did not mean the elimination of the government-owned factories, only that the private sectors of society could now run their own businesses legally on the condition that they pay taxes. In

[14] Flad (2011).
[15] *HS* 8: 252.
[16] *Yantie lun* 1: 1.
[17] *HHS* 90: 2991.

25. Salt production in Sichuan. Scene from a molded brick. Courtesy of Institute of History and Philology, Academia Sinica, T683.2 (27004)

other words, both state-owned as well as private industries existed side by side, a practice that would continue throughout most of the later history of China (Fig. 25).

WINE

It might seem curious that wine (i.e., rice wine) production should also be among the list of state monopolies proposed by Emperor Wu, since the making of wine was an ancient practice, and a common drink item that each family would have the know-how to produce.[18] Yet since at least the Qin dynasty, it seems that the government had put some restraint on the selling of wine by the farmers in their homes. A paragraph in the "Statutes on Agriculture" says: "Farmers who live in the village are not allowed to sell wine. Those who do not heed the order shall be banished. If the field overseer, officer in charge of manufacturing, and the personnel office did not tend to the matter, the fine is two *jia* (甲)."[19] Because the officer in charge of manufacturing was involved,

[18] Poo (1999).
[19] Li and Zhao (2011: 106–107).

it is reasonable to assume that the prohibition must have something to do with the practicalities of taxation.

The government monopoly on wine production that Emperor Wu initiated was, therefore, another measure that seriously disrupted the usual lifestyle of the common people. Given the nature of the product, that is, one had to contain the wine in heavy jars, which were not easily transported beyond the local community, government-managed wine producers would find it difficult to move the product over long distances, if that was the intention of controlling the price and curtailing private profits.

If we look at it from the point of view of the common people, it was fortunate that the government monopoly on wine production was lifted after the Debate on Salt and Iron. Unlike the production of salt and iron, which involved some specialized technical know-how and large equipment that not every household could afford to have, the production of wine was relatively simple, and we have yet to identify any merchants who were known to have made an enormous profit by selling wine. Thus the initial decision of making wine production a state monopoly was apparently ill conceived.

It is obvious that among the industries discussed earlier, some, such as salt, iron, lacquer, or high-quality silk, are most likely to have been produced with a high concentration of capital, labor force, and technical know-how that no ordinary farmers would have possessed. Yet there is still an array of simple handcrafted objects that could be produced by farming households and sold as merchandise at local markets. Clothes, of lower-quality silk and hemp, pottery, furniture, even foodstuffs such as dried meat or farm produce, could also be sold at market in exchange for money, which could in turn be used for purchasing the tools or salt that an ordinary farming community could not produce for itself. The farming community, although depending on agricultural production to provide its main source of income, by no means lacked commercial connections with towns and cities, where the more advanced industrial products could be bought and farm produce could be sold. Farm handicrafts could also be collected by enterprising merchants and sold elsewhere to make a profit. A "Statute of Market" in the Zhangjiashan legal texts stipulates clearly the dimension of the clothes to be sold in market, suggesting that it was a common phenomenon that small vendors or merchants sold their merchandise on the local market, and the government was trying to regulate the dimension of the textiles, presumably for taxation purposes.[20]

[20] Barbieri-Low and Yates (2015).

COMMODITY PRICES

At a time when people's daily sustenance was provided by the produce of the field, when the variety of manufactured goods for sale was limited, and when currency was scarce, the meaning of commodity prices to Han people may have been different from that of people in modern society. It is true that the more money one has, the more things one can purchase. Yet the goods produced in the family workshops that existed in the countryside could have been bartered and exchanged through nonmonetary means.[21] Thus at the village level, we can see fewer commercial activities based on the monetary system. Nonetheless, enough evidence exists that shows the value of goods based on currency.

In order to have a sense of the reality of daily life in terms of the ability of people to purchase the goods they needed, we need to have two kinds of information: the price of merchandise and the income level of an ordinary household. Needless to say, the documents which we have are limited and fragmented. Nevertheless, economic historians have painstakingly reconstructed a general picture by which we can imagine what the life of a consumer was like in the Han period.

Among the things one could purchase, land and a home were probably the most expensive and most important items. According to transmitted historical sources as well as archaeologically excavated texts, we can at least establish some reference to land prices in certain areas and at certain time periods. In the Eastern Han, in the capital Luoyang area, the price of land was between 4,000 coins and 3,000 coins per *mou*, whereas in the southwestern regions, in the Sichuan area, for example, we have references ranging from 2,000 to 500 coins per *mou*, this being significantly lower than in the Luoyang area. In the western borderlands, as expected, land was vastly cheaper, and one record has 100 coins per *mou*. The price of the land was also related to its fertility, or whether there was easy access to water sources and transportation.

As for houses, we have records ranging from 10,000 coins to 1,000,000 coins, with a similar pattern that houses close to the capital were generally worth more than those located in the border areas. Since the measurement unit of houses was not as fixed as that of land, we see a large fluctuation in prices, probably due to the actual size of the houses.

For those who needed to purchase clothes, the prices and choices were many. Linen cloth was the cheaper kind, ranging from 220 to 750 coins per *pi* (50.82 × 924 centimeters), while silk of various qualities could range from 300 to 1,000 coins per *pi*.

[21] *Yantielun* 6: 430.

The price of grain was also at the center of attention for government officials and the common people, as it was often the indicator that showed whether the society was under stress, or whether the people's lives were relatively comfortable. In the Han period, the price of grain generally fluctuated between several dozen coins to a hundred coins per *shi*. It is understandable that, owing to the cost of transportation, the price of grain in the border areas would have been higher than in the areas of grain production. In the Eastern Han, grain prices were generally higher than those in the Western Han. Needless to say, during times of war or natural disaster, the price would inevitably have increased.

The price of cattle was generally high, as we have a record of 15,000 coins per head in Sichuan, and around 2,000 to 4,800 coins at the western border fortress of Juyan. The price of horses was understandably higher than that of cattle because of their military and transportation value. Records at Juyan show that the price of horses ranged from 4,000 to 9,500 coins per head. Goats, on the other hand, were considerably cheaper, at about 250 coins per head at Juyan. When we look at the price of some of the foodstuffs, there is a record of 140 coins per *shi* for wine, 3 to 9 coins per *jin* for meat, and 36 to 40 coins per head for chicken.

There may be doubts about the accuracy and general applicability of the commodity prices quoted here. It is true that the information gathered from transmitted texts such as the *History of Han* is most likely a rough estimate that could provide us only with some vague ideas of the relative value of the commodities. Fortunately there are also quite a large number of excavated texts, especially from the western region, where Han military settlements were located, that provide us with realistic and first-hand records about many sorts of commodity prices. Other kinds of excavated texts are gathered from funerary texts and tomb stelae. Thus, without claiming that we could reconstruct the commodity prices of a period or an area over a long period of time, we could at least say that we know for certain that at certain points of time and space, people had to buy what they needed by paying the prices we have seen in the texts. When we could also find out the income level of the people who were paying these prices for their purchases, we would gain an insight into whether their lives were comfortable or not.

INCOME AND EXPENDITURE

Not only we modern observers wish to have a sense of the living conditions of the people of the Han as a general assessment of the well-being of the society, the ancient authors also took an interest in this matter, even if for different purposes. At the end of the Warring States period, when interstate competition was strong, the strength of a state often depended on whether the people could live comfortably and happily. According to a passage in the *History of Han*, the general financial situation of the average farming household in the state of Wei during the late Warring States period was:

> Nowadays a farmer with a family of five, working with a field of one hundred *mou*, could harvest one and half *shi* of grain per *mou* (per year), thus total one hundred and fifty *shi*. Minus ten per cent tax of fifteen *shi*, the remainder is one hundred and thirty five *shi*. For food, one person consumes one and half *shi* per month, five persons would consume ninety *shi* per year. This makes the remainder forty five *shi*. One *shi* equals thirty coins, which makes one thousand three hundred and fifty coins. Minus the cost of community seasonal celebrations and sacrifices of three hundred coins, the remainder is one thousand and fifty. For clothes, three hundred coins per person, five persons would cost one thousand and five hundred coins per year, thus there is the deficit of four hundred and fifty. These do not yet include those unfortunate cases of medical and funerary cost, plus taxes that need to be submitted to the government.[22]

Despite this rather simplified estimation of the income and expenditure of the average farming family, an obvious conclusion from this assessment is that it would be a difficult task for the average farming family to make ends meet.

The foregoing quotation refers to a time before the Qin-Han period, yet the situation in the Western Han was probably not much different. According to another account in the *History of Han*, for a farming family of five, about two adults would labor in a field of no more than 100 *mou*, and the yearly harvest would be no more than 100 *shi* of grain.[23] While 100 *shi* might be a little less than expected, one should not take it literally. It has been estimated by economic historians that in the Han period, a farming family with 100 *mou* could harvest roughly about 200 *shi* of grain. An adult farmer would on average consume about 3 *shi* of grain per month. Calculations based on documents found in the western border area indicate that for a family of five, the yearly grain consumption was about 150–160 *shi*, while a family of four would consume about 114–124 *shi*. We also need to consider the cost of salt, as it was a necessary item of consumption. It has been calculated that the cost of salt was about (measured by the grain price) 4.32 *shi* for a family of four, and about 5.4 *shi* for a family of five. Thus, staple food (discounting vegetables, wine, and meats) and salt alone would cost about 118–128 *shi* for a family of four and about 155–165 for a family of five. If the family income was 200 *shi*, this means that only 35–45 *shi* was available for the other purposes of a family of five. Because the price of grain was about 100 coins per *shi* at the higher end, the family would have no more than 3,500–4,500 coins left to spend during the whole year. It needs to be remembered that there were still various taxes (poll tax, property tax, etc.) to be paid before this money could be used to buy any merchandise.

22 *HS* 24a: 1125.

23 *HS* 24a: 1132.

By the foregoing simple estimation, a family of five with 100 *mou* of farm land – and we know that many farmers owned less than 100 *mou* – would have a very difficult task to keep a balance of income and expenditure. Other kinds of income-producing work had to be sought, be it doing ad hoc work for rich families, or producing handicrafts for sale.

In contrast to the farmers, people who were able to find a job in the government could usually expect to have better living standards, that is, by receiving a salary and other privileges that came with the position. But let us look at their official income only, since any other forms of income gained because of their position would not be on record. Although there were about 18 to 20 levels of salary, in general the Han officialdom could be divided into four grades: those with the highest pay (2,000 *shi*–below 2,000 *shi*), usually the ministers and governors; those with the middle pay (600 *shi*–1,000 *shi*), the middle-ranking officials; those with the lower-middle pay (200 *shi*–400 *shi*); and those with the lowest pay (below 200 *shi*), the clerks and bailiffs. A monthly salary of 2,000 *shi* was roughly equivalent to about 60,000 coins in the Western Han and about 35,000 coins in the Eastern Han, while that of 200 *shi* amounted to about 2,000 coins in the Western Han and about 3,000 coins in the Eastern Han. Thus it could be seen that the salaries of the Eastern Han high-ranking officials were less than those of the Western Han, while the salaries of the lower officials were just the opposite. This was due to the fact that it was recognized in the late Western Han and the early Eastern Han that the salary of the lower officials was too low to sustain a livable life, which was bad for their morale and a major cause of corruption. Thus several times the government increased the salaries of the lower officials, and reduced those of the higher officials.

The hardship of the lower officials was once described by the Eastern Han scholar Cui Shi (c. 100–170 CE), who was also the author of the "Monthly Ordinance for the Four Peoples":

> During the tyranny of the Qin, [those ruling elites] acted against the righteous way and gathered wealth for themselves, while treating their subjects as slaves. The Han Dynasty rose but did not change the Qin's institution. Thus although the county officers bear the responsibility of the vassals, their salary was like that of the gate keeper. Allow me to make an example. The monthly salary [of the county official] was 20 *hu* 斛 (= *shi*), which equals 2,000 coins. Even if the official wishes to be thrifty, he should still have a servant. If he has no slave, he would have to hire a person. The salary of the servant is about 1,000 coins, the cost of meat etc. is 500 coins, and tinder, salt, vegetable cost another 500 coins. Two persons would consume 6 *hu* of grain, the rest could barely feed the horse, how could he supply clothes for the winter and summer, and the seasonal sacrifices, plus wine and food for guests? Not to mention taking care of the parents and providing for the wife and children.[24]

[24] *Zhenglun* 7: 149.

Cui Shi thus blamed the low salaries of the lower officials as the reason for the corruption in the government:

> If one does not provide for his parents, it is not filial; if one does not provide for his wife and children, he shall have no descendant. As one could not make ends meet by providing for one's parents and family, and as one could not be as righteous as Boyi and Shuqi, who would want to starve to death? Therefore there happen the crimes of selling official titles and bribing jail guards, and the evil of bandits acting as officials.[25]

Another critic of the low salaries of the local officials commented that:

> The local officials and state clerks have meager salaries. Their carriages and horses and clothes are all provided by the people. Those who are upright take what they need, those who are corrupt fill their houses. They pick from the best and transport over the country, with endless hustles and bustles, and costly exchanges of visits and sending-offs, damaging the government business and hurting the people.[26]

Now, if the salary of the lower officials was meager, what about that of the common soldiers and clerks? Texts found in the western borderland tell us that a common soldier at a border fortress received a monthly ration of 3.33 *shi* of grain, his wife received 2.1 *shi*, a male child (aged seven and up) 2.1 *shi*, a female child (aged eight and up) 1.6 *shi*, while a boy under six got 1.6 *shi*, and a girl under seven got 1.1 *shi*. One could calculate that for a family of five, the monthly income could be no more than 12 *shi* of grain per month, which equals about 1,200 coins, much lower than that of the low officials. In a word, it seems that those soldiers and their families who lived in the western borderlands generally had a hard life, which would make the life of the farmer something to be envied. But the general picture should not be mistaken: throughout the Han, whether in the farming villages or in the borderlands, those who were in the lower strata of society, be they farmers or soldiers, led a harsh if not unbearable life. They could perhaps have had enough to eat, but they were always short of cash. It was difficult for them to accumulate wealth.

In contrast, the life of the rich was another world. As a late Eastern Han scholar Zhongchang Tong 仲長統 (180–220 CE) observed:

> The residences of the rich people consisted of hundreds of rooms, enormous lands that fill the countryside, with thousands of slaves, and tens of thousands of clients. They use ships and wagons to sell merchandise all over the country, and they stack up merchandise in the warehouses all over the city.[27]

[25] *Zhenglun* 7: 149. For Bo Yi and Shu Qi, see Chapter 9.

[26] *HHS* 61: 2017.

[27] *Changyan* (2012: 265–66).

> When the system of nine-square field changed, the rich people began to do business. Their warehouses were distributed over the provinces and commanderies, their fields were extensive and comparable to the enfeoffed kingdoms. They did not have any official appointment, but they could secretly don the costume of court officials. They were not the Head of Five in the local household registration, yet they possessed the service of thousands of households and great cities.[28]

It is not surprising that people should have tried to improve their income by engaging themselves in some form of business. Thus the famous line depicting this situation in the *Records of the Grand Scribe*:

> When a poor man wishes to seek for wealth, farming is not as good as craft work, craft work is not as good as commerce, and doing embroidery is not as good as selling goods at the market gate. These are petty professions, yet they are what the poor depend upon.[29]

The best place to find a niche in these petty professions, no doubt, would have been in the city. As another critic, Wang Fu 王符 (83–170 CE), commented: "Nowadays at Luoyang the number of people who engage in the petty professions are ten times those of the farmers, while the number of people who engage in devious deeds and idle pursuits are ten times those of the merchants."[30]

IDEOLOGICAL CONSTRAINTS

One would suspect that the life of a farmer could not have been an all-happy one, that is, some obviously fared better than others for a variety of reasons: the location of their fields, the condition of their soil, the accessibility to irrigation, farming techniques, tools, and, not least of all, their personal diligence and luck – even without the disruption of natural or human disasters. But these lucky situations might not have been the shared lot of most of the farmers. It is only after the foregoing investigations that we could be sure that these speculations are close to the reality.

Production, consumption, income, expenditure – apparently these concepts mean different things to people of different social and economic status and at different times. As we have mentioned a number of times in our discussion about the political and economic situation, during the Debate on Salt and Iron held at Emperor Zhao's court, both sides argued that their way was the one that would be of greater benefit for the people and the state. They argued for and against the government control of prices and government monopolies

[28] *Changyan* (2012: 279).
[29] *SJ* 69: 3274.
[30] *HHS* 49: 1633.

of the vital industries such as salt and iron that affected the development of the economy and the livelihood of the people. It could be said that neither side had a perfect solution, since what they did was to simplify the reality and polarize different views.[31]

What are their commonly shared values, if any, besides the rhetoric of benefiting the people and the state? It would seem that a shared view on both sides was that there were the "essential" professions for people to pursue and the "trivial" occupations that should be discouraged. Thus in the transmitted text of the *Debate on Salt and Iron*, the Scholar says: "The most urgent matter now is to rid of the ill of hunger and cold, stop the monopoly of salt and iron, dismiss the privileged, and distribute land, so as to encourage [the farmers to engage in] the essential task and cultivate mulberry and flax, and explore the potential of the earth." While the Official says: "Now the official foundries are producing farming tools so that the people could work on the essential task and not engaging in the trivial business, thus people would not be hurt by hunger and cold. What is the harm of the monopoly of salt and iron?"[32]

In fact, ever since the Warring States period, the theory or rhetoric that some of the elite/intellectuals propagated was that the government should encourage the people to engage in the essential work and not be attracted by the trivial occupations. The so-called essential work was for the farmers to stay and work on the land, and to produce enough food for themselves and pay their taxes in full and on time. The Legalist politicians such as Shang Yang or philosophers such as Han Fei, or even the First Emperor of Qin, all espoused the idea that "to rule a country, those who could gather together the strength of the people and concentrate on pursuing one goal would become strong; those who could engage in the essential and prohibit the trivial would become rich."[33] Or, as Han Fei put it: "The policy to rule a country by a wise king is to reduce the people who engage in crafts and commerce and work as itinerant workers, and make their position lower, so as to encourage people to work on the essential task [of agriculture] and less on the trivial things."[34] Many similar opinions on the importance of encouraging people to engage in the "essential" and not on the "trivial," i.e., crafts and commerce, were expressed by a number of Han ministers, authors, and emperors. Thus we see from the Legalists, such as Shang Yang and Han Fei, to the Confucianists, such as Wang Fu, that they all stood by the idea of dividing the people's occupations into two opposing categories: those of the "essential," and those of the "trivial." It was perhaps only in Wang Fu's writing that

[31] Loewe (1974).
[32] *Yantie lun* 6: 430.
[33] *Shangjun shu* 8: 81.
[34] *Hanfeizi* 19: 455.

we see a recognition of craftsmanship and commerce as having their own "essential" aspects as opposed to the "trivial" aspects:

> The way to enrich the people is to uphold agriculture and silk farming as the essential work, and to regard seeking other employments as the trivial. The artisans are to regard utility as the essential and the ingenious decorations as the trivial; the merchants are to regard the smooth exchange of merchandise as the essential, and the stocking and speculation as the trivial.[35]

Thus at least Wang Fu did not exclude craftsmanship and commerce from "the essential" professions.

What is of interest is that this habit of argument, that is, of dividing the various occupations that people could engage themselves in as being either "essential" or "trivial," might have hampered a more realistic and flexible way of understanding the complex interrelations between the different components of the economy. By stigmatizing certain occupations and products as trivial, it denied the chance that these "trivial" occupations could lead to innovations that would improve the overall performance of the so-called "essential" occupations. What happened in the end was that those who argued about economic policies tended to employ the terms "essential" and "trivial" as value judgments that served to justify their own claims and to denigrate their opponents' views. Moreover, they tended to confuse the actual policy with the execution of the policy, since a good policy could well become an evil if executed by the wrong people or in the wrong way. Thus the two sides were basically debating about human errors. They tried to prove themselves more credible by pointing out the deficiencies of their opponents, not by proving how they could ensure that their policy could be successfully carried out by avoiding human errors and greed. Both sides seemed to promote the interest of a certain segment of society: the officials for the state treasury and personal positions and wealth; the scholars for the interests of the local magnates and landowners who alone could have the means to engage in the private salt and iron industries. We could not say for sure whether these behind-the-scene motivations were what propelled the debate, yet it is worthwhile pondering whether both sides perpetuated the simplistic division between the essential and the trivial, thus hindering the understanding of the complex nature of economic activities that should not be reduced to an either–or choice or strategy.

Economic historians have pointed out that, despite the paramount importance of agriculture as the foundation of the subsistence of society, there were always certain commercial and industrial activities that constituted the organic structure of the economy. Interestingly, while studying the Debate on Salt and

[35] *Qianfu lun* 1: 15–16.

Iron or the economic situation of the Han dynasty, some modern Chinese historians could be said to be embodying the sentiments of their own time. In the early 1950s and 1960s Chinese historians often praised the policy of government monopolies of salt and iron initiated by Emperor Wu and continued by Emperor Xuan. In the 1990s and thereafter, scholars began to praise the views of the Scholars, that is, propagating the laissez faire policy, against the government control of economy, and for the development of private businesses.[36] Readers who have some knowledge of Chinese history during the second half of the twentieth century should readily be able to see the connection between scholarly concern and contemporary political and social issues.

Now, if we detect that there was an ideological constraint in the Han dynasty's intellectual circles about the ways of achieving economic prosperity, what would be the implication for the development of science and technology, which, if we follow the logic of the scholars, or perhaps also of the officials, falls into the category of the "trivial" engagements? We will explore these problems in the following chapter.

[36] For example, Liu Jiagui 2008.

SEVEN

PRACTICAL TECHNOLOGY

The unification of the empire, initiated by the First Emperor of Qin, and continued by the Han, brought about some fundamental changes to the nature of the mental landscape of the people who lived on that vast stretch of land. However, as with any historical change, the changes did not appear overnight, but only gradually, little by little, some faster, some slower, but eventually all moving toward a realization, at least to certain members of the elite who were familiar with the larger picture, that the state was now vastly larger than any state that had ever been known to the people on the East Asian continent. Whether or not the population was aware of this at the time, we have to assume that there must have been some conditions under which this vast state was able to be held together and its continuous existence sustained. By these conditions we do not mean the ruling apparatus such as the bureaucracy and military force, whose importance no one would deny. What interests us here is the type of knowledge and technology that people at various levels of society, from the peasants to the county officials, to the commandery government, as far as the court at the capital, would have depended on daily, within their own realms. This knowledge and technology manifested itself in the metric system, the currency, the transportation system, and, not least, in the writing system. All these, as can be easily demonstrated, point to a fundamental principle of standardization and universalization of some basic forms of technology that was able to increase the efficiency of the transference of materials and ideas, and ease the way of governance.

Under Qin rule, China as a more or less homogeneous cultural unit began to take shape. The improved situation for travel led to the development of commercial activities, as it became easier to transport merchandise over long distances. The exchange of information and technology between different parts of the empire may well have fostered a more homogenized world view for the people. Fragments and versions of daybooks used mainly for daily activities, for another example, have been found over a large area, from the western border at Gansu to the area of Changsha, Hunan, which again testifies to the extent of the communication system based on a common writing script, as well as the relatively unity or similarity of the popular customs.[1] Taking medicine as another example, knowledge of recipes previously used or practices at a certain location became available to other places and could be collected and studied, leading to the advancement of medical knowledge. The development of medicine in general during the Han period led to the formation of the *Inner Canon of the Yellow Thearch*, the most important medical work that had a paramount influence on Chinese medicine over the next two millennia.[2] A number of medical texts found in the early Han tombs at Mawangdui testify to the transition of medical knowledge, which, together with other texts passed down through centuries, provide us with rich information about the medical practices that people might have followed during that time. These include various aspects of the treatment of illness, as well as the kind of illnesses that people could have contracted in their daily lives. Similarly, knowledge about other kinds of practical technology was also circulated around the country. In sum, this chapter tries to introduce the formation of a new world view by giving an account of the development of practical technology in the context of daily life.

MEASURING SYSTEMS: WEIGHT, LENGTH, VOLUME

The Warring States philosopher Zhuangzi once commented that the way to stop people from fighting each other for profit was to destroy the measuring instruments, for without measurement, value could not be established. Without value, people would not fight for profit.[3] Being a philosopher with great literary talent, Zhuangzi was able to use graphic metaphors to make his point; that is, the obsession with material gain destroys the harmonious life of a society. When there is no instrument of measurement, or even the idea of

[1] See Harper and Kalinowski (2017).
[2] Brown (2015).
[3] *Zhuangzi* 4b: 353.

measurement, to measure the "valuable stuff," then there would be nothing to incite people's greedy nature, and peace would prevail. Of course, Zhuangzi was using a metaphor to comment on human nature and suggest the origin of some ethical issues in society. This is in tune with the famous motto of the Daoist philosopher Laozi: "Do not show the desirable things, so that people will not be unsettled of mind."[4] Although a little extreme, and harking back to a prestate or even pretribal society, Laozi seems to have realized that the appearance of the idea of measurement had led to the development of institutions related to profit-seeking and management, which he thought were against the carefree and conflict-free existence in the ideal world that he imagined. Looking from an opposite angle, the Legalist philosopher Han Fei also realized the importance of measurement, yet he turned around and advocated the idea that measurement was a vital tool for controlling the people: "The ruler holds the instruments of length and volume, so as to measure and divide his subjects. Therefore the establishment of a measuring system is the most precious thing for a ruler."[5] It can be argued that here, as well as in many other occasions, the term *duliang* (度量), literally "measuring length and volume," could be understood as a metaphorical expression of "judgment"; that is, judgment involves careful measuring and weighing. It nevertheless indicates that to establish a standard measurement is important for the government. Thus the *Zhanguoce* (*Discourses of the Warring States* 戰國策) summarizes the rise of the power of Qin:

> Lord Shang worked for Duke Xiao (of Qin) to standardize the weight system, adjust the measuring system, and balance the weight, and reorganized the fields, and to teach the people to farm and fight. Thus when the military force was used, the territory was extended; when the military force was at rest, the state became rich. Therefore Qin had no enemy in the world, and established authority among the vassal states.[6]

This confirms the idea that in order to control and to rule a society in an orderly fashion, there should be an underlying system of measurement to assess the costs and effects of any policy related to the sustaining of the state and society. Thus when the First Emperor ordered the standardization of the system of weight and measure, the transportation system, and the writing system, following his unification of the country, it signified the dawn of an era in which the state was able to, or tried to, exert its power to regulate the life of the people in an almost imperceptible way.

For example, a farmer who lived in the early Han dynasty, around the time of Emperor Wen, in the area of present-day Hubei, was likely to have been

4 *Laozi*, chapter 3; cf. Lau (2001: 7).

5 *Hanfeizi* 2: 51.

6 *Zhanguoce* 5: 335.

informed by his local officials that there were some regulations concerning his farming activities that he needed to follow:

> For agricultural fields [of one mu area, being] 1 double-pace wide by 240 double-paces long, make lengthwise field paths. For every mu [approx. 461 square meters], there are to be two lengthwise field paths and one cross-wise road. One hundred mu make one ҭqing. For [each] ten qing, make a lengthwise road; the road is to be two zhang [approx. 4.62 meters] in width. Always in the seventh month of autumn, remove tall grasses from the lengthwise crosswise roads. In the ninth month, make a great clearing of the roads as well as the dangerous sloping spots. In the tenth month, construct bridges, repair embankments and dikes, and clear out [obstructions at] fords and bridges ...[7]

It might be surprising that the government took such a detailed interest in how the roads in the fields and countryside should be built and maintained. Yet if we look at other regulations found in the same corpus of legal documents, it will become apparent that an extremely pragmatic master plan was behind such kind of regulation, with the intention of micromanaging the farming community. One would have no difficulty in recognizing this as the manifestation of the Legalist mentality that was adopted by the Qin state, and inherited by the Han government and generalized to become a part of the administrative routine for centuries to come.

All this micromanagement would have been impossible to carry out, however, without a commonly accepted and observed measuring system. The farmer would have to have an idea of how large an area is a *mou*, and how long is a "step," since it could not have been just anyone's "step." The length of *chi*/foot was also standardized and retained by each farming family; otherwise it would be impossible to sell the silk cloth that the family produced in the market, for there was a strict regulation of how wide a piece of silk cloth should be:

> For a case of trading or selling cloth whose breadth is not a full two chi and two cun (approx. 50.6 centimeters); confiscate it. For one who is able to arrest or denounce [a person engaged in such trade]: give it (viz. the cloth) to him. For fine or tough cloth made from kudzu, plain while-silk banners, deep-purple selcage, vermillion silk strips, woven woolen fabric, fine, while ramie cloth, crepe silk, and bamboo-fiber cloth, do not apply this statute.[8]

The measurements for weight and volume, similarly, were equally important for the daily operation of the farmers. The payment of taxes, for one, was often based on a certain amount of grain and produce measured in volume and

[7] *Zhangjiashan*, 42; Barbieri-Low and Yates (2015: 698–99).
[8] Barbieri-Low and Yates (2015: 723).

weight. On other occasions, however, coins or the knowledge of the worth of certain objects measured by coins were needed for certain payments. A statute concerning the payment for fodder and hay stalks, as a form of land tax, has the following stipulations:

> When taking in hay and straw according to [the number of] qing [of agricultural fields], take in three shi [approx. 60 liters] of hay per qing [approx. 4.61 hectares]. In Shang Commandery, where the land is poor, take in two shi [approx. 40 liters] [of hay] per qing. In every case, [take in] two shi of straw [per qing]. Order each [household] to submit what it has from this year's harvest. Do not take in stale [hay or straw]. For one who does not obey the ordinances: fine four liang [approx. 62 grams] of gold. When collecting and entering hay and straw, each county is to assess what it will use of hay and straw in one year, to satisfy the county's needs. Should there be a surplus [i.e., after the county has satisfied its needs], let it take in fifty-five case per qing [of agricultural fields] in order to match [the tax on] hay and straw. One shi [approx. 20 liters] of hay matches fifteen cash, and one shi of straw matches five cash.[9]

According to a Statute on Robbery:

> The illicit profit from a robbery valued in excess of 660 cash: tattoo [the criminal] and make [him of her] a wall-builder or grain-pounder; from 660 to 220 cash: leave [the criminal] intact and make [him or her] a wall-builder or grain-pounder; not a full 220 to 110 cash: shave [the criminal] and make [him of her] a bond servant or bondwoman; not a full 110 to 22 cash: fine four liang [approx. 62 grams] of gold; not a full 22 to 1 cash: fine one liang [approx. 15.5 grams] of gold.[10]

Thus although for the farmers taxes were mostly paid in kind, i.e., by submitting grain or fodder, there were still occasions when coins were needed. In sum, all these operations would have depended on a unified measuring system.

The enforcement and implementation of a unified system, however, was more easily said than done. Owing to the vast size of the country and local customs, each place would probably have its local measurements. What the government needed was to collect taxes in kind according to the official system of weight and measure issued by the government. Yet one of the most difficult problems was the measurement of volume and weight. Unlike the measurement for length, which is easy to judge by sight alone, the accuracy of the size of the measurement vessels for volume and the plumb bob for weight could not easily be detected, which was the origin of fraudulent transactions. Perhaps exactly because of the possibilities of fraud, there was a constant urge by the government to enforce the surveillance of the measuring system used

[9] Barbieri-Low and Yates (2015: 697).
[10] Barbieri-Low and Yates (2015: 463).

by people, and, not unimaginably, by the government offices themselves, and the great landlords who received rental income from their tenant farmers.

In fact, the manipulation of the volume of measurement vessels could work both ways; that is, one could use larger vessels to buy grain and use smaller vessels to sell grain, in order to gain profit with the difference. In some instances, an ambitious entrepreneur or official could deliberately use smaller vessels to buy grain, while using larger vessels to sell grain – and letting people know of this "benevolent act" – so as to give favor to the buyers – mostly peasants and commoners – in order to win over their support.[11] Either way, it was a fact the people had to live with even until modern times. That is, there could be certain manipulations within the measuring system when it came to transactions of farm or industrial products. As demonstrated by the numerous official documents that enumerated issues concerning various kinds of calculation by numbers, the Qin and Han governments certainly seem to have realized that precise numerical control of numbers, whether in production, consumption, transaction, or transportation, was the key to efficient and successful management of the state.

TIME MEASUREMENT

Besides the measuring of concrete things, of length, volume, or weight, there is also the measuring of the more abstract, the invisible, that is, time. One can imagine that in an agricultural society the telling of time was closely tied to nature. Sunrise and sunset usually give a general guideline of the progress of day and night. Yet finding a method to further divide up the day and night was a much more complicated matter. Should one divide the entire day equally into a number of portions, or divide daytime and nighttime separately? This had to do with people's realization that the lengths of day and night are not always the same. In fact people of the Qin and early Han periods adopted a system that divided the day into twelve hours, corresponding to the twelve earthly stems. It is also suggested that, according to historical documents and excavated administrative records, a system that divided the day into sixteen hours was also in use. One recent study indicates that the sixteen-hour system was probably in use at least until the late Western Han period, while the twelve-hour system, although attested to as early as the Qin, or even earlier, was most likely to have been adopted for general use only since the Eastern Han period, and was passed down throughout the rest of Chinese history. The important point is that, however the day was divided – twelve hours, sixteen hours, with each division having equal length or not – the names of the divisions are all given according to practical descriptions such as dawn, rooster call, sunrise, breakfast,

[11] *Zuo Zhuan, Duke Zhao*: 1235–36; see a similar example in *Huainanzi* 18: 1306.

mid-day, sun-slanting, sunset, dinner, rest, and midnight. They could tell the relative positions of certain time sections of the day in relation to other time sections, but not the exact lengths of the sections. For this, one would have to rely on the time-keeping instruments.

As is well known, many early civilizations learned to use some versions of the sundial to tell the time, and China was no exception, as the use of the sundial could be found as early as the Shang dynasty. By Qin and Han times, a number of different sundials with different accuracies were in use, and quite widely in society. In the countryside, at every *ting*-station, there would have been a sundial post erected to allow people to tell the time. These would be the more common ones, but less accurate. In the government offices, more finely made instruments based on the principle of the sundial were used. It is known that in the imperial library of the Han court, there were books on the make and use of sundials, indicating that there must have been a serious demand for them. It is also known that by the Han period the practice of dividing the length of a day into 100 sections (*ke*, a carved mark on the dial) was already in use, which made every section approximately 14.4 minutes. This term *ke* is still used today as a time counting unit, representing 15 minutes. Any time period smaller than the section, however, could not be differentiated effectively. Despite this, the sundial could be very accurate at least once a day, which is noontime, when the sun is directly above the dial and no shadow is to be observed.

In addition to the sundial, there was also the water clock, which was based on the principle of draining water regularly and evenly out or into a container with marks. When the water level falls or rises, the water level shown on the marks could tell the passing of time. As with the sundial, the construction of water clocks could vary from simple to more complicated ones, from clay pots that peasants used at home to bronze cast sets that only the rich family and the government offices could afford to use. An example of the draining water clock was a bronze vessel, dated to 27 BCE, with a height of 47.9 centimeters, weighing 8.25 kilograms. A drain tube at the bottom of the vessel indicates that it is a draining water clock. A much bigger water clock, with a height of 79.3 centimeters, weighing 74 kilograms, was found in the tomb of a prince, possibly the son of Emperor Wu, Liu Fu, who died in 87 BCE.

The advantage of the water clock over the sundial is obvious, as it could be used both during the day and at night, and the carvings could be made finer, when technological issues such as the humidity and the quality of the water used could be controlled. But this does not mean that the sundial was superseded by the water clock, since the sundial is much more mobile than the water clock and thus could adapt to different situations when accuracy was not the absolute concern. In fact, often the sundial and the water clock were used in combination, as the water clock gives a finer division of time, while the sundial serves as a correction of the water clock once a day at noon.

Administrative documents found in the Western fortresses indicate that, at least in the military settings, the telling of time was quite a serious business. Records about the transportation of mail and other articles were written down in detail, often indicating the exact time that the document left and arrived from one office to another, the distance traveled, and whether or not the courier delivered the mail on time. As early as the late third century BCE, in the legal documents discovered in a Qin tomb at Shuihudi, there is a "Statute on the Forwarding of Documents (*xingshu lü*)" in which it is clearly stated that "When transmitting and receiving official documents, one must record the date and time of dispatch and arrival, in order to reply in time to make mutual reference. If the document is lost, one should immediately report this to the office. One should not send slaves, old and weak and untrustworthy people to deliver the documents."[12] This Qin regulation apparently was still in effect during the Han, as a similar statute was found in the corpus of legal documents of Zhangjiashan.[13]

Documents found at the Western border fortresses contained a large amount of such kinds of routine records. One such text reads, "First Month, day of *wuwu*, mid-night, soldier Shang of Linmu transmitted [a document] to soldier Sheng of Chengao. On the day of *jiwei* (i.e., next day), soldier X of Dangqu delivered [the document] to soldier Hai of Shouxiang. The distance was 98 *li*, normal traveling time 12 hours. Over schedule two hours and two-tenths of an hour."[14] One could only imagine that such careful recording must have been designed out of a certain necessity in the bureaucratic system, to control the operation of daily affairs. The importance of time keeping, therefore, should be understood in the context of this bureaucratic mindset.

CALENDAR SYSTEM

Beyond keeping time for daily activities, for the life of a farming community, the most important regulating system would be the yearly calendar. As with many early civilizations, people living on the East Asian subcontinent had developed a way to observe the astronomical phenomena in order to determine the revolution of the seasons and the progression of the years. Besides recognizing the various constellations and their relationship with seasonal cycles such as the solstices, the calculation of the length of the years as 365 ¼ days was similar to the Julian calendar adopted by the Romans in 43 BCE.[15] The intercalary leap year, the most characteristic way of day keeping, was the

12 *Shuihudi*, 61.
13 Barbieri-Low and Yates (2015: 729–52).
14 Gansu sheng wenwu kaogu yanjiusuo (1990: 547).
15 Pankenier (2013).

invention of the sexagenary system, where the twelve "heavenly stems" and ten "earthly branches" combine to form a sixty-day or sixty-year cycle, which has been in existence at least as early as the Shang dynasty and has been in use ever since until modern times. During the Warring States period, a number of calendars based on the 365 ¼-day year were in use; the difference between them was mainly where to place the beginning of the year. For example, the Xia calendar placed New Year's Day at the first day of the First Month, while the Shang calendar placed it at the first day of the Twelfth Month.[16]

When the Han dynasty was established, as with many other institutions, the calendrical system of the Qin was adopted, until the time of Emperor Wu, when the calendar could not keep pace with the actual movement of the heavenly bodies. Emperor Wu commenced a calendrical reform in 104 CE and the result was a system that was highly accurate and adaptive to the agricultural cycle, with intercalary months and years to adjust the correlations between the four seasons and the twelve months, and the twenty-four seasonal nodes, which became the foundation of agricultural activities throughout later history. New Year's Day, more importantly, was fixed on the first day of the First Month, following the Xia calendar.

Although by the time of Emperor Wu specialists in astronomy were making very precise calculations of the movements of the heavenly bodies in relation to the construction of a more accurate calendar, in terms of the daily lives of the farmers, the twenty-four seasonal nodes, each for about fifteen days, were of paramount importance, as they provided clear and precise indications for agricultural activities. The names of these seasonal nodes are self-explanatory and provide a very graphic description of the changing of the seasons.

Spring	Spring's Beginning (Lichun 立春)	Rain Water (Yushui 雨水)	Stirring of Hibernating Insects (Jingzhi 驚蟄)	Spring Equinox (Chunfen, 春分)	Clear and Bright (Qingming 清明)	Grain Rain (Guyu 谷雨)
Summer	Summer's Beginning (Lixia 立夏)	Small Grain Full (Xiaoman 小滿)	Grain in Ear (Mangzhong 芒種),	Summer Solstice (Xiazhi 夏至)	Slight Heat (Xiaoshu 小暑)	Great Heat (Dashu 大暑)
Autumn	Autumn's Beginning (Liqiu 立秋)	Stopping of Heat (Chushu 處暑)	White Dew (Bailu 白露)	Autumn Equinox (Qiufen 秋分)	Cold Dew (Hanlu 寒露)	Frost's Descent (Shuangjiang 霜降)
Winter	Winter's Beginning (Lidong 立冬)	Light Snow (Xiaoxue 小雪)	Great Snow (Daxue 大雪)	Winter Solstice (Dongzhi 冬至)	Slight Cold (Xiaohan 小寒)	Great Cold (Dahan 大寒)

[16] Sivin (1969); Needham (2004, Vol. 3, 390–480).

It can be seen that these nodes are based on the solar year, as the integration of solstices and equinoxes indicated. These terms in their successive order indicate that people had established the relationship between the gradual changing of weather and the corresponding agricultural activities, and integrated them into the calendrical system, so that farmers would know what kind of weather patterns to expect at each season, and what activities they should be preparing to engage in. Needless to say, on that vast continent, farmers who lived in the north would experience quite different weather patterns than those who lived in the south. During the Han period, the area south of the Yangzi River was not well developed; thus we do not know if farmers there had the knowledge of the seasonal nodes. Still, the precision of the "weather forecast," if we could use this term, was extremely accurate and practical in the Central Plain area. Later, the imperial government would make the publication of calendars the responsibility of the state, for this provided important guidance for farming society.

TRANSPORTATION SYSTEM

With the establishment of the measuring system and time measurement, the elements of managing a state efficiently become possible. Yet this management would have to depend on physical conditions for the effective transmission of messages and materials over a long distance. The transportation system, therefore, was crucial for the operation of the state as well as the circulation of goods and materials throughout the country. With the unification of the country under the First Emperor of Qin, it became possible for people to travel for a longer distance. Although the physical conditions of the roads and waterways were far from safe, some indications tell us that long-distance travel was beginning to become a regular activity, which must have brought about a change to the mental picture of the world that people lived in, even if most people in the countryside would rarely have had the chance to engage in travel.[17]

Before unification, of course, all the various competing Warring States developed transportation systems within their own borders. In the state of Qi, for example, there were official post stations along the main road, at intervals of thirty *li*, for the purpose of providing food and lodging for travelers and their horses.[18] By "post" we of course do not mean the post in the modern sense, but only a system to transmit official documents and personnel. The famous Duke Wen of Jin was also highly praised by historians for his efforts in building hostels and roads in order that travelers and envoys from other states could travel easily and rest comfortably.[19] Another story, dated to 541 BCE,

[17] Yates (1994, 2001).
[18] *Guanzi* 7: 368.
[19] *Zuo Zhuan*:1186.

mentions that a road between the states of Qin and Jin was equipped with post stations at intervals of ten *li*, and by changing carriages at each station, the messenger was able to travel a thousand *li* with great speed.[20] If there is any doubt about the accuracy of this story, the early Western Han legal documents found at Zhangjiashan should dispel it with a degree of certainty. In a Statute on the Forwarding of Documents (*Xing shu lü*), the following sentences are to be found:

> Every ten *li* [approx. 4.16 kilometers], establish one courier station. From the Yangzi River in Nan Commandery, south to the southern boundary of Suo County, every twenty *li* [approx. 8.32 kilometers] [establish] one courier station ... In Beidi, Shang, and Longxi [commanderies], [establish] one courier station every thirty *li* [approx. 12.5 kilometers]. Where the terrain is precipitous and narrow, and courier stations cannot be established, one may adjust the distance according to the convenience of the location.[21]

Although the statute does not mention every place in the empire, it could be reasonably assumed that the post system, and with it the road transportation system, was established all over the country, with local variations of the distance between the post stations. The variation seems to be based on the density of population along the route (Fig. 26).

Overall, the foundation of a vast road system was laid in the unified Qin dynasty, and further developed during the Han. As could be seen on the map, by connecting the existing major routes linking the capitals Chang'an and Luoyang to the cities to the east, south, north, and northwest, Chang'an and Luoyang are located at the center of the web of communications. Many of the nodal points of this web were those cities that were already important commercial and political centers before the unification of the empire.

How fast were people able to travel? Since the speed of travel depends upon the means of travel, the condition of the road if there is any, and the weight that the traveler carries, it is difficult to produce a general estimation. Yet precisely because of this, people cared about the speed of travel. As we have seen previously, records of the transmission of official documents paid attention to the precise time of the dispatch and arrival of the document, and the distance traveled, so that it is possible to calculate the speed of travel. According to a record of document transmission by a foot soldier at the fortress of Juyan at the Western border, "For a distance of 97 *li* [approx. 40.25 kilometers], the normal travel time is 8 hours and 3 divisions. Actual travel time: 7 hours and 2 divisions." Given a six-hour (twelve in modern hours) working day, the

20 *Zuo Zhuan*:1214.
21 Barbieri-Low and Yates (2015: 739).

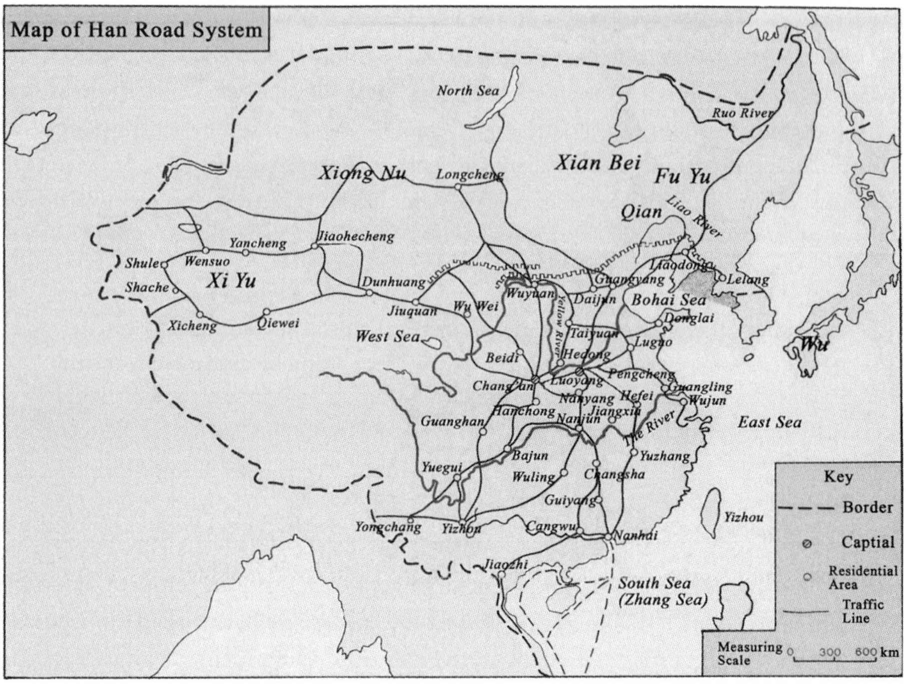

26. Map of the Han road system. After Zhou Cheng 周成 ed., *Zhongguo Gudai Jiaotong Tudian* 中國古代交通圖典 (Beijing 北京: Zhongguo shijieyu chubanshe 中國世界語出版社, 1995), 13

standard daily travel speed would be 68.7 *li* [approx. 28.5 kilometers] while the actual speed was 79.2 *li* [approx. 32.8 kilometers].

The fact that a standard travel time was provided in the document to measure against the actual travel time indicates that there was an officially established standard speed of travel. According to a study, during the Han period, a soldier carrying a full load of equipment could travel for about 30 *li* (c. 12.5 kilometers) per day. With a light load, a soldier could travel for 50 *li* (c. 20 kilometers) per day. And for travel without carrying a load, one could reach 70 *li* (c. 29 kilometers). In an emergency, the travel speed could reach 100 *li* (c. 41 kilometers) per day.

Although traveling on foot might have been more flexible, with fewer constraints with road conditions, travel by carriage or on horse would serve quite different functions. Obviously, for transportation of goods and equipment, carriages and wagons played an important role, as did animals such as horses and cattle. According to documents found at Juyan, an empty cart could travel 70 *li* per day, while a loaded cart could travel about 50 *li*. The load of an average cart could be between 25 and 35 *shi*. Of course carts or wagons came in different sizes and styles, including four-wheeled carts, double-shaft carts, and single-wheel carts, and animals were used to carry cargo, including horses, cattle, donkeys, mules, and camels. Needless to say, traveling on horseback would be the fastest method. The famous mathematical treatise *The Nine Chapters* (九章算術 *Jiuzhang suanshu*), commonly assumed to have been composed and edited over a long period of time and reaching its present form during the Eastern Han period, contains some examples that use the speed of travel as questions for calculation:

> A fast horse and a slow horse set out from Chang'an to Qi. Qi is 3000 *li* away from Chang'an. The fast horse travels 193 *li* on the first day, and this increases by 13 *li* every day thereafter. The slow horse travels 97 *li* on the first day, and decreases by 0.5 *li* every day thereafter. The fast horse reached Qi first, and turned around to meet the slow horse. Question: how many days after setting out would they meet, and how many *li* would each travel?"[22]

We are of course not to believe that the speed of the horses in the hypothetical question is realistic, yet compared to the speed of the foot soldier and the cart, it would not be surprising if the starting speed was fairly authentic.

In addition to land travel, waterways were also an important means of transportation. Most of the known waterways during the Qin and Han periods were located in northern China, whereas waterways south of the Yangzi River were not yet fully developed. The Yellow River and its various tributaries were therefore the major arteries of river transportation. From many known names of the ferry crossings along the rivers, we can see the interconnectedness of water and land transportation. However, as will be discussed in the text that follows, this does not mean that the water systems south of the Yangzi River were not explored. In fact, as part of the efforts to integrate the water transportation system, the Qin and Han governments made a considerable effort to build canals, another type of important hydraulic engineering project, that had a great impact on the waterway system of communication. Some of the more famous canals, such as the Honggou Canal that connects the Yellow River system with the Huai River system, the Hangou Canal that connects the Yangzi River system and the Huai River system, and the Lingqu Canal that connects the Xiang River system and the Zhu River system, played a key role in connecting and integrating the vast country into a unified water transportation system.

Whether traveling by land or by river, it was vitally important to have some kind of guidance, such as a map. Lacking the modern technology to produce land surveys, map making in ancient times would have been a very difficult task. It was a most extraordinary event in the history of science that a map drawn on a wooden board, dated as early as 239 BCE, and found in a Qin dynasty tomb in the present Gansu Province, shows traces of mountains, rivers,

[22] Song (1987).

ferry points, and roads. Although being somewhat rudimentary and formulaic, it nevertheless could have been of significant help to travelers.[23]

However, maps could also be drawn on cloth. A famous story contained in the *Record of the Grand Scribe* tells the story of the assassination attempt against the King of Qin (later the First Emperor of Qin) by Jing Ke, an assassin from the rival state of Yan. Pretending to defect from the state of Yan, Jing Ke presented a map of a piece of territory that belonged to Yan as a gift. The knife that was intended to be used to assassinate the king was wrapped in the map, apparently made of silk or linen, to avoid being discovered by the guards. Thus, when Jing Ke approached the king, he unrolled the map and at the end of the roll, the knife emerged, which he grabbed and tried to stab the king (Fig. 27). This assassination attempt failed; otherwise the history of China would have been radically changed forever.[24] This story nevertheless created a most appropriate proverb for describing the exposure of conspiracy or ill intention: "When the map is unrolled, the knife emerges (*tuqung bijian* 圖窮匕見)"

More samples of maps, drawn on silk cloth, were found in the Mawangdui tomb no. 3, buried 168 BCE (Fig. 28). One of the maps shows the road and river systems, settlements, and the mountain ranges of the area of southern Changsha Kingdom and the adjacent Nanyue Kingdom, the present Guangdong Province. The fact that the main features of the map approximate the actual geography of the area indicates that the concept of scale must have been employed in the process of map making. This would not be too surprising given the fact that the Han people had by this time developed rather sophisticated mathematical skills, as evidenced by the construction of the calendar systems as well as the appearance of *The Nine Chapters*.[25]

During the process of the expansion to the south, the Qin had already utilized the river systems of the area south of the Yangzi River, such as Yuan River, Xiang River, Gan River, Xin River, and Zhu River. When Emperor Wu sent an army to suppress the kingdom of Nanyue, the army also utilized the Zhu River system.[26] The Mawangdui map that shows the Xiang River and its tributaries as well as the river system of the Nanyue Kingdom is a clear indication that, well before Emperor Wu's time, detailed maps with military implications had been produced and remained in the possession of regional military officials, which corroborates what we have learned from traditional sources.

Another map found in the Mawangdui tomb no. 3 is a specialized map of the military settlements of the Changsha Kingdom, which is of particular interest

[23] He Shuangquan (1989).
[24] *SJ* 34: 1561; 86: 2534–35.
[25] Needham (2004, Vol. 3: 552).
[26] Wang (1994: 168–70).

27. Jing Ke's assassination attempt on the King of Qin (middle row). Courtesy of the Institute of History and Philology, Academia Sinica, T683.2 (27404)

for our understanding of the practice of map making at that time. It could be inferred by the existence of different kinds of maps that people then were already very familiar with the idea of using maps for different purposes. This of course resonates with the known geographic texts such as the "Tribute of Yu" (*Yugong*) and the geographic treatises found in the *History of Han* and *History of Later Han*, and such specialized works as *Commentary on the Classic of Rivers* (*Shuijing zhu*). All these meticulous descriptions of the geographic features would be hard to imagine without the help of some form of map at hand. It has been shown that these maps represent a high achievement in mapping and surveying methods during this time, which offers another piece of evidence for the extent to which the Han state focused its efforts on gaining control of the land and its resources. This is why, during the Han period, whenever a

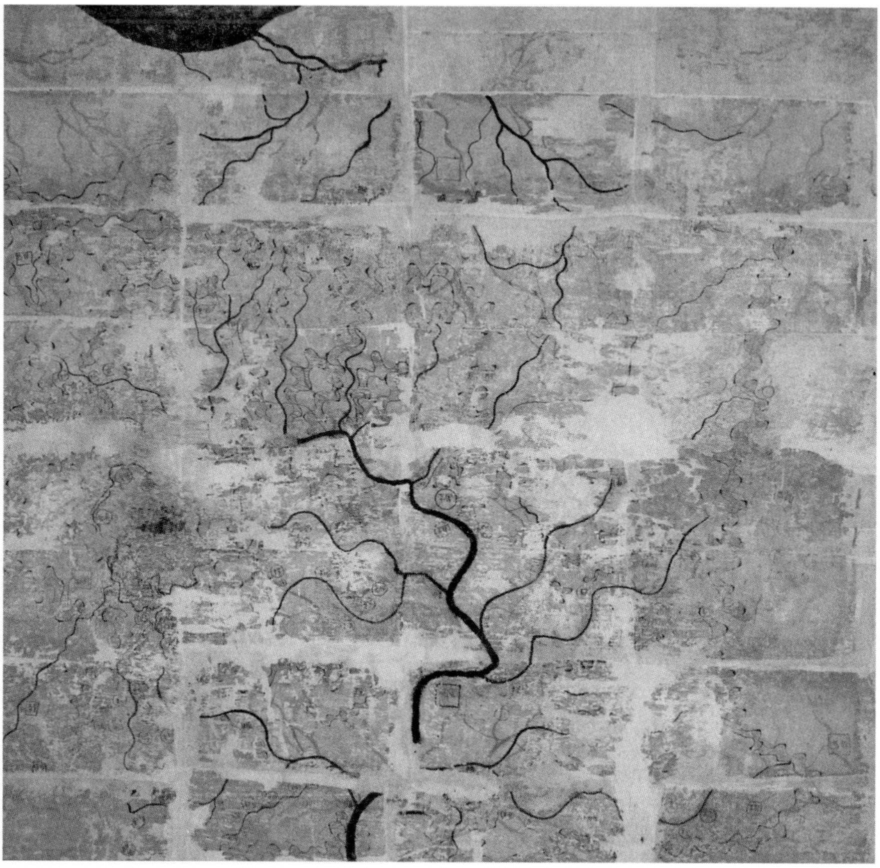

28. Map unearthed from Mawangdui tomb no. 3. Courtesy of Hunan Provincial Museum. Source: Fu and Chen eds., *Mawangdui Hanmu wenwu*, 151

new emperor ascended the throne, the presentation of a map of the territory that the emperor ruled was part of the important enthronement ceremony.[27]

Perhaps nowhere in the early documents was the use of maps in government administration demonstrated so well as what is found in the *Rites of Zhou* (*Zhouli*). In the chapter on the Earth Office, the Master of Public Works is in charge of the maps of the state and uses them to assess the extent of the land, and to recognize the forests and mountains, rivers and lakes, and many kinds of geographic features, as well as the location of cities and towns. When there were disputes about land property, maps were to be employed to settle them.[28] The mere mention of the use of maps, no matter if the offices presented in the *Zhouli* were more or less an idealized construct of an ideal

[27] *SJ* 60: 2110.
[28] *Zhouli* 18: 689–92.

government, indicates an overall concern about efficient governing with exact measurements.

Was the map an important part of common people's daily lives? It can be assumed that road maps could be directly useful for individuals when traveling, but it is more likely that, during the Han and even later centuries, whether they were for transportation, for military defense, or for controlling the territory and assessment of taxation, maps were controlled by the government officials, to which the tomb owner of Mawangdui no. 3 must have belonged. Nevertheless, the map was the graphic manifestation of the mental and physical control of the state, and as such, it affected people's daily life in an imperceptible way.

MEDICINE

Of all the technologies that had to do with daily life, medicine was probably the most intimate and vital one. In the royal divination records from the Shang dynasty, the diviners asked whether the king or some members of the royal family would recover from certain illnesses. They also wished to know which spirit had caused the illness, so that propitiating measures could be implemented. However, the actions that they undertook to manage the illnesses were certainly more than divination and propitiation. One of the important features of medical science during this time, and continuing down to the Qin and Han periods, was the fact that an empirical and practical understanding of treatment of illnesses based on experience and cumulative knowledge of materia medica was gradually enveloped in a philosophical theory based on the idea of *qi*/ether/energy as the basic substance of the myriad objects in the universe; the idea of *yin* and *yang*, the fundamental principle of the binary structure of the universe; and finally the Five Phases theory, which laid out the operational principle of the universe by assigning everything to one of the five elements: metal, wood, water, earth, and fire. The relationship between the five elements could be one conquering the other; thus metal conquers wood, wood conquers earth, earth conquers water, water conquers fire, while fire conquers metal. Or, their relationship could be one generating another; thus metal generates water, water generates wood, wood generates fire, fire generates earth, while earth generates metal. This operational principle could explain (ideally of course) not only how everything in the universe is related to everything else, but also what takes place within the human body. A healthy body is one in which all the elements in the body (i.e., the internal organs which correspond to one of the five elements) are in balance. When one of the elements becomes stronger or weaker than the others, the balance of the body will be affected, and illness would occur. The treatment, therefore, is to try to help suppress or enhance the irregular element/organ and restore the balance, and therefore the health, of the body. The body, therefore, is seen metaphorically as a microcosmos. This microcosmos is also part of the macrocosmos; thus it resonates with what happens in the natural world. Such a theory has been termed "natural philosophy"[29] or "correlative cosmology."[30]

This theory developed during the Spring and Autumn period and gradually matured during the course of the Warring States period. One can understand that there is a certain amount of truth in the idea that a harmonious world is a world with balance, and a healthy body is a body that maintains equilibrium in all aspects; every limb and every organ operates smoothly without a hitch. Attempting to fit every detail into the Five Phases theory, however, is a much more challenging task, not only for physicians, but also for the intellectuals and politicians who found it appealing to employ it to explain the change of dynasties. A natural philosophy thus became the guideline for natural science (e.g., medicine), and political science (e.g., the legitimation of dynastic succession). The result, as can be expected, was a natural science enveloped and conditioned by a particular philosophy, and a political science constantly adjusting the standards of the application of the Five Phases theory.

As was true with many aspects in life, reality is much more complex than written words can record. The progress of the knowledge of medicine, despite having the need to conform or to help develop what *yin–yang* and Five Phases theory prescribed, expanded in all directions. As the range of concern for health maintenance and treatment of diseases was almost limitless, the early Chinese medical practitioners actively studied various types of cures for a number of different diseases; developed recipes for treatment; and compiled essays on the principles of physiology, pathology, diagnosis, and treatment. It was probably during the Warring States period that medical treatises began to be collected, one among them later known as the *Inner Canon of the Yellow Thearch* (*Huangdi neijing* 黃帝內經). This text, or a version of it, was mentioned in the "Bibliography Treatise" in the *History of Han*, which means that such types of medical texts were in existence at least during the late Western Han. The received version of the *Inner Canon* came entirely from later sources.[31] Known as the foundational text of traditional Chinese medicine, the *Inner Canon* represents an integrated account of various medical treatises and theories. A basic theory in the *Inner Canon* is the idea of the "12 vessels" or "channels" (*mai* 脈) in the human body. This theory maintains that there are twelve channels of *qi*/vapor/energy, which are called *mai*, often translated as "vessel," in the human body. They are invisible to the human eye, and are certainly not blood veins, but are related to the inner organs of the body.

[29] See Harper (1998: 11).
[30] Graham (1986).
[31] Sivin (1993:196–215); Unschuld (2003: 1–7).

Along these channels there are a number of points, which correspond to the functions of the inner organs, and the points are the locations to apply acupuncture or cauterization.[32]

It has long been observed that the received text of the *Inner Canon* is the result of numerous editions throughout the ages, and therefore not the work of a single author, let alone the legendary Yellow Thearch. This has been further validated by the discovery of medical texts that were found in the Mawangdui tomb no. 3, dated to early second century BCE. In the Mawangdui manuscripts, there are four treatises on the subject of "*mai*/vessel." Two of the treatises mention eleven vessels in the human body, while in the *Inner Canon*, and indeed in all subsequent medical texts, there are twelve vessels. Thus the Mawangdui texts could have represented an earlier stage of the development of the "vessel" theory. The Mawangdui texts did not mention acupuncture, again an indication of the early date of the texts, although we cannot rule out the possibility that acupuncture theory already existed at this time, except for the fact that so far no textual evidence has been found.

The Mawangdui medical manuscripts also allow us to have a closer view of the kinds of diseases or illnesses that people might have suffered in their daily lives. A text now identified as the "Recipes for Fifty-two Ailments (*wushier bingfang* 五十二病方)" lists about 103 diseases, covering internal medicine, surgery, gynecology, pediatrics, as well as 283 recipes for curing diseases, and employed 247 different kinds of materia medica.[33] Recipes and treatments for various wounds, infant spasms, convulsions, dog bites, leech bites, snake bites, scorpion bites, burns, urine ailments, warts, seizures, and hemorrhoids clearly show the kinds of diseases people contracted at that time. One example describing treating metal wound reads as follows:

> To alleviate the pain of a metal wound. Take one portion of thoroughly dried fruits of *ji* (capsella), scorched until blackened and seared; and two portions of *zhu* (atractylodes) root, peeled and seared. Blend the two substances together. Take one three-fingered pinch reaching to the knuckles and put the medicine into one brimming-full cup of pure liquor. Stir and drink. For those who do not (usually drink), use one half cup of liquor. Having drunk it, after some time there is no pain. If the pain returns, drink the medicine following the same procedure. If there is no pain, do not drink the medicine. (Take) the medicine before eating or after eating as you wish. While treating the ailment, do not eat fish, pork, horseflesh, turtles, snakes, odorous foods, and *mazhu* greens. Do not approach the inner (chamber). When the ailment desists, (you may do things) as before. While treating the ailment, there are no temporal (restrictions). Prepare enough medicine to treat the ailment. After

[32] See Liu Yanchi (1988, chapter 4).

[33] Zhou and Xiao (1989: 49).

> formulating the medicine, store it in a silk pouch. When preparing the *zhu* (atractylodes), allow it to dry by putting it in the sun or by using some other means, then prepare. Excellent.[34]

While medical historians of China endeavor to find out if the recipes could indeed be proven effective, there seems no doubt that the instruction given here came from a long tradition of empirical knowledge about materia medica. The instructions to the patient about when to take the medicine and prohibition against certain behavior also indicate that the medical practitioners had developed a sophisticated understanding of the relationship between medicine and physiology. A number of medical texts on physical exercise and health hygiene discovered in the Mawangdui tomb no. 3 demonstrate that by the early second century BCE, the medical practitioners had developed not only sophisticated pharmacological knowledge, but also a nuanced understanding of the human physiology, a theoretical explanation of the cause of disease, and a sophisticated philosophy of health. One of the texts, *The Union of Yin and Yang* (*He yinyang* 合陰陽), was actually a manual that describes the physical reaction of the male and female body during sexual intercourse, with detailed description of the sexual positions and principles of engagement, obviously with the aim of promoting a healthy sex life. It shows the most detailed knowledge of human physiology and objective understanding of sexual behavior that had ever been written in the ancient world, let alone in China.[35]

From a daily life point of view, the Mawangdui medical texts represent a kind of technical knowledge that had a great impact on the quality of life for those who were able to have access to such knowledge. Given the fact that the texts were probably written only by specialized physicians and for the use of those who had the leisure to read and practice, or to have the privilege of having the service of medical specialists, we could not say that it was a field of public knowledge. Yet the implication of this kind of knowledge for the development of traditional Chinese medicine was profound, and as such, had a direct influence on people's daily lives. Meanwhile, the reality of the medical situation of the society at large was probably not at all comparable with that of the noble households. At numerous occasions, the government dispensed medical help to the people when natural disasters or epidemics struck and public health declined.[36] These facts indicate that medical knowledge and the supply of medicine were usually not adequate in local societies. Moreover, illnesses were treated with local recipes intermixed with various magical spells. In fact, in the Mawangdui text "Recipes for Fifty-two Ailments," magical spells were prescribed to cure a number of ailments, which indicates that in the early

[34] Zhou and Xiao (1989: 62). Translation: Harper (1998: 228–29).

[35] See Goldin (2001: 46–47).

[36] *HS* 12: 353; *HS* 75: 3172; *HHS*: 254, 294,296, 332, 334, 342.

Western Han it was not uncommon even for the elites to resort to magical treatment of diseases. The general belief in the efficacy of the medical skill of the *wu*-shaman, as well as in the power of spirits and ghosts in the entire Han period, was confirmed by numerous examples, including commoners and people of upper social echelon.[37] We shall address this aspect of daily life in Chapter 10.

[37] Lin (2009).

EIGHT

LEISURE AND ENTERTAINMENT, GAMES, AND FESTIVALS

FESTIVALS RELATED TO THE AGRICULTURAL CYCLE

With the unification of the country, in theory if not in practice, the reform of the calendar system in the reign of Emperor Wu gave the population a further general time guideline for annual agricultural activities. As is the case with most traditional societies, the agricultural activities and festivals associated with the harvest tended to form the backbone of life for the common people. The Chinese term for festival is *jie* (節), literally "section" or "node," which refers to the various nodal points of the annual cycle, such as the twenty-four nodal points that mark the changing stages of the agricultural cycle. Related to these twenty-four nodal points are various festivals that celebrate the important moments of the agricultural cycle.

According to the transmitted texts, people of the Zhou dynasty were already celebrating various seasonal festivals that marked the stages of the agricultural cycle. A passage in the *Book of Poetry* describes the religious activities of the noble families as follows:

> [The ice-house was opened] in the days of the fourth month, early in the morning,
> Having offered, as a sacrifice, a lamb with spring onions;
> In the ninth month, it is cold, with frost;
> In the tenth month, they sweep their stack-sites clean.
> The two bottles of spirits are enjoyed,
> And they say, "Let us kill our lambs and sheep,

> And to go to the hall of our prince,
> There raise the cup of rhinoceros horn,
> And wish him long life, – that he may live forever."[1]

Although the poems are embellished and quite reserved in tone, they are traditionally seen as representing seasonal celebrations during the Zhou.[2] Indeed it is worth pondering if it was possible that the elite of an agricultural society would not honor the age-old tradition of the peasants and try to forge a set of more "cultured" or "civilized" festivals for people to enjoy. In fact, this idea of changing or reforming customs – usually the undesirable, more vulgar ones – of the commoners according to an ideal, i.e., the Confucian ideal, remained one of the concerns of the ruling elite from the Spring and Autumn period onwards. The evidence to show the consequence of this train of thinking, toward the end of the Warring States period, was an extraordinary document, the *Monthly Ordinances* (*Yueling*), first laid out in *the Master Lü's Spring and Autumn Annal* (*Lüshi chunqiu*), and later incorporated into the text of *Book of Rites* (*Liji*). It is an idealized political program that takes into account the seasonal changes of the weather and prescribes corresponding human activities, so that the state, the officials, and the common people would know how to conduct their activities according to the movement of the seasons. The observation of the seasonal changes and the appropriate agricultural activities was, of course, based on the accumulated wisdom of the agricultural society. The corresponding political and social actions, however, were constructed following the reasoning of the Five Phases theory.

During the Han era, with the consolidation of the empire, and the implementation of a unified calendar, the disparate local traditions gradually became integrated into a larger, empire-wide system: the various celebrations of seasonal agricultural activities became commonly shared annual festivals.

Beginning from the First Month, there was the New Year's celebration, to inaugurate a new year and to seek the blessing of the ancestral spirits. It was, and still is, the most important annual festival of the Chinese people. During the Han, not only the government, from the imperial court to local magistrates officials, but also the common people would celebrate New Year's Day.

At the imperial court, the various officials would dress in new garments and according to their rank, file past the emperor to pay homage and recite congratulatory eulogies. In the houses of the common people, the head of the household would lead his family members in making sacrifices to their ancestors, followed by a banquet made up of the most extravagant dishes to celebrate the passing of the old year and the coming of the new.[3]

1 Legge (1960, Vol. 4: 232–33).
2 A classic study of the poems is Granet (1932).
3 Bodde (1975); Peng and Yang (2001).

The preparation of the New Year celebrations, however, started at least a month before New Year's Day, with the stocking up of all sorts of food, plus an exorcistic ritual to cast out any evil spirits accumulated during the course of the year. This was the Great Exorcism (*danuo* 大儺), a ritual with ancient roots that was performed at various levels of society, with different elaborations of a central theme, i.e., to expel the evil spirits that could have hidden in the dark corners of the palace, or inside the house. In the Eastern Han period, this ritual evolved into an extensive performance that dramatized the struggle between the exorcist and the demonic spirits. In the modern period, the *no*-ritual drama is still preserved in many places in China, especially some of the southwestern provinces.[4]

Following the New Year's Day celebration was the Beginning of Spring, on which day officials, from the central government through to the local county, would have to dress in green garments and go to the eastern suburb and reverently welcome the coming of spring, symbolized by a boy dressed in green, the symbolic color of spring. The deity to be worshipped with a sacrifice was the Green Thearch of the East. The emperor would dispatch gifts to all the officials to celebrate the beginning of a new season. As this celebration was probably adopted by the Han government only during the Eastern Han period, without much evidence of the application of this event in the countryside, it seems to have been more of an official ceremony than a state-wide festival.[5] However, this does not mean that in the local society people did not perform certain rituals to celebrate the new season.

As a continuous celebration of the coming of spring, there was the celebration of the First *Ding*-day of the First Month. The first *Ding*-day refers to the first day of the month that has the *ding*–X combination of the sexagenarian system of day-reckoning, "X" being one of the twelve branches. The emperor and court officials would make a sacrifice to the Southern and Northern Thearchs and imperial ancestral shrines, followed by a visit to the mausoleums of the emperors Gaozu 高祖 (first emperor of the Western Han) and Guangwu 光武 (first emperor of the Eastern Han). Correspondingly, the common people would make a sacrifice to their family ancestors and the deity of travel and pray for a good year to come.

With the passing of the seasons, people periodically celebrated festivals or rituals such as the First *si*-day of the Third Month, the Fifth day of the Fifth Month, the Summer Solstice, the Autumn Equinox, the Winter Solstice, and finally the *La*-Day 臘日 in the Twelfth Month, toward the end of the year, which was a day for family reunions and the beginning of the preparation for the coming new year.[6] Most of the festivals involved sacrifice to ancestors and/

4 Bodde (1975: 81–82); Qu and Qian (2003: 159–99).

5 *HHS*, "Liyi zhi"; "Jisi zhi"; Peng and Yang (2001: 629–30).

6 Bodde (1975: 223 ff.).

or deities, for the purposes of propitiation for blessings, an abundant harvest, and good health and luck. Often family members would gather to feast and enjoy each other's company, and to be entertained by various performances or games.

We could surmise that as people celebrated the seasonal festivals, besides the outwardly more serious or utilitarian ceremonies and sacrifices, these occasions would also be an opportunity for the consolidation of lineage and family ties, not only by paying homage to common ancestors and protective deities, but also by gathering and feasting together. As scholars of festivities have long observed, in a traditional, that is, agricultural, society, the rhythm of the annual activities needed to be highlighted by periodical festivals, so that people could relax and relieve the tensions that would accumulate from hard physical labor in the fields.[7]

Unlike the early modern European carnivals, or the ancient Roman Bacchanalias,[8] when the existing social order sanctioned by the church or state was temporarily suspended to accommodate extravagant celebrations and wanton behavior, festivals and ceremonies of the Han period, at least from what was expressed in the – inevitably ideologically sanctioned – transmitted texts, were less of a "reverse of order" kind of festivity, but, on the contrary, a festivity that celebrated the established family values and hierarchical order of the society, and the necessity of following the prescribed order of activities. This situation was made even clearer when we consider that the festivals were prescribed under the ideological umbrella of the "Monthly Ordinances," whether the official Ordinances contained in the *Book of Rites*, or private ones such as the *Monthly Ordinances of the Four Peoples* (*Simin yueling*) that the Eastern Han scholar Cui Shi composed for his family estate. The term "ordinance" itself reveals an overall plan and the execution of an ideologically driven program, with the aim of producing a "harmonious society" that could hardly expect or appreciate any irregularity. Such observation, one might add, is not based purely on reading the texts alone, but with "in field" evidence. A version of the *Monthly Ordinances* dated to 5 CE was found among the documents excavated in the far western border garrison of Dunhuang, which served as an imperial edict for the daily activities of the communities there, even though the content of the Ordinance might not be in accord with the general environment of the desert area in which Dunhuang was situated.[9]

One of the festivals, however, might have carried with it the remnants of an ancient mating ritual: the Gaomei, or the Supreme Matchmaker (or Intermediary).[10] References to this ritual are scarce, but since it was recorded

[7] Burke (1994: 178 ff.); a classic discussion is Huizinga (1950: 10–11).
[8] For a classic study of carnival, see Bakhtin (1984); also see Le Roy Laudrie (1979).
[9] For the text, see Li and Zhao (2011: 188–210); Sanft (2009).
[10] See discussions in Bodde (1975: 243–62); Poo (1998, chapter 3).

in the *Yue ling* (*Monthly Ordinances*) and *Zhou li* (*The Rites of Zhou*), it received due attention by scholars as early as the Eastern Han period. *The Rites of Zhou* describes the duty of *meishi*, the Matchmaker, as follows:

> … in the month of mid-spring, to order the gathering of men and women. At this time, there is no restriction on those [couples] who run off [*ben*] together. Those who ignore this order without just cause are to be punished.[11]

A passage in the *Monthly Ordinances* says:

> In this month (the mid-spring), the dark-colored birds arrive. On the arrival day, one should make a *tailao* [ox, sheep, pig] sacrifice at the shrine of *gaomei* [Supreme Matchmaker]. The Son of Heaven attends the occasion personally; the queen leads the nine consorts there. Then those who were mounted by [*yu*, i.e., have had intercourse with] the Son of Heaven are treated with proper ritual. They are given bows, cases, and arrows, in front of the shrine of *gaomei*.[12]

These two references have prompted some intensive discussions among modern scholars, Chinese as well as Western Sinologists.[13] The gist of the focus was to see the references to *gaomei* as an ancient sexual rite performed at the beginning of spring. However, while it is true that the text of the *Rites of Zhou* suggests an official policy (certainly an idealized one) to allow young people to mix freely and choose their partners, it does not explicitly refer to any "sexual rite" despite a certain sexual overtone. The passage in the *Monthly Ordinances*, on the other hand, refers to a fertility ritual, with symbolic actions and objects such as the giving of bows, cases, and arrows, performed by the ruling family with the hope to procure offspring, thus connecting *gaomei* to a certain fertility deity. Again, even though some scholars wanted to see *gaomei* as evidence of a "sexual rite" in ancient China,[14] there is insufficient evidence to support this theory. On the contrary, we see that the supposedly "free spirit" implied by the so-called "sexual rite" was absent from the celebration of the *gaomei*, as it was a state-sponsored activity; that is, the government gave orders to allow young people to meet and choose their partners.

In sum, the example of the *gaomei* shows that even during the Han period, people were unable to fully understand the origins of some the festivals transmitted from the distant past.

[11] *Zhouli* 26: 1040–45.
[12] *Lüshi Chunqiu* 2: 34–35; *Liji* 15: 473–75.
[13] Granet (1932); Kaltenmark (1966); Poo (1998: 31–33).
[14] For example, Granet (1932).

29. Entertainment scene. Courtesy of the Institute of History and Philology, Academia Sinica. T683.2 (27281)

ENTERTAINMENT ACTIVITIES

In order to celebrate the festivals, it is only natural to expect that people would offer many sorts of activities and performances. Banqueting was probably the most basic way to celebrate any festival. In addition, musical performances and dances, and shows that presented special talents, were sponsored by those who were able to afford them (Fig. 29).

Following the improvement of the economic situation of the country, seventy years after the establishment of the new dynasty, when horses and cattle filled the streets and alleys, grain in the storage was spilled and spoiled, and strings holding coins in the treasury became rotten,[15] the Han Emperor Wu began to enjoy the fruits of the labors of his ancestors on all fronts. With the building of the new palaces in the capital, an extension of the frontiers to the northwest and south underway, the imperial powers reached a new height, and life in the palace was more than luxurious. One could easily imagine that the capital would be the most favorable place for every type of entertainment to thrive. A famous court official Dongfang Suo (東方朔) once gave Emperor Wu a direct warning about the latter's wanton and extravagant behavior and its negative impact on the people. The emperor was known to be extremely delighted with watching cockfights, kick-ball games, and horse and dog races. Obviously such pursuits were not the invention of the emperor but belonged to the fashion of the time.[16] Even before the time of Emperor Wu, during the reign of Emperor Wen, a person named Wei Wan was recruited to the rank of palace attendant (*lang* 郎) because of his prowess at chariot racing.[17]

[15] *SJ* 30:1420.
[16] *HS* 65: 2858.
[17] *SJ* 103: 2768.

The famous writer Zhang Heng (78–139 CE) once described various games performed in the capital of Chang'an with the emperor as a spectator:

> When the Grand Equipage visited the Lodge of Peaceful Joy,
> They pitched A-rank and B-rank tents, and the emperor donned a halcyon-plume coat.
> He gathered precious treasures for play and amusement,
> Mixed the rare and beautiful with the wasteful and extravagant.
> He went down to the broad arena with a far-ranging view,
> And observed the wondrous feats of competitive games.
> Wu Huo (a giant) hoisted cauldrons;
> A Dulu climber shinnied up a pole.
> They "rushed the narrows" and performed a swallow dip,
> Their chests thrusting at the sharp spear tips.
> They juggled balls and swords whirling and twirling,
> Walked a tightrope, meeting halfway across,
> ...
> Amazing magicians, quicker than the eye,
> Changed appearances, sundered bodies,
> Swallowed knives, ate fire,
> Darkened the arena with clouds and mist.
> They drew on the ground and created rivers,
> That flowed like the Wei-river, coursed like Jing-river.
> ...
> And then:
> They assembled the show wagon,
> From which they hoisted a tall banner on a pole.
> Young boys displayed their skill.
> Up and down doing glides and flips.
> Suddenly, they threw themselves upside down, catching themselves with their heels;
> Seemingly they were cut asunder and connected again.
> One hundred horses under the same bridle,
> Raced side by side, as fast as their feet could carry them.
> As for the tricks performed at the top of the pole-
> There was no end to their numerous postures.[18]

With highly fanciful diction, this long passage describes something like a circus show the modern descendants of which would have a hard time matching: acrobats performing all kinds of feats in the air, on the pole, or on the tightrope; magicians performing tricks; jugglers tossing balls and knives; giants lifting heavy weights (cauldrons); animals trained to perform tricks; marksmen shooting arrows; wrestlers fighting each other; people in masks acting out dramatic stories; and singers and dancers providing soothing entertainment (Fig. 30).

[18] Knechtges (1982, Vol. I: 227–35).

30. Music and acrobatic performance. After Zhongguo huaxiangshi quanji bianji weiyuanhui, *Zhongguo Huaxiangshi Quanji*, Vol. 1, 152–53

While the emperor enjoyed the performances in the palace or in the imperial garden, similar performances, perhaps with less extravagant display, would be given to the nobility or wealthy merchants, in their mansions or courtyards. For the ordinary citizens, itinerary troupes performing in the marketplace would be the most common way for them to enjoy some eye-catching spectacles. Some of the tricks, especially magical shows, sword swallowing, fire eating, and various forms of music and dance, were brought in from outside of the western and southwestern borders as the result of Emperor Wu's expansionist policy.[19]

Textual and archaeological evidence shows that entertainments of many varieties were performed at banquets or friendly gatherings. One common type of performance would have been that of comic performers, who usually combined dramatic performance with jesting "talk shows" or even clumsy acrobatic actions designed to elicit laughter. Some of the performers were dwarfs, for the obvious fact that their physical features tended to cater to the audience's interest in something comical. A number of famous dwarf performers were renowned not only for telling jokes, but also for the use of satirical stories to remonstrate with those in power. It was because of their rare talents that Sima Qian devoted a chapter in his *Records of the Grand Scribe* to these performers.

A large number of representations of performing arts can be identified on the wall paintings and decorative tiles found in the tombs of the Han period. Scenes depicting dancers, jugglers, acrobats, musicians, wrestlers, and jesters were very common motives, indicating a general aspiration for an enjoyable life in the hereafter. Funerary figurines of musicians, dancers, and jesters are among the favorite paraphernalia of the tombs of the rich (Figs. 31–33).

One of the more extravagant performances was the "carriage show," which was often depicted on the decorated tomb bricks of the Eastern Han period.

[19] Yü (1967: 202–19).

31. Dancing woman, painted terra-cotta. Courtesy of National Museum of China. Source: Zhongguo meishu quanji bianji weiyuanhui ed., *Zhongguo Meishu Quanji, Diaosu bian*, Vol. 2, 62

One of the scenes shows two chariots driving from left to right. A person riding on a horse in front of the chariots is carrying a flag, signifying a certain performing troupe behind him. To the left of the rider is a marksman, on horseback, bending to shoot an arrow at a certain target. The first chariot is controlled by a driver. A pole is erected in the middle of the chariot. At the top of the pole, a man is hanging upside down by his feet. On each of his outstretched arms stands a person. Below in the chariot, a second person behind the driver is holding a rope that is connected at a slanting angle to a person crouching on top of the pole on the second chariot. An acrobat is walking on the rope, performing a delicate balancing act. Two drivers on the second chariot are looking at the acrobat and controlling the speed of the horse, apparently in order to keep a desired distance from the first chariot, so that the rope between the two chariots could be drawn in a tight position. The scene depicts actions that defy the common sense of physics. The hanging man on the first chariot would have to be an incredibly strong person to be able to

32. Decorated brick. Two male jugglers performing at the upper right; two spectators, one man and one woman, sitting on the mat to the upper left. Two male musicians playing mouth organs to the lower left, and a female dancer dancing at the lower right, accompanied by a male dancer in the middle. Eastern Han. Sichuan Chengdu City Museum. Courtesy of the Institute of History and Philology, Academia Sinica, T683.2 (27002)

33. Carriage show on brick. After Nanyangshi wenwu yianjiuso 南陽市文物研究所, *Nanyang handai huaxiangzhuan* 南陽漢代畫像磚 (Beijing 北京: Wenwu chubanshe 文物出版社, 1990, fig. 115)

support one person on each arm in an upside down position. It seems virtually impossible for a person to do so even in an upright position. Again, one person holding a slanting rope at each end and being able to support an acrobat is a highly questionable feat, not to mention the fact that the rope is stretched between two running chariots at a 45-degree angle.

While we probably should not take the depictions on the bricks or the wall paintings literally, just as we should not take the textual descriptions literally, we can certainly gain a general impression as to the great skill of the performers, the varieties of the shows, and the festive sentiments that the pictures tried to convey.

As there are always two aspects of each phenomenon, those who enjoyed the performances might enjoy a social status that would be very different from that of those who provided the performances. Who were the performers? It is most likely that specialized troupes, skilled in performing one or several shows, were employed by the court and the rich families. Other troupes were probably like wandering troubadours seeking employment from one neighborhood to another. Otherwise, among the alleys and in the countryside, semi-amateur or amateur performers would perform to supplement their living as the opportunity presented itself.

There is not much doubt, however, as to the generally low status of the performers. The relatively risky actions to which some of the performers subjected themselves might indicate a fair amount of desperation in trying to earn a living. Dwarfs or people with certain deformities, as mentioned earlier, could have been forced to join the circus to earn a living. Children of the lower orders or destitute families often also tried to make a living by joining or even being sold to the troupes. When land communication with the Western regions began to flourish, foreign talents were introduced into China, as many of the performers were imported from the West.[20]

DAILY PASTIMES

As for the daily pastimes that people enjoyed by themselves rather than watching others perform, we are able to identify a number of games that were played by the male members of society. These include *liubo*, a board game aided by twelve sticks, six red and six black, and six dice. Funerary figurines showing the *liubo* game were also not uncommon. What is intriguing is that the game seemed to have gained a certain sacred aura, as some of the tomb paintings featured *liubo* being played by winged immortals (Fig. 34). Unfortunately the exact playing procedure has been lost. Textual evidence and archaeological

[20] See Xiao (2010: 269–71).

34. Decorated brick, showing a *liubo* board and two immortals. Courtesy of the Institute of History and Philology, Academia Sinica. T 283.2 (26971)

35. Arrow throwing. Courtesy of the Institute of History and Philology, Academia Sinica, T683.2 (27288–2)

finds of the board indicate that the game had probably been in existence at least since the Eastern Zhou dynasty.[21]

Another popular game, again played by men and often depicted on decorated tomb bricks, is the *touhu*, or "arrow throwing," which consists of throwing arrows into a jar (Fig. 35), apparently a game quite similar to the modern game of darts.

For the more sophisticated and perhaps also more leisured class, the board game of *weiqi* (literally "encircling chess"), known today as "Go," by far the most prestigious board game in China, Japan, and Korea, with professional players, was already a favorite pastime among the elite. An ancient text *Yinwenzi* contains a description of the nature of the game: "For those who

[21] See Song and Miao (2010: 8 ff.).

seek intellectual gain, it is like playing *weiqi*. In the play, whether it is advance or retreat, take or give, attack or abandon, all depend upon one's own decision."[22] The famous Eastern Han historian Ban Gu (32–92 CE) wrote an essay on the principles of the game, which he compared with various aspects of the ways of government and military tactics. Another scholar, Ma Rong (79–166 CE), also wrote a rhapsody on the game and compared its principles to tactics for warfare.[23]

In contrast to board games, a more physical pastime was the game of kick-ball. Legend has it that the Yellow Emperor invented the game to train the soldiers by stuffing the stomach of the defeated archenemy Chiyou and allowing the soldiers to kick it.[24] In the Han period, the game was very popular among all levels of society. From the courts of the emperors to noble families, to the streets and alleys of the towns and cities, the game could be played by adults and children alike. The fact that the "Treatise on Bibliography" in the *History of Han* preserved twenty-five chapters on the game of kick-ball indicates that it was a very serious pastime, although these were still classified as among the military works.[25]

By far the most popular game, in an agricultural society at the level of the common people's daily lives, would have been the cockfight (Fig. 36), the modern descendant of which was made famous by the anthropologist Geertz.[26] As cocks were readily available in ordinary households, the game was a form of low-cost entertainment, although given the fact that the rich and the nobility were also infatuated with the game, the stakes could be very high. Even before the establishment of the unified empire, a description of the city of Linzi of the state of Qi has the following words indicating the popularity of the cockfights and the games of *liubo* and kick-ball: "The city of Linzi is very rich and strong, people there were all fond of playing flute and *se*-zither, plucking *qin*-zither and hitting at clay drum, playing cockfight and dog race, and gaming with *liubo* and kick-ball."[27]

It is also revealing to learn how much effort and fortune could have been invested in a simple game and became a kind of extravaganza among the rich and the powerful. At the end of the Eastern Han, the famous writer Cao Zhi 曹植 (192–232 CE), the son of the great strategist Cao 曹操 (155–220) who practically ended the Han dynasty and helped his son Cao Pi 曹丕 (187–226) to ascend the throne of the new dynasty of Wei, wrote about the cockfight at a banquet: "Playful guests sitting by the long dinner table, they leisurely watch

22 *Yiwen leiju* 74: 1272.
23 *Yiwen leiju* 74: 1271.
24 *Taiping yulan* 754: 3349.
25 *HS* 30: 1761.
26 Geertz (1973).
27 *SJ* 69: 2257.

36. Cockfight. After Zhongguo huaxiangshi quanji bianji weiyuanhui, *Zhongguo Huaxiangshi Quanji*, Vol. 6, 140–41

the cockfight in the hall. The heroes are enhancing their might, their wings flipping about. They wave their feathers and incite the clear wind, their fierce eyes shining bright red. Beaks fall with the fallen feathers, spurs often injured during the fight."[28]

Among all the figures or scenes about performances or games for pastime, it is noticeable that no women were depicted as playing any kind of games. The most that we could say is that women might have danced for their own pleasure in a domestic environment, as some scenes on tomb bricks might indicate. Textual evidence also shows that during family and friend gatherings, women and men could rise up and dance when emotions were high. In a letter written by an Eastern Han scholar, Yang Yun 楊惲 (? –54 BCE), to his friend, we find a rare account of dancing in a domestic environment:

> My family originates from the Qin area, thus I can sing Qin style songs. My wife is from the area of Zhao and is good at playing the zither. We have several maid servants who can sing. When after a drink of wine, the blood rushes to the face, we raise our heads, beat the pots, and hum some melodies ... Then we can flounce our robes and laugh, and throw our sleeves and look up, and stamp our feet and rise up dancing. This is certainly seen as quite wanton and ruthless, and I do not know why it is not allowed.[29]

We might have quoted this paragraph out of context, since this description of domestic partying was meant to be sarcastic, as the author, Yang Yun, the grandson of the Grand Scribe Sima Qian, wrote this letter to his friend to express his grievance during a time when he was dismissed from the office because he had spoken some unwelcome truth to Emperor Xuan. This letter later got him in trouble and he was executed. There is no reason, however, to doubt what he described as less than a realistic picture. Nevertheless, the fact that no women were shown playing any kind of games in the scenes displayed

[28] Zhang Pu (1990, Vol. 2: 20); *Yiwen leiju* 91: 1585.
[29] *HS* 66: 2896.

37. Women enjoying fish in a pond. Courtesy of the Institute of History and Philology, Academia Sinica, T683.2 (1042 02905–5)

in the tombs does not mean that women did not play games at all or that there were no games for women. Such a fact also suggests that we should look for and try to understand the prevailing social ethics and gender ideology during this time by noticing what was not displayed in the material or textual sources (Fig. 37).

Festivals, entertainments, and pastimes – these were and still are what most people aspired to enjoy in order to brighten up their daily lives, which, for the commoners under a well-organized political regime, were subject to seemingly endless drudgery and obligation. It is certainly true that people in the poor countryside could still from time to time find a way to amuse themselves, such as beating pots and pans and singing in unison, or slaughtering a goat or two and pouring a pot of wine to alleviate their hardship. All these, together with what they could have thought or felt, have mostly fallen into oblivion, never to be recovered. The precious images we have examined in the foregoing might indeed supply us with some idea of what was current or fashionable in society when people wished to remember what an ideal life could have been as they pass on to another form of existence. After all, most of the images came as part of the funerary paraphernalia. The decorated bricks or reliefs adorned the tomb chambers, presumably to accompany the deceased and to remind him or her of the happy times on earth, or, perhaps more likely, the happy life that was to come. It would also be unrealistic to assume that whatever pictures were depicted or objects buried in the tomb represented the actual life experience of the tomb owner. Moreover, it is almost impossible for us to detect any unhappy moment among the thousands of tomb paintings or decorated bricks. The collective images we observe are that of a festive, joyous, and carefree world. The fact that winged immortals are often depicted among the figures in the paintings and reliefs indicates that the scenes are not necessarily meant as portraits of reality, but symbolic representations of an ideal life to come.

Confronted with this one-sided representation of certain moments in the life experience of the people, therefore, we need to find some counterbalance, some evidence that could reveal to us the feelings and emotions of the most common type, even if only a glimpse. It is important that a quest for an understanding of life as people really lived it should refrain from an overambitious reconstruction of this experience. As we shall see in the following chapter, evidence for it could be found in texts of many genres such as biographies, poems, letters, even in certain types of funerary texts.

NINE

GLIMPSES OF EMOTIONAL LIFE

One of the attractions of studying history is to learn about the life experience of people from other eras and places. By getting in touch with the emotions and feelings of people long gone, we are able to establish a certain connection between ourselves and the ancients, regardless of the distance of time and space. Of course, we do not wish to commit the anachronistic and romantic error of overlooking the historical context in which our subjects were situated.

In search for the intangible but real part of the lives of the ancients, we need to remember that it is extremely rare that any historical record would contain extensive accounts of people's private feelings; this is because the main purpose of these historical works was to record the public events or roles that people played in these events. Only rarely did flashes of personal emotions leave their traces. There were, of course, conversations and speeches in the sources, and they deserve to be taken seriously, even though there could be doubts regarding their authenticity as far as what they purported to represent, for they are far more difficult to verify than those public deeds that can more or less be corroborated or confirmed by tangible records. Yet in another sense, one can accept the truthfulness of these sources as representing the feelings and emotions of the people that the authors deemed realistic in those particular historical circumstances. Examples from the traditional accounts as well as from newly excavated texts can provide some vivid evidence about the emotional lives of the people. By examining these examples, we are given a chance to see cultural values in action – whether or not according to the ideal principles. It is all the more important that we try to bring the reader face to face with the emotional lives of the people, so as to allow the reader to have access to the people as real persons.

THE EMPEROR

What was it like to be an emperor, the One under heaven? According to a famous story, when Shusun Tong, the able minister of Liu Bang, the founder of the Han dynasty, organized court ritual so that, in contrast to the chaotic brawling at the preceding court, the various officials knew their places and stood still in absolute silence during court audiences, Liu Bang burst out, saying, "Today I finally know what it feels like being an emperor!" However, this feeling of power, prestige, authority, joy, and contentment that came from a man of the lower orders should be counterbalanced by another episode when Liu Bang, late in his reign, returned to his hometown during a time of rebellion that threatened his regime. He summoned some old acquaintances and feasted. When enough wine had been consumed, Liu Bang stood up and sang impromptu, as the Grand Scribe Sima Qian wrote:

> "A great wind came forth; the clouds rose on high. Now that my might rules all within the seas, I have returned to my old village. Where shall I find brave men to guard the four corners of my land?" He made the children join in and repeat the song, while he rose and danced. He was deeply moved with grief and nostalgia, with tears streaming down his face.[1]

We, of course, should not question where Sima Qian obtained his quotations of Liu Bang's words and the information about his homecoming feast, because such questions could be asked about every chapter he wrote. We should be only temporarily content with the idea that Sima Qian did his best to obtain official and private documents and fleshed out his stories with some imaginative reconstructions. In any case, the song expressed a feeling of bittersweetness. On the one hand, Liu Bang returned bearing all the glory of an emperor to his hometown where he had been a nobody before, and thus his mood was celebrative. Yet deep in his heart he also felt loneliness, because his regime was still unstable and under attack from disgruntled subjects, and he was not sure whether he could successfully put down the rebellious forces. The episode described through the brush of the Grand Scribe Sima Qian was obviously a deliberate attempt to try to capture the feelings of a sovereign who was too often seen as a power player devoid of any fine and delicate emotions. Liu Bang's wariness of being alone in the power game was perhaps quite common

[1] *SJ* 8:389. Translation: Watson (1968: 114).

among the emperors, although different personalities would certainly have had different ways of dealing with their emotional needs.

Emperor Wu, for example, had a successful reign, and was remembered by later generations as the great sovereign who extended the country's borders and defeated the encroaching Xiongnu nomads from the west and established the Han as one of the most successful and glorious dynasties in Chinese history. Yet, according to Sima Qian, underneath the magnificent façade, he was an extremely superstitious person who longed for immortality and was fearful of evil spirits. He was rather dispirited in his final years after his favorite consort Lady Lee died, and grew increasingly suspicious of the people surrounding him, even of his own son. This infirmity of mind gave opportunities to the power mongers at court, which finally led to the tragic case of witchcraft that marked the infamous end of his otherwise glorious reign.

The event started as a case of searching for the culprit of witchcraft in the palace who allegedly intended to hurt the emperor, which resulted in a full-blown civil war between the heir apparent and other factions at court and ended with the suicide of the empress, the crown prince, and the execution of a host of high officials.[2] With a broken family and a shattered government, Emperor Wu could not be said to have lived a life with contentment of heart.

THE EMPRESS

Life in the imperial household was naturally the envy of the world, yet not until one experienced the cruel fact that power struggles could be most deadly at court would one finally realize that more material wealth and power might not bring simple happiness or peace that ordinary people might have had.

In the struggle for power in the inner court, women could often play a significant role in shaping events. Those who lost out in the struggle would no doubt be subject to a miserable life. For example, after Emperor Liu Bang died, his jealous dowager, Empress Lü, placed his favorite concubine, Lady Qi, under house arrest and made her pound rice for a living. Lady Qi lamented in her toil and sang to herself: "My son is a king, and his mother a slave, pounding rice from dawn to dusk, and being friends with death. We are three thousand *li* apart, who could tell you this?"[3] It seems that Lady Qi was also singing to the deceased Emperor Liu Bang, whose spirit was thousands of miles away, a common expression for describing the whereabouts of the soul of a deceased person. According to the *History of Han*, Lady Qi's son, the king of Zhao, was a capable person and the favorite son of Liu Bang. Liu Bang wanted him to succeed to the throne, yet because

[2] Loewe (1974, chapter 2); Cai (2014).

[3] *HS* 97a: 3937.

Liu Bang's principal wife the Empress Lü had already given birth to the heir apparent who had the legitimate right to succeed to the throne, the plan did not succeed. Fearing that the king of Zhao might rebel, Empress Lü secured her power by murdering the king of Zhao and sending his mother Lady Qi to prison after the death of Liu Bang. When somehow she heard of Lady Qi's song, which she considered a complaint, she cut off Lady Qi's limbs, blinded her, damaged her hearing, cut out her tongue, and put her in a dungeon for several months. Then she asked the newly enthroned Emperor Hui, her own son who was only seventeen years old, to observe the mutilated body of Lady Qi, and called her a "human hog." When Emperor Hui found out that she was Lady Qi, he cried with great grief and was ill for more than a year. He then sent a message to the Empress Dowager, saying, "This is not what a human being should do. Though I am your son, I could never rule the world again!"[4] He thus abandoned himself to debauchery and refused to take charge of the government, and died when he was twenty-four. Such was the historian's way of capturing the powerful and sad emotions of a young man.

Such a story, not a very complimentary one, attributed to the house and the immediate family members of the founder of the Han dynasty, can, despite all possible decorum and the refined tone, still powerfully transmit to us the tragic human drama and the intense emotions that affected the victims, as well as the stout and cold-hearted Empress Dowager, who was probably the earliest epitome of female manipulators in court intrigues in Chinese history that was matched only by the Empress Wu Zetian of the Tang dynasty.

THE PRINCESS

In the early years of the Han dynasty when the Xiongnu was too strong for the Han to confront it militarily, marriage alliances and economic exchanges were the policy options chosen by the Han rulers. From 200 to 140 BCE, for example, ten princesses were sent to the Xiongnu leaders as wives in exchange for peace.[5] During the time of Emperor Wu, although his military campaign against the Xiongnu was successful, relationships with other nomadic people to the north had to be maintained through peaceful means. One such marriage alliance happened with the Wusun tribe. Emperor Wu sent Lady Liu Xijun to be the wife of King Kunmo of Wusun, in order to maintain good diplomatic relations. Lady Xijun had a very difficult life because she was much younger than King Kunmo, and did not know the local language. Her story became

4 *HS* 97a: 3938.
5 Cui (2005: 631–88).

known to the Han court, and she had purportedly written a song expressing her sorrow and her longing for home:

> My family married me to the far corner under heaven,
> Far away in a foreign country with the King of Wusun.
> Round tent is my house, and fur blanket my wall.
> Meat is my food, and yogurt my drink.
> I think about my land every day and my heart grieves,
> I would rather become a yellow crane and fly back home![6]

Lady Liu spent her life among the Wusun people, and after the death of Kunmo, she was forced to marry his grandson, according to the nomadic custom. Her story was only one among a number of ladies who were sent to the foreign lands and had their happiness sacrificed under the Han policy of marriage alliance.

THE CONCUBINES AND COURT LADIES

Some other court ladies, although they were not sent out of the country, nevertheless ended up deep in the cold palace and suffered another kind of loneliness and despair. Ban Jieyu 班婕妤 (c. 48–c. 6 BCE), once the favorite concubine of Emperor Cheng (37–33 BCE), later lost favor because of the intrigues of another, Lady Zhao Feiyan, and was forced to retreat to the dark corner of the inner palace to serve the dowager empress, a fate suffered by so many court ladies before and after her. As an educated person, and coming from a prominent literary family (she was the great-aunt of Ban Gu, the author of the *History of Han*), she was known to have left some poems to express her grievances. One such poem, the "Rhapsody of Self Commiseration," has gained a lasting reputation as one of the earliest female writers' masterpieces. Her great-nephew Ban Gu duly recorded the poem in her biography. The poem describes her rise and fall from imperial favor, and ends with the following words:

> I am hidden in the dark palace, secluded and still:
> The main entrance is shut, the forbidden gates barred,
> Dust lies in ornate halls, moss covers jade stairs,
> In its courtyards, green grass thickly grows.
> Broad chambers are somber, curtains darkly drawn,
> Through empty window gratings the wind blows biting cold.
> It stirs curtains and gown, blows red chiffons;
> Swish, swish, the sound of rustling silks.
> My soul flies away to some secret, quiet place;
> My lord no longer favors me with his presence –

[6] *HS* 96b: 3903–904.

who could feel honor in this?
I look down over the vermilion walkway
And recall where my lord used to tread.
I look up at his cloudenshrouded chamber
And twin streams of tears pour down my face.
With pleasant expression, I look at those around me;
Pour a winged goblet to dispel my sorrow.
I think how one is born to life,
Only suddenly to pass as if drifting in a stream.
Already I've enjoyed eminence and honor,
And lived a life of unmatched blessings.
I shall cheer my spirit, enjoy myself to the full,
For good fortune and felicity are hard to predict.
"Green Jacket" and "White Flower" –
From ancient times, such has been the state of affairs.[7]

"Green Jacket" and "White Flower" are two poems from the *Book of Poetry*. The former talks about the subversion of a concubine to oust the rightful wife; the latter refers to the corrupted king You of Zhou dynasty who demoted his virtuous queen.[8] Thus Ban Jieyu ended her poem by comparing her experience to historical precedences, to reconcile her grief. Although translation can never accurately reproduce the sentiments of the original, we can nevertheless gain the gist of a court lady's lamentation about aging and the loss of imperial favor. To our modern tastes these might not necessarily strike a chord of resonance, yet during a time when it was a great advantage, socially and economically, for any woman to become the concubine of the emperor, and with the prospect of becoming the mother of the future emperor, the fall from favor was like a fall from heaven down to earth. Great expectation often brings deep disappointment. Ban Gu's decision to record the story of his great-aunt and preserve her writings was probably meant not only to honor her memory, but perhaps also intended to show an aspect of the cruel reality of the inner court. Many kept their hopes high, but only a few lucky ones got close to what they wished for, and often not without bitter struggle and intrigues. Ban Jieyu's fall from favor was exactly a case in which the manipulative Lady Zhao Feiyan outmaneuvered all the other ladies surrounding Emperor Cheng, and had them expelled one by one.

GENDER RELATIONS

We can perhaps trust that Lady Liu's song was her composition, and that Ban Jieyu's poems were written by herself, but there were many more anonymous

[7] *HS* 97b: 3985–87. See Sun Chang and Saussy (1999: 20).
[8] According to Yan Shigu's annotation. *HS* 97b:3988.

poems in the female voice where we cannot be sure of the authorship, and this poses problems of interpretation. In the *Book of Poetry* (*Shi jing*詩經), the earliest collection of poems in Chinese literature from the Zhou dynasty, there are already some famous expressions of female sentiments:

> Ever since Bo went eastward,
> My hair had been like rush in the wind.
> Certainly there is perfume and toilet,
> But for whom should I make up?[9]

This poem, though vividly expressing the emotional state of a wife longing for her husband by describing her apathy toward doing her daily toilet while he is away from home, could only raise the inevitable question of authorship and agency: could this be the words of a woman, or that of a sympathetic man who was trying to exercise his literary skill? If it was the latter, what could the motivation be for a man to try to emulate the emotional state of a woman? And for what purpose? This poem could be seen as the beginning of the appearance of a literary genre in Chinese literature that concentrated on the subject of "women's sorrow," which was basically a type of male construction of female emotions.

A group of anonymous poems, traditionally titled the "Nineteen Ancient Poems," generally dated to the Eastern Han or even earlier, provide some more samples of this problem of authorship. In one example, "A guest came from afar," the poet has the following words:

> A guest came from afar,
> Bringing me a roll of brocade.
> Ten thousand *li* apart from each other;
> Old friend's heart still presents tender care.
> Embroidered with two lovebirds,
> Made into a lover's quilt.
> Filled with floss not to be forgotten,
> Fringed with inseparable knot.
> When lacquer is thrown into the glue,
> Who could separate the two?[10]

As we do not know who the author was, our understanding of the poem must vary according to our assumption of the gender of the author. Should the author be a woman, we could be looking at some original sentiments of a literate woman, because Ban Jieyu had testified to their existence. If, on the other hand, the author was a man, what could have been the intention of his writing, and what could this phenomenon have meant in terms of the emotional world of the ancients? These are interesting questions that we need to ask with ever more caution. Was a male author assuming the female voice out

[9] *Maoshi zhenyi* (1976, 3:11).
[10] Ma Maoyuan (1969: 174).

of a desire to portray objectively a certain female sentiment? In that case, the poem could be factual and historical; that is, the author was trying to represent a sentiment that he witnessed and wished to preserve his impression by writing it down. Was a male author assuming the female voice only to express what he imagined a loving wife would or should have felt when her husband was away? In that case, the constructed female voice was not a reflection of the female mind, but the male desire for an ideal gender relationship: a loving and loyal wife waiting faithfully for the return of her husband.[11]

What, then, would be the ideal type of a loving husband? A group of poems and letters exchanged between a husband and his wife provide us with some examples. Qin Jia 秦嘉, a clerk serving in the Longxi (the present-day Gansu) Commandery, was sent to the capital Luoyang to present the annual accounting record. He was detained and given an official job, and thus was forced to stay in Luoyang for the rest of his life. His wife, Xu Shu 徐淑, after she received his letters, poems, and gifts, wrote back to him to express her loving feelings. Qin Jia was not a famous person, nor was he a high official, but the poems and letters were preserved because of their extraordinary quality of literary style and tender feelings. In one of his letters to Xu Shu, Qin Jia wrote:

> The carriage returned empty, and I am very much disappointed. It is because we are separate far from each other, and my feelings cannot help but be immersed in a sad mood. I happen to have this bright and nice mirror with exquisite decorations that is rarely found. I like it very much, therefore I am giving it to you, together with a pair of precious hair pins that are worth a thousand gold, a pair of shoes with dragon and tiger patterns, four kinds of incense, each weighs one *jin*, and one simple zither that I used to play. The bright mirror could reflect your image, the hair pin could shine on your head, the incense could make your body fragrant and clean, and the zither could please your ear.[12]

Xu Shu returned the letter with one of her own:

> You have graced me with your message, and bequeath me with various gifts. Such warm regards and kindness is beyond my expectation. The mirror is brilliantly decorated, and the pins are exotic and ingeniously made. The incense is precious, and the zither is even better. To give rare gifts to a common person, and to send what you treasured to me, this could not be so unless there is deep and rich feelings. Looking into the mirror and holding the hair pin, I recall the moment when we were

[11] For the problem of the ideological background of the representation of women in early China, see Raphals (1998). For a general study of women in early imperial China, see Hinsch (2002). As for the problem of female literacy, there is no doubt that educated women in the elite families could learn to read and write. Even women in the lower social strata would have opportunities to become "literate" since there are different degrees of literacy, not only for women, but also for men in general. See Yates (2011: 364–67).

[12] Quan Shanggu Sandai Qinhan Sanguo Liuchao wen (1958, Vol. 1, 66: 834a).

> together. Playing the zither and humming the poems, my longing clogs in my heart. You asked me to use the incense to make my body fragrant, and use the mirror to make up my face. This is actually an overstatement and does not capture my feeling. The ancient poet once expressed the feeling of "hair was like rush in the wind," and Ban Jieyu had the grief about not receiving her emperor. So zither playing would have to wait until you come back, and mirror looking would have to wait until you return. Without seeing your figure, the precious hair pin will not be used, and until I wait for you in the bed curtain, the incense will not be lighted.[13]

The letters certainly captured the mood of the couple, separated by forces that they could not resist. The reserved but rich emotion that Qin Jia expressed by sending some items for the lady's personal use was natural and unobtrusive; the highlight of the drama comes with Xu Shu's reply that she would not use the items until her husband comes back. Thus the items were suddenly elevated from nice gifts to symbols of fervent love and determination. Without Xu Shu's reply, Qin Jia's letter and gifts would never have been remembered as something worth preserving.

Despite certain problems remaining concerning the life story of these two, the letters were somehow preserved and collected into literary anthologies such as the *New Lyrics from the Jade Terrace* (*Yutai xinyong* 玉臺新詠). The existence of handwritten copies of the letters found in the Dunhuang collection of manuscripts further testifies to their popularity even in fourth- or fifth-century China.[14] Of course, we cannot be sure if indeed Xu Shu, and not Qin Jia or someone else, was the author of the letters that bear her name. For us, the letters depict a self-fulfilling ideal relationship between husband and wife. The pattern, however, could still be seen as rather conventional: the wife awaits her husband despite all kinds of adversities and difficulties.

Occasionally, however, we hear a strong female voice in contrast to the more soft and passionate language of a loving wife. A poem in the collection of Han Office of Music (*yuefu* 樂府) has some powerful lines:

> Someone I was longing for is south by the great Ocean.
> What have I prepared to send you?
> A tortoise hair pin with two pearls,
> And decorated with jade.
> Now I hear that you have another love,
> I smashed the hair pin and burned it.
> I burned it and let the wind blow it away.
> From now on I think of you no more.
> Lovesick ends with you.[15]

[13] Quan Shanggu Sandai Qinhan Sanguo Liuchao wen (1958, Vol. 1, 96: 990b–991a).

[14] Instituta vostokovedeniia (Rossiiskai akademii nauk), Sankt-peterburgskoe otdelenie ed (2001: Vol. 16).

[15] *Yuefu Shiji* (1979, Vol. 1: 230).

Here a resolute woman takes decisive action to cut off an episode of a fruitless love affair and move on without remorse. Thus, even if this was written by a man, the encouragement for women to be brave and forthcoming in expression their feelings, and be independent from the emotional support of men, may provide us with a more nuanced view of the emotional world of the women of that era.

We are, in fact, much more familiar with the ideal images of women than with their real sentiments. The famous *Biographies of Arrayed Women* (*Lienu zhuan* 列女傳), written by Liu Xiang (劉向 77–6 BCE), the great Confucian scholar, preserved stories about a number of exemplary women who demonstrated extraordinary spirit in preserving the female virtues promoted by Confucian teaching. A look at the categories would suffice to show the ideological propensity: virtuous and sagacious, benevolent and wise, devoted and obedient, honorable and righteous, etc.[16] As a contrast to these praiseworthy womanly virtues, the author also devoted a special chapter on those mischievous and evil women who were one way or another the cause of disasters, and, of course, the bad examples who should be denounced. Thus Liu Xiang's biographies of famous women were written with the purpose of exalting Confucian virtues, instead of celebrating female emotions. This overarching Confucian ideology was also the guiding principle for Ban Zhao 班昭, the great-niece of Ban Jieyu and sister of Ban Gu. She wrote the "*Commandments for Women*" (*Nüjie* 女誡) as her advice to the female family members.[17] The main points are: be humble in conducting daily businesses, be obedient and devoted to the husband, be reverent and discreet, be virtuous, soft spoken, and refrain from gossiping, and befriend in-laws such as brothers- and sisters-in-law. It seems that Ban Zhao's treatise on womanly virtues, if carried out to the letters, could pretty much suppress the subjectivity of women. We can, fortunately, still obtain glimpses of the feelings of some women through sources such as the poems discussed earlier.

THE DISILLUSIONED LITERATI

The Han dynasty was the first regime in Chinese history to open up government positions to all, and therefore any man could theoretically have the chance of gaining government employment with the hope of obtaining a good life. Still, the road to such a goal was not easily reached. There were always more people competing for a limited number of positions, and there were always intrigues and setups once one was involved in the power game. This simple fact was, however, not always crystal-clear to people who were

[16] See Raphals (1998); Kinney (2014).

[17] *HHS* 84: 2786–91.

young and full of energy and aspirations. Most, to be sure, would more or less suffer the obstacles and setbacks with perseverance and compromises during their careers. Yet there were also uncompromising individuals who fought the impossible fight and who ended up disillusioned and defeated. For a talented person, this could become an acute disappointment when his talent went unrecognized and was wasted. One such prominent example is Jia Yi賈誼 (200–168 BCE), a literary genius and shrewd political strategist who lived during the reign of Emperor Wen. His famous essay on the cause of the downfall of the Qin dynasty powerfully advocated benevolence and compassion in governing the people that is meaningful reading, even today. Many of his ideas regarding the structuring of the government and the strategy for dealing with powerful vassals were influential after he died. At the height of his promising career, he was sabotaged by jealous colleagues at court, and was sent away from the power center to the kingdom of Changsha to be a king's tutor. He felt deeply disillusioned and feared that his life might not last in the damp and hostile environment, especially because it was where the famous poet Qu Yuan屈原 (c. 343–278), who had also been banished from the court because of politics, had committed suicide. He thus expressed his sorrow and fear through a rhapsody entitled "Mourning Qu Yuan":

> Despite receiving the benevolent favor, I am banished to Changsha. I heard that Qu Yuan threw himself into the Miluo River. Therefore I asked the river to carry my message and reverently in mourning of you, sir. You have suffered endless slanders and finally lost your life. What a tragedy that you were born in a wrong era, where the noble phoenix was low in hiding, while the treacherous owl flies high. Those mediocre people gained high position and have their way because of sycophancy and flattery, the sagacious and talented were demoted and the righteous were put upside down. All the people thought the sages were evil, and bandits virtuous; the famous Moye sword as rusted, while the lead knife sharp. Unable to exercise your talent, you met this unexpected disaster. It is like throwing away the precious Zhou Dynasty bronze *ding*-tripod, and treasuring the clay pot; or like riding on poor cattle and using a limping donkey to pull the carriage, while pure breed stallion was in front of the salt cart ...[18]

Jia Yi used these bitter metaphors to mourn the unfortunate fate of Qu Yuan, and at the same time to mourn his own, which was similar to that of Qu Yuan, as both were unable to fully employ their talent to serve their country because of the jealousy and sabotage of those "little men" who were bent on destroying any talent that would reveal their own mediocrity. Such strong

[18] *HS* 48: 2223.

emotions and condemnatory words, had they been heard by those in power, would probably have incited further persecution from his opponents.

Yet Jia Yi's lamentation about his own ill fate was not a lone voice. Just as he expressed his frustration by mourning Qu Yuan, his biography was written by another person who also suffered injustice and humiliation for being honest and straightforward – the historian Sima Qian himself. The *Records of the Grand Scribe*, the foundation of Chinese historiography and the ultimate model for generations of historians, the incomparable and irreplaceable source for the history of early China until the reign of Emperor Wu, was written by a man who suffered the most humiliating punishment a man could have, even more than death itself, that is, castration.

Sima Qian held the position of "Grand Scribe" at the court of Emperor Wu and was composing his magnum opus when an event happened that caught his attention. This was the time when Emperor Wu was engaging in military expeditions against the nomadic Xiongnu. The battles raged fiercely and both sides suffered huge losses. In one of these expeditions, the Han general Li Ling 李陵 (?–74 BCE) led 5,000 soldiers and ventured deep inside Xiongnu territory and waged successive battles that heavily damaged the Xiongnu defense. Yet because of the lack of support from other Han military leaders, he was finally captured by the Xiongnu after fighting to the last man.[19] Li was a well-known general with a very good reputation as an excellent leader and a loyal subject. His defeat casted a dark shadow over the mind of Emperor Wu and created a huge controversy at court. Sima Qian, although not a close friend of Li according to his own account, presented his views to the emperor and tried to soothe the latter's anger and frustration by saying that Li was after all a loyal and capable general who had made important contributions, and that his defeat was not his own fault. What was unexpected was that the emperor, and perhaps those who were jealous of Li, took Sima Qian's words as slandering the Grand General Wei Qing 衛青 (?–106 BCE), the supreme commander of the Han army and the brother-in-law of Emperor Wu, who did not send troops to support Li Ling when Li was trapped behind enemy lines. Sima Qian was punished for this crime and paid heavily by accepting the sentence of castration instead of death. Why did he do that? Why not commit suicide, as many before him had done who would not accept such humiliation? It was an extremely hard decision to make at the time when the sentence of castration symbolized the annihilation of a man's manhood and reputation, and even that of his family. Sima Qian was of course extremely frustrated for the rest of his life. Yet he managed to cope with his frustration and lived to write his *Records of History*, which was the only reason for him to stay alive. In a letter that he

[19] *SJ* 109: 2877–78.

sent to a friend by the name of Ren An, who criticized his decision to live rather than to die, he had the following words:

> Although I was weak and wanted to survive in disgrace, I was also very much aware of the distinction between what was or was not proper thing to do, and how could I allow myself be trapped in this great humiliation [i.e., castration]! And even the ordinary male or female servants and slaves could take their own lives, how could I not do so in the insufferable situation that I was! The reason why I decided to suppress my feelings and live disgracefully, and did not avoid all the humiliations, was because I had some unfinished goal in my heart, and I loathed that if I died my literary work would not be known to future generations.[20]

Indeed it was because of his decision to endure his personal humiliation and agony, and to complete what his father had started, that Sima Qian finally fulfilled his wish to bequeath his work to later generations. One could say that the *Records of the Grand Scribe* was more than a record of history: it was a monumental literary testimony to Sima Qian's personal sentiments and his bird's eye view of the vicissitudes of generations of human drama, of success and failure, love and hate, benevolence and malevolence, friendship and betrayal, war and peace, and, not the least of all, life and death. When we say that the historical works, including *Records of the Grand Scribe*, *History of Han*, and *History of Later Han*, did not provide with us much material about the emotional life of the people, we are of course making a simplified statement. As these three histories were basically the works of single author, they inevitably bear the imprint of the personal character of each one. Often the authors' emotions and sentiments, if not the emotions of the characters in the stories, could be captured in the way in which they presented their stories.

Sima Qian's *Records*, for example, opens the biographies section with the biography of Boyi 伯夷 and Shuqi 叔齊, two sons of the Lord of Guzhu, at the end of the Shang dynasty.[21] Their father wished to make Shuqi the heir apparent, and when he died, Shuqi wanted to hand the position to his elder brother Boyi. Boyi declined because he did not want to defy his father's command, and thus he ran away from his country. Shuqi also ran away because he did not want to be the lord. Thus the people of Guzhu made the middle son the lord. When Boyi and Shuqi heard that the Duke Chang of Zhou was famous for his benevolence toward elders, they went to Zhou to seek a living. When they arrived, Duke Chang had died, and his son rebelled against the corrupt Shang dynasty and established himself as King Wu of Zhou, and began to attack the Shang. Boyi and Shuqi wished to persuade King Wu not to commit this unethical act of rebellion against the sovereign. King Wu respected

20 *HS* 62: 3733.
21 *SJ* 61: 2121 ff.

their loyalty but did not listen to them. After the establishment of the Zhou, they went into voluntary exile and died of hunger by not accepting employment from the Zhou.

Sima Qian then goes on to use the example of the fate of Boyi and Shuqi to elaborate his view of the cruel fact of history: often the evildoers lived happy and peaceful lives, while upright gentlemen suffered unexpected and undeserved disasters. He casts his doubt: "If there is the so-called heavenly way, is it like this or not?"[22] Sima Qian did not have an answer to the problem of theodicy, nor did he advance his view to say that the Zhou dynasty was not legitimate because he praised Boyi and Shuqi. But throughout his work, he did not shy away from describing the injustice suffered by the virtuous and honorable, even at the hands of the other honorables such as King Wu of Zhou, as if to use these stories to alleviate his own dilemma and grievances.

Yet if we think that Sima Qian should have gotten the support of his fellow officials or friends, we will be surprised to find out that things are, as always, more complicated than we expected. We only need to read Ban Gu's comment on Sima Qian's biography to find out that he was not entirely in agreement with what Sima Qian had stated, although Ban Gu copied almost word for word much of Sima Qian's account of the history of the Western Han until the reign of Emperor Wu. According to Ban Gu,

> Sima Qian's writing about the history of Qin and Han was quite detailed. Yet the way that he chose from canonical texts and histories and picked accounts from different sources contains many omissions, or even contradictions ... And he often expressed judgments different from that of the sages, as when he discussed the Grand Way he put the Yellow Emperor and Laozi before the Six Confucian Canons; when talking about knight-errants he put down the gentlemen and promoted the cunning aggressors; when talking about the economy, he adored the powerful and the rich and despised the deprived poor. This is where he was short-sighted ... Even with his wide knowledge and erudition, Qian could not depend upon his wisdom to preserve himself ... As for his self-commiseration, it was the like of the lament of the eunuchs. For it is only the clever and wise who could preserve his life, as the poem says, and it is very difficult to achieve that.[23]

Thus Ban Gu gave a mixed comment on Sima Qian's life and work. Nor did he share Sima Qian's sympathy for Jia Yi. For him, Jia Yi had actually fared quite well, being promoted to high position in his early twenties. There was nothing regrettable about Jia Yi's life story: "Jia Yi died young. Though he did not advance to the high position as a minister, one cannot say that he did

[22] *SJ* 61: 2125.
[23] *HS* 62: 2737–38.

not have his chance."[24] Obviously, many more anonymous but talented young men had lived a far more miserable life than had Jia Yi. Thus although we might not have many examples of direct records of expressions of emotions and sentiments in the stories preserved in the histories, we can actually feel the personal predilections and biases of their authors. What seem to be plain statements often contained a rich deposit of strong emotions and sentiments.

A SOLDIER'S LETTER TO HIS MOTHER

It is natural that we expect the educated to express their subtle feelings and remorse with delicate words, but that could not have been the way or the emotion that common people would have expressed if they had had the chance. A rare find in a Qin tomb of the late third century BCE gives us the opportunity to glance into the life of a common soldier and his communications with his brother. It was the time of the war that the King Zheng of Qin (later the First Emperor of Qin) waged to conquer the six states and ended the Warring States period. A Qin soldier named Heifu, together with his brother Jing, wrote home to their brother Zhong, inquired about their mother, and asked her to send them new garments.

> On the day Xinsi of the Second Month, Heifu and Jing write to inquire Zhong whether mother is fine. Heifu and Jing are fine. The day before Heifu and Jing were separated, now we are together. Heifu asked scribe Yi to write: "Send Heifu money, and ask mother to make summer clothes for us. When this letter arrives, mother could find out if the fabrics of Anlu are cheap and could be made into garments. If so, mother should certainly make them and send along together with the money. If the fabric is expensive, then just send the money, Heifu can buy fabrics here. Heifu and fellow soldiers are on duty at Huaiyang. The attack of the rebellious city could last long. One does not know if one will get hurt. Wish that mother could send more money to Heifu. When this letter arrives please reply, and let us know whether the Family Assistance Honor Rank (*xiangjia jue* 相家爵 [reward due to a soldier's bravery in battle]) has been dispatched to our house, and let Heifu know the situation … Is mother fine? Has she thanked the officials for the Family Assistance Honor Rank? Inquire earnestly for Heifu and Jing the well-being of aunt and sister, … Inquire earnestly for Heifu and Jing if Jixu of the Eastern room is fine, inquire earnestly for Heifu and Jing the matter with Ying Jishi, whether it is settled? Inquire for Heifu and Jing if Luying of Xiyang and the old gentleman Yan Zheng of Bianli are alright… Jing inquire earnestly if his bride Yuan is fine. The new bride should strive to serve her father-in-law…[25]

[24] *HS* 48: 2265.

[25] Yunmeng Shuihudi Qin-mu bianxiezu (1981: 25).

The letter demonstrates with a straightforward fashion the concern of the sons for their mother, friends, and relatives. In its plain way the letter describes a close-knit local community. Not only are family members addressed, but certain neighbors or acquaintances are also included in the round of well-wishing. Given the possibility that the letter might have been written by a professional letter writer in the army, for presumably most of the soldiers were illiterate, the sentiments expressed in the letter still carry an undeniable weight since the content and the names mentioned had to come from the mouth of the soldier Heifu and his brother Jing.[26] A solid feeling of simple but warm emotion could be felt from the repetitive inquiries about the well-being of family members and acquaintances. It also shows that for them to ask for money from home while on duty at the frontline was nothing unusual. One could therefore surmise that the material situation of the soldiers during that time might not be particularly comfortable. A small detail is that the mother seems to be the decision maker of the household, as she could decide on matters of family finance, while her husband, the "father-in-law" of the bride of Jing, seems to still be alive. The mother, in the letter at least, appears to be the focus of concern of the brothers, as she is the foremost person in their inquiries. The filial piety of sons for their mothers in traditional China could be an entire subject of study[27]; so too was the property right of the wife.

FILIAL BONDS

We have discussed gender relationships, including the relationship of husband and wife, and observed some other cases, both typical and uncommon. For other kinds of family relations, such as the parent–child relationship, or that between siblings, we are constrained by the available evidence. Few documents, literary or otherwise, have been preserved through which we can probe into the feelings between parents and children, or between siblings. The letter of Heifu, discussed previously, presents a single insight into a moment of exchange between brothers and their concern for their mother and siblings. Moreover, examples remain only examples; they are not able to represent the general situation but only the possibilities of what might have happened.

One well-known example in the history of Han literature that expressed a mother's dilemma and agony of facing the choice to abandon her children for her own freedom was attributed to Cai Yan 蔡琰 (176?–early third century), daughter of the famous scholar-official Cai Yong 蔡邕 (133–192). According to the very simple description of her biography in the *History of Later Han*,[28] Cai

[26] Yates (2011).
[27] See Hsiung (1994); Knapp (2005).
[28] *HHS* 84: 2800; Owen (2006: 232 ff.).

Yan received a good education because of her family background. During the chaotic period at the end of the Eastern Han, when the warlords fought for power, she was captured, around 192 BCE, by a group of nomadic mercenaries and was forced to become the wife of a chieftain of the Xiongnu people. She stayed with the Xiongnu for twelve years and bore two sons for the king. Her story was then heard by Cao, the most powerful warlord who controlled the Han government, and Cao decided to pay a heavy ransom for her to come back. Since her sons, being Xiongnu princes, could not return with her, she was placed in a dilemma. She finally had to give up her sons with deep remorse and returned to her homeland. In the *History of Later Han*, the author included a poem that described her life experience, beginning with the time when rebellions caused havoc and the country was in total chaos. Then she talked about the time when she was kidnapped by the nomadic soldiers and carried on horseback to the west:

> The troops that came were all Hu and Qiang,
> They cursed the wilds, surrounded the cities,
> Wherever they went, all were destroyed.
> They butchered and beheaded, left not one person behind.
> Corpses were propped up against one another,
> Men's heads were strung from the horses' sides,
> Women and girls, brought behind the horses,
> In a long march we went west into the Passes,
> ...

After a period of time living in the foreign land, she finally was saved and had the chance to go back to her homeland:

> O Heaven, what fault have I committed?
> To meet such trouble and calamity.
> The frontier wilds are different from China,
> There is little propriety in their customs.
> Where I lived there was much frost and snow,
> Nomad winds rose in spring and summer.
> They blew my clothes flapping,
> Whistling, they entered my ears,
> Stirred by the times, I thought on my parents.
> ...
> I chance to be blessed by a wish of the times,
> My own flesh and blood came to meet me.
> I had been released myself,
> But I had to abandon my children.
> Natural relations are bound to a person's heart,
> I brooded on parting, never to meet again.
> We would be separated forever in life and death,
> And I could not bear to take leave of them.

My son came forward and embraced my neck
And asked: "where are you going, mother?
People say that you have to go away,
That you certainly will never return again.
Mother has always been gentle and caring,
I wonder how you can now be so unkind.
I am not yet fully grown,
How can you not show concern for me?"
Hearing this made my organs fail within me,
I was confused and felt foolish and mad.
Weeping, I caressed him with my hand,
I was due to set out, then turned back unsure.
There were also others of my own age
Who sent me off and said their goodbyes.
They envied how I alone got to return,
Shouting in woe, their voices were shattering.
Because of this, the horses stood hesitating,
Because of this, the carriage did not roll.[29]

The sad language that we read in the poem and the violent expressions of the emotional bonds between the sons and the mother are extraordinarily direct and powerful. It is perhaps true that it will take a dramatic event such as what Cai Yan had experienced to prompt a corresponding literary expression to recapture the emotion. The poem has since been remembered in the history of Chinese literature as the most powerful female voice against the cruelty of war and the suffering of the common people. Of course, here again questions have been raised concerning the authorship of this poem. Because the *History of Later Han* was composed around the mid-fifth century by Fan Ye 范曄 (c. 398–445), 200 years after Cai Yan's time, the poem does pose certain historical problems. Without further speculation, there should be no doubt that the poet had successfully preserved the emotional world of a daughter, a mother, and her sons during that fateful moment in their lives. Many more families were torn apart during that dark period when the world they knew was turned upside-down. The voice of Cai Yan, even if only a mouthpiece, embodied generations of sufferers' emotions and sentiments that stood against the relentless muffling and erosive waves of time.

Less dramatic examples of filial bonds, on the other hand, could provide us with testimonies of commonplace emotions in an ordinary situation, and therefore be even closer to the daily experience of a given era. In the year 170 CE, a child named Xu Aqu died at the age of five. His tomb

[29] For the full translation, see Owen (2006: 234–37).

was well supplied with elaborate decoration, and a stela with the following inscription:

> It is the Jianning era of the Han,
> The third year since our emperor [*i.e.*, Emperor Ling] ascended the throne.
> In the third month of wuwu,
> On the fifteenth day of jiayin,
> We express our grief and sorrow
> For Xu Aqu our son.
> You were only five years old
> When you abandoned the glory of the living.
> You entered an endless night
> Never to see the sun and stars again
> Your spirit wanders alone
> In eternal darkness underground.
> You have left your home forever;
> How can we still hope to glimpse your dear face?
> Longing for you with all our hearts,
> We came to pay an audience to our ancestors;
> Three times we increased offerings and incense
> Mourning for our deceased kin.
> You did not even recognize [your ancestors],
> But ran east and west, crying and weeping.
> Finally you vanished with them,
> While still turning back from time to time.
> Deeply moved, we, your father and mother... [inscription damaged]
> To us all delicacies have become tasteless.
> Wan and sallow,
> We have exhausted our savings [to build your shrine and make offerings],
> Hoping your spirit will last forever.
> ... [inscription damaged]
> Visitors,
> When you come here and see dust on this grave,
> Please sweep it without delay.
> Your kindness will make the deceased happy.[30]

We do not know who the parents were, but judging from the fact that a decorated tomb was built for a child of a mere five years, we could surmise that the family was not too poor. Furthermore, and perhaps even more impressively, is the rare affection devoted to the child. Whoever composed the epitaph had captured a deep sense of loss and disillusion with any hope of an afterlife. The parents, while mourning for their deceased son, also expressed their despair

[30] Kinney (1995: 79–80).

regarding the hard reality of the division between life and death. What one could expect of the latter was only eternal darkness.

If we look at the textual sources we have, it would be a shock to realize that, perhaps with the exception of Cai Yan's poem – which was extraordinary in every sense – almost nothing could be found in the area of the expressions of parent–child affection. First, just as women's lives and emotions were ignored in the official histories, children, or parent–child relationships, were not a major concern when authors engaged in presenting the more "important" events of the state. When children appeared in the writing or came to the attention of the authors, it was mostly because they, the children, were part of the education program to produce good Confucian gentlemen.[31] The same could be said regarding the pictorial sources. Except perhaps the tombstone of Xu Aqu, on which were two boys playing in front of Xu Aqu, who sits on a mat like an adult enjoying the show, we can hardly find any representation of children playing in Han tomb paintings and reliefs.[32] The world represented by texts and pictures was by and large the world of the adults. The example of Xu Aqu is probably the exception that proves the rule.

Yet one sentiment expressed in Xu Aqu's epitaph was surely universal: the fear of the inevitable fate that awaits all, that is, death, the unknown darkness. Depending on the age and circumstances that one faces, death, or the frailty of life, was on the mind of many, yet it could be expressed by only a few talented writers. It was perhaps not a coincidence that, when the rate of literacy became higher, and when enough momentum was gathered in the collective literary expression, that lamentation about the brevity of life and the unpredictable course of fate became the subject of poetic creation. One such poem captures the gist of many similar works:

> One's life is less than a hundred years,
> Yet constantly mindful of millennia of sorrows.
> Day is short and night painfully long,
> Why not take a candle and roam about?
> Make merry while there is time,
> How could one wait for the future?
> The fool is stringent about spending,
> Only to be mocked by later generations.
> There are immortals such as Prince Qiao,
> Yet one could hardly expect to become one.[33]

31 Kinney (1995); Knapp (2005); Hsiung (2005).

32 The most frequently depicted image of a child, actually a boy dressed in an adult's clothes, is the image of Xiang Tuo 項橐, the boy that appears in the stock scene of "Confucius meets Laozi." According to scattered references preserved in ancient sources such as *Zhangguo ce*, *Huainanzi*, and *Shi ji*, Xiang Tuo was a boy of seven years, known for his wisdom and knowledge, and Confucius once visited him and learned from him. See Xing yitian (2004: 313–25).

33 Cf. Owen (2006: 181). For the topic of "human life is short," see Owen (2006: 327 ff.).

After experiencing all the vicissitudes of life, the loss of loved ones, the shattering of self-esteem, the sufferings of the just, the triumph of the evil, and finally the imminent arrival of old age, it was perhaps natural for many to muse about death and burial, and the world beyond. In the context of our pursuit of daily life experience, the great equalizer for every living soul would be death. No one comes back to tell us about the experience of death or the world after death; it is known to us only through materials left for us when people prepared for that inevitable end of life. Yet how people viewed death, prepared for burial, and imagined the world after death were all manifestations of their attitudes toward and their expectations of life, and therefore part of their daily life experience, as we shall explore in the next chapter.

TEN

DEATH, BURIAL, AND THE HOPE FOR A HAPPY AFTERLIFE

Despite a love of life and caring for physical well-being, the inescapable reality is that the grave is the final destination and death the great equalizer. The realization of this fact, however, does not have to lead to a total resignation. Instead, the life beyond the grave has caught people's imaginations. The grave, then, became the gate to another kind of existence. This necessitates the burying of the dead and the building of a tomb. Just as the birth of a new life, therefore, death, funeral, and burial are daily events in the lives of common people. How people bury their dead and build their tombs, furthermore, is informed by their culture, their view of life and death, and the relationship between this and the netherworld.

Ancient China provides us with abundant material to study these rich burial customs and the ideas associated with it. As we shall see in the following, studies of Han dynasty tombs have established the evolution of burial styles and the sociocultural factors that lie behind the changes. While the Confucian officials wanted to promote a moderate way of handling funerals, the ordinary people had their own agendas and customs. Numerous transmitted as well as newly excavated texts indicate that people held a range of views about what would happen after death, and what kind of preparations and actions would be appropriate for it. Such actions, with rituals and rich funerary paraphernalia, were designed with the hope to reach a happy life beyond for the dead. However, the imagination of a life after death was not the only way to deal with death. The idea of immortality, of a deathless existence removed from mundane life, had its root in the pre-Qin era, developed during the Qin-Han transition, continued into the post-Han period, and became an integrated element of the newly developed Daoist religion. Moreover, the introduction of Buddhism into China during the later Han period inaugurated a long-lasting transformation of Chinese society that had changed the character of Chinese culture, and had great impact on ideas concerning life, death, and the afterlife. The exploration of Buddhism in China, however, lies outside of the present volume.[1] This chapter, therefore, proposes to examine several related issues that had important significance to the understanding of context in which the culture of death was developed. We shall begin by examining the idea of the soul and the netherworld, followed by discussions of the development of tomb styles, burial customs, and funerary rituals, culminating in the desire to reach a happy afterlife and the possibility of defying death and achieving immortality.

THE SOUL

Studies of the concept of ghost in early China based on received texts and newly excavated manuscripts demonstrate that the term *gui*, usually translated as ghost, could refer to the soul or spirit of a variety of beings: some are human dead, some are other animate or inanimate things.[2] Among these some are unfriendly to humans for different reasons. On the whole, it was widely accepted, both among the elite and the common people, that the human dead usually would become ghosts, whether malicious or not. When a ghost receives proper burial and sacrifice, he becomes the ancestor of his descendants, and should theoretically rest in peace. Those that did not receive proper burial and sacrifice, on the other hand, could become evil ghosts (厲 *li*) and have the potential to haunt or harm people, because they were not treated properly.

Thus the Chinese understanding of the nature of spiritual beings always contains a certain ambiguity: the difference between a ghost/*gui* and a god/*shen* is not their nature or power, but whether or not they can perform certain benevolent or miraculous deeds that could prompt the people to revere and worship them. Those ghosts that could demonstrate their power by performing worthwhile deeds stand a good chance to be apotheosized. Those that could only do harm, however, continue on as evil ghosts. To complicate the matter further, terms such as *hun* 魂, *po* 魄, *ling* 靈, *or shen* 神 can also refer to the post-mortem or spiritual existence of the dead. The term *shen*, in addition, could refer to a deity, or the spirit, regardless of whether it is the spirit of a person, a god, or a ghost. Although still a subject of debate, in the pre-Qin period at

[1] See Poo et al. (2017).
[2] Poo (2004).

least, *hun* referred to the soul of the dead that rose up to the heavens, while *po* referred to the physical aspect of the dead that remained in the underground, but of course it was different from the corpse itself.[3] Thus *hun* and *po* may refer to two different aspects of *gui*/ghost, perhaps analogous to the Egyptian *ba*, *akh*, and *ka*.[4] However, the distinction among *gui*, *hun*, *po*, *ling*, and *shen* was blurred in the Han period, as they were often used synonymously in combinations such as *hunpo*, *guihun*, *linghun*, *shenling*.[5]

There are, to be sure, many questions that can be asked about ghosts: What did they look like? How did they affect people's lives? What was their relationship with human beings? What was their role in the belief systems? How did they affect literature, art, and how did they transform people's ideas of the world? What makes them malicious or terrifying, and what makes them also vulnerable? Why did people begin to talk about ghosts in a benign manner? As some of these questions have been studied elsewhere,[6] here we can simply suggest that the assumption that ghosts or souls existed constitutes the foundation for a society to develop all kinds of customs and institutions related to death and afterlife. Of course, there were always doubts about the existence of ghosts. Questions such as whether ghosts and spirits were actual beings or simply figments of imagination were debated. But on the whole such debates did not affect the prevailing social custom, as we shall discuss in the following.

WHERE HAVE ALL THE GHOSTS GONE?

In early China people referred to the world after death as the "Yellow Spring," which originally meant underground water, but metaphorically referred to "the netherworld." The term was widely used in Chinese literature, but rarely had people given any clear description. It remained a dark place, both physically and conceptually.[7]

That the netherworld should be a dark place was not an uncommon idea, and in the late Warring States period, the term "Dark City (*youdu* 幽都)" was mentioned as the place where souls might travel to. Textual evidence of the Dark City suggests that it was not a widely used term except in literary texts, though this does not mean that the concept of the netherworld as a dark place was not a prevalent one. References in other ancient cultures often point to a similar idea of a dark netherworld. The ancient Mesopotamians, for example, believed that the world of the dead was a dark and cold place, ruled by the deities Ereshkigal and Nergal.[8] The ancient Greek conception of the netherworld

3 Yü (1987); Poo (1998); Brashier (2011).
4 Eyre (2009).
5 Poo (1998: 62–66; 163–65).
6 Poo (2004).
7 Wu (2010).
8 Bottéro (2001: 107–108).

was also a gloomy place, where the souls of the dead existed in a pale and shadowy form.[9] The darkness of the netherworld was a concept retained well into the Eastern Han period.

On the other hand, an extremely interesting text found in a third century BCE Qin dynasty tomb tells us about the resurrection of a man named Dan. In the story the deceased claimed that he "lived" in the tomb for three years before he received a special order from the Controller of Life (*siming* 司命), a deity who was in charge of the roster of people's life spans, to release him from the confinement of the tomb and return to the land of the living. He further said that the dead did not like to wear many clothes, nor did they enjoy any kind of food offering that was swimming in sauce.[10] We do not know the exact intention of this story, but the plot indicates that it could be understood as a kind of satire about the injustice that ordinary people often suffered and how they were punished for crimes they did not commit. In this case, even the official in the divine realm can make mistakes. The sloppy food offering that the ghost detested, moreover, reflects the reality of the so-called filial piety: offerings to ancestors were sometimes performed in an indifferent fashion.

However, although the tomb was the abode of the dead, whether it could be seen as the only place for the dead is still uncertain. For apparently when the term Dark City was used to refer to the netherworld, it meant a place that was more than the tomb itself. Indeed texts found in tombs dating from the early Han dynasty referred to the world of the dead as simply "underground," which, if understood as the counterpart of "above ground," could refer to an entire "world." This assumption has actually been confirmed by funerary texts that contain official titles such as "Lord of Underground" or "Assistant Magistrate of the Underground" that suggest a certain bureaucratic organization similar to that in the world of the living.[11]

From the use of the term "underground," and the associated bureaucracy, we can detect an overall change in the conception of the netherworld from a dark and unknown place to a "society" that seems to be a replica of the world of the living. Within this trend, toward the Eastern Han, a number of specific places emerged as the abode of ghosts. The most important place was no doubt Mount Tai, in present-day Shandong Province, the sacred mountain on which the ancient rulers were said to have ascended in order to make sacrifices and receive the Mandate of Heaven. It was perhaps due to this special connection with Heaven that Mount Tai gained a sacred status as a place to communicate with the unseen world ruled by the Lord of Mount Tai.[12] Apparently this

[9] See Bremmer (1983); Finucane (1996: 4–28).
[10] Harper (1994).
[11] Poo (1998, chapter 7).
[12] Chavannes (1910); Liu Tseng-kuei (1997); Yü (1987).

place was considered the counterpart of the worldly capital of Chang'an, as a funerary text reads: "The living belong to [the jurisdiction of] Chang'an to the west; the dead belong to [the jurisdiction of] Mount Tai to the east."[13] In the late Han and the subsequent eras, Mount Tai was often regarded as the destinations for ghosts – until they were replaced by the Buddhist idea of hell, or *diyu* (地獄), literally "underground prison."[14]

While we can admit to a general idea of the netherworld as a place somewhere below the ground, certain graphic elements found in the Han tombs indicate that the scope of people's imaginations might not have been confined to the underground only. A well-known example is the silk banner discovered in tomb no. 1 at Mawangdui (Fig. 38).[15] This T-shaped silk painting is about 205 centimeters long, with a width of 92 centimeters for the upper part and 47.7 centimeters for the lower part. In the middle of the painting stands an old lady who, staff in hand, is being greeted by two servant-like figures, and has generally been identified as the tomb owner Lady Dai herself.[16]

Since its discovery, the meaning of the painting has been the subject of numerous scholarly debates. Despite different interpretations, most scholars agree that the picture depicts the spiritual world where the deceased might travel to or live in, since clearly many of the things and characters depicted in the painting do not belong to the world of the living.[17] Some scholars maintain that the painting should be divided into three parts; the upper part represents heaven, the middle part represents earth, and the lower part represents the netherworld. The deceased Lady Dai, who stands in the middle section, was therefore aspiring to ascend to heaven.[18] However, it is also possible to understand the painting as a representation of the state of existence of the deceased, not necessarily in heaven or in the netherworld, since there is really no indication to see Lady Dai as being ready for or in the process of traveling to any destination. She could very well have been standing in her next life, in a world inhabited by the various creatures and personnel. It is probably out of our modern mindset that scholars are inclined to see the painting as some kind of "learned" statement of the composition of the cosmos, which might not have been what the painter or designer of the painting had in mind. Instead, a more modest way to imagine the purpose of the painting would be to see the elements represented in the painting as a gathering of various traditions and myths about the world beyond, and most importantly, an auspicious place.

13 Liu (1997).
14 Teiser (1994).
15 Loewe (1979).
16 Loewe (1979: 30–59).
17 Loewe (1979); Wu (1992, 2010).
18 Loewe (1979: 34–35); Wu (1992); Wu (2010: 130–31); Tseng (2011: 166ff.).

38. T-shaped painting on silk from Mawangdui tomb no. 1. Courtesy of Hunan Provincial Museum. Source: Hunan sheng bowuguan, Zhongguo kexueyuan kaogu yanjiusuo eds., *Changsha mawangdui ihao hanmu* (Beijing: Wenwu chubanshe, 1973,Vol. 1, fig. 38)

There is no doubt, however, that such visions revealed in the painting were not the creation of any individual painter, but the culminating result of a long decorative tradition widely shared in society. Not only did the painting have a duplicate found in the Mawangdui tomb no. 3, which was identified as belonging to the son of Lady Dai, but another similar silk painting was found in a Western Han tomb at Shandong Jinqueshan, located thousands of miles from Changsha. In this painting, elements such as the sun and the bird, the moon and the toad, the tomb owner and her entourage, and the coiled dragons are all present.

In sum, all this evidence gives us some idea of how the Mawangdui painting preserved for us a view of the collective imagination of the world after death that was graphically represented in the tombs. These paintings depict not only various activities that the deceased is supposed to participate in; the appearance of the mythical figures and auspicious animals also indicates that the tomb was no longer a confined space to contain the body of the dead, but a completely new world in which the deceased could roam about at leisure.[19] If we still use the term "netherworld," this might not be understood as a simple "underground" world that implies only darkness and eternal confinement. Instead, the netherworld can mean a world beyond, a place with many fantastic features, and a place for another form of life.

HOUSE OF ETERNITY

No matter where the soul of the dead may have been conceived to travel to or stay in, it all started from the tomb, since it is by burying the dead that society was able to complete the life cycle, and return to the normal order that the death of a member had disrupted. If the tomb was regarded as the living quarters of the dead, then a look at the tomb itself might reveal some clues as to people's conception of life in the netherworld. How to bury the dead in a society, however, is not an individual decision. Every era and every society would have had a more or less prevailing convention for burying the dead. Moreover, burial customs rarely changed in early societies, and if they did, the cause would have been something significant. This is certainly true in the case of ancient China.

From as early as the Shang dynasty, the principal method of burial was the so-called "vertical shaft wooden casket" tomb, which means that the tomb chamber was in the shape of a vertical pit dug in the ground, and that the coffins and caskets were placed at the bottom of the pit (Fig. 39). The caskets were often packed with carbon and clay as a means of waterproofing, before being covered with soil. Sacrificial animals or humans were often found either in the main burial pit, or in nearby pits, while funerary objects were placed inside the casket or coffin to accompany the deceased in the next life. Above the tomb, there would usually have been an earth mound, with trees planted

19 Finsterbusch (1966); James (1996); Lai Guolong (2015: 161–87).

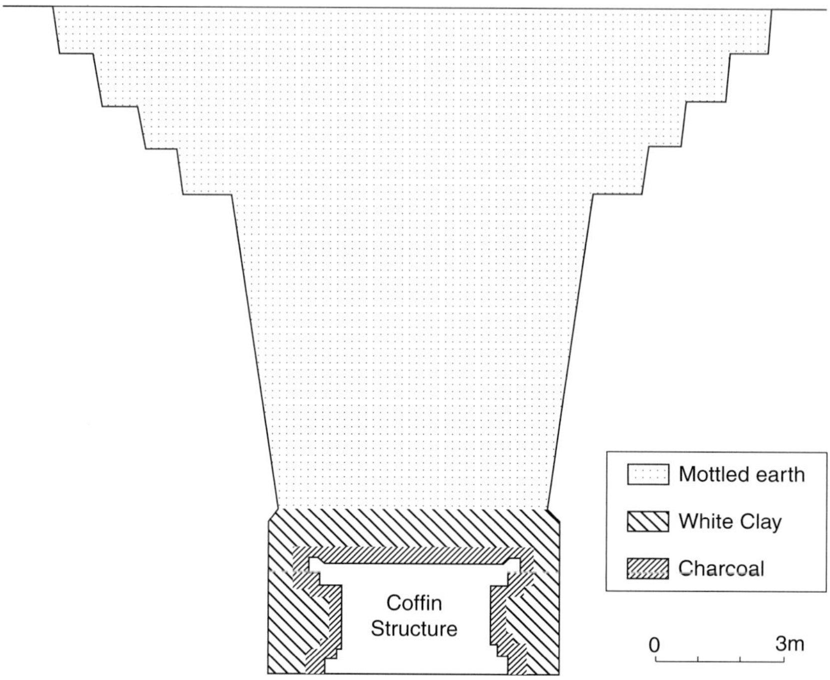

39. The profile of Mawangdui tomb no. 1. Courtesy of Hunan Provincial Museum. Source: Hunan sheng bowuguan, Zhongguo kexueyuan kaogu yanjiusuo eds., *Changsha mawangdui ihao hanmu* (Beijing: Wenwu chubanshe, 1973, Vol. 1, fig. 3)

on top, as markers of the position of the tomb. Funerary shrines would sometimes have been erected on top or in front of the tomb.[20]

As would be expected, depending on the social and political status of the deceased, different degrees of elaboration were given to the tombs, and a set of rules for burial were applied, theoretically, to all members of society, from the rulers to the commoners. According to the ideal burial custom set out in various ancient texts,[21] the king's burial had seven layers of coffins and caskets, a prince had five layers, an official had three, and a gentleman had two. Corresponding to the number of coffins and caskets, a certain number of funerary objects would be supplied; the number of the ramps of the tomb also followed a hierarchical order.

From the Warring States period onward, as a consequence of the disintegration of the Zhou feudal system, a new burial style emerged, which is the so-called horizontal brick chamber tomb (Fig. 40).[22]

Simply put, instead of a vertical pit with the casket at the bottom, the new style was a chamber – made either of stone slabs, large bricks, or small bricks.

20 Wang (1982: 175 ff.).
21 Huang Xiao-fen (2003); Wu Hung (2010:17 ff.); Lai (2015: 55–97).
22 Lai (2015: 55–97).

40. Brick tomb, Chongqing, Han dynasty. Courtesy of Chongqingshi Wenhua Yichan Yanjiuyuan 重慶市文化遺產研究院, "*Chongqingshi Jiangjinqu Yandungang Handai zhuanshimu fajue Jianbao* 重慶市江津區煙墩崗漢代磚室墓發掘簡報," *Sichuan Wenwu* 四川文物 4(2014): 47

Although the chamber was still buried underground, it was usually approached from a horizontal direction, with a ramp leading to the gate of the tomb. It therefore bears an undeniable similarity to the house of the living. As time went by, the structure of the tomb became more elaborated, often consisting of side chambers, or several chambers along a central axis. This tendency to imitate the house of the living was enhanced with the addition of decorative wall paintings and reliefs, similar to the way in which houses of the living were adorned.[23] The funerary objects found in the tombs, instead of the ceremonial bronze vessels that indicated the political status of the tomb owner such as a king, a prince, a minister, or a gentleman, were mostly real or surrogate objects of daily use, including all kinds of utensils and implements, and figurines of

[23] See Xing (1986).

various types, representing farms, fields, animals, or household servants that were supposed to serve the deceased in the world below. Thus it is reasonable to conclude that the collective social imaginings of the netherworld shifted from a predominant concern with the sociopolitical status of the deceased to a concern with a comfortable life in the netherworld.

To understand the reason behind the change in burial style, we need to look at what had happened in society during the time of change. One obvious suggestion would be the tremendous social and political changes that occurred during the Warring States period. It was a period of the decline of the old aristocratic society dominated by the Shang–Zhou imperial lineages, and the rise of a more egalitarian society wherein personal effort, not blood descent, could lead to success (see Chapter 3). Under these circumstances, the old symbols of social status, i.e., the ritual bronze vessels, were gradually replaced by items that could reflect personal achievement, family wealth, and a comfortable life.[24] Such a change, of course, could not have been the conscious decision of any individual, but a gradual change in the collective mentality that could be detected and surmised only through an observation of a long trend. Parallel with the social change, moreover, was a change of shared imagination of the netherworld based on the emerging bureaucratic society. A concept of bureaucratic netherworld is possible only when the world of the living was already bureaucratized. The evidence from the early Han, such as the various underground officials mentioned earlier, might not have reflected the completion of this bureaucratization of the netherworld, but it certainly portrayed one that has all the signs of a unified empire.

LAVISH BURIAL AND SOCIAL CONVENTION

One of the most spectacular examples of extravagant burial in the entire Han dynasty would be the famous Mawangdui tomb no. 1, the tomb of Lady Dai, wife of Marquis Dai, dating from about 160 BCE (Fig. 41). Some simple figures can show the extraordinarily luxurious construction of the burial: the tomb pit, in the ancient style of vertical pit wooden casket, was about 20 meters long, 18 meters wide, and 16 meters deep, roughly a four-story high space the size of a basketball field.

At the bottom of the pit was built a wooden casket, or *guo*, which contains a three-layered lacquer coffin of the tomb owner, Lady Dai. The entire structure of the *guo* measures 6.72 × 4.88× 2.8 meters, and consumed a total of more than 200 cubic meters of fine wood. In view of the thickness of the wood, it is estimated that the trees employed were more than 2 meters thick in diameter.

[24] Lai (2015: 97).

41. Mawangdui tomb no. 1 pit during excavation. Courtesy of Fu Juyou 傅舉有, *Buxiu zhi Hou: Mawangdui Hanmu Kaogu Dafaxian* 不朽之侯: 馬王堆漢墓考古大發現 (Hangzhou 杭州: Zhejiang wenyi chubanshe 浙江文藝出版社, 2002, 9)

The content of the funerary objects was even more surprisingly splendid. Among the more than 750 items found in the tomb are a great many "real" objects, including many fine lacquer wares and more than 150 items of silk clothes, shoes, gloves, socks, bags, scarves, as well as musical instruments. The exquisite quality of the silk products has completely altered our knowledge of the weaving industry of the early Han, as discussed in Chapter 6. Among the forty-eight bamboo-woven containers found in the tomb of Lady Dai, thirty contained food. These included staple foods such as rice, wheat, corn, millet, soybeans, and fruits such as plums, pears, persimmons, jujubes, oranges, and melons. Other agricultural produce included taro, ginger, lotus root, mustard seeds, and various meats of animals such as cattle, sheep, dogs, pigs, horses, rabbits, chickens, ducks, geese, quails, cranes, swans, swallows, and various kinds of fish. All of these were apparently for the enjoyment of Lady Dai in the afterlife.

While the rich burial of Lady Dai and her family members might have been only "conventional," as noble families in the empire were used to provide their deceased members with such lavishness, whether such a practice was appropriate in the eyes of contemporary society is another matter. According to the regulations of the time of Emperor Jing (156–141 BCE), when a person of the rank of marquis died, his family could enlist no more than 300 people to work on the tomb.[25] Lady Dai died before this regulation was promulgated. One of

[25] *HS* 5: 145.

the excavators of her tomb recalled that, when they cleared the burial pit in 1972, about 100 or so workers toiled for 60 days to remove the earth before they reached the burial chamber. The earth removed from the burial shaft totaled more than 6,000 cubic meters.[26] One can surmise that the amount of work devoted to the construction of the tomb could only have been more stupendous than that of the excavating process.

Criticisms against lavish burials, to be sure, were often expressed by the intellectuals.[27] As opinions emerge not without reasons, it should be clear that the criticisms are good indicators of the prevalent social customs. In fact, very few in ancient China could give up any form of burial and accept Zhuangzi's position: "I use the Heaven and the Earth as my coffin, the sun and moon as the jade, the stars as pearls and gems, and the myriad of creatures as my funerary goods."[28]

The Confucians in general favored the "middle way," and therefore would not condone extravagance. Yet they also stressed the importance of rituals and ceremonies, which, when taken seriously, had the tendency to become more and more elaborate. In the *Debate on Salt and Iron*, which we have mentioned several times previously, the conservative party of the scholars vehemently criticized contemporary social practice:

> People nowadays do not care and respect the [parents] when they are alive, but when they die, they [the descendants] use lavish funerals to compete with each other. Although they do not express any grief, as long as they spend a great amount of money on a lavish burial, people will praise them as being filial sons, and they will win fame in the country and be praised in their hometown.[29]

The funerals of the rich and famous in society, as the criticism goes, were examples that encouraged the common people to follow suit. During a funeral, people often came to the residence of the deceased, demanding that the family should supply them with lavish banquets, even entertainment and performances of various sorts. If they were not satisfied with the service, they began to criticize the unfortunate family for not being generous enough.[30] Readers who are familiar with early Greek history can quickly see that such desire for a lavish burial was perhaps not peculiar to Chinese society, as witnessed in Solon's legislation against lavish funerals.[31]

According to Wang Fu, people liked to have lavish funerals and weddings mainly because they wanted to display their wealth and social status, or, at least,

[26] Hou Liang 1994: 13–14.
[27] Poo (1990).
[28] *Zhuangzi* 10a: 1063.
[29] *Yantielun* 6: 354.
[30] *Yantielun* 6: 354.
[31] Alexiou (1974: 15–22).

the appearance of them.[32] Thus the vast majority of the people in society continued to supply their tombs with luxury items so long as they were able to do so. Despite repeated imperial decrees and criticisms against lavish burials throughout the Han dynasty, there were plenty of cases that ignored the official admonitions.

Despite the aforementioned situation, we should perhaps not regard the custom of lavish burial as being wholly out of a desire to flaunt family wealth or to pursue a good name for being a filial son, often under peer pressure. A grain of wishful thinking could always have existed in people's minds regarding the fate of the dead and life in the netherworld. As the Eastern Han skeptic Wang Chong (20–98 CE) comments:

> Ordinary people, on the one side, have these very doubtful arguments [about whether ghosts exist or not], and on the other … note that the dead in their tombs arise and have intercourse with sick people whose end is near. They then believe in this, and imagine that the dead are like the living. They commiserate with them, [thinking] that in their graves they are lonely, that their souls are solitary and without companionship, that their tombs and mounds are closed and devoid of grain and other things. Therefore they make dummies to serve the corpses in their coffins, and fill the latter with provisions, to gratify the spirits. This custom has become so entrenched and has reached such lengths, that very often people will ruin their families and use up all their property to pay for the coffins of the dead.[33]

Thus even if the act of a lavish burial was largely the result of social pressure, one could not deny the possibility that some people also genuinely believed that it was for the benefit of the dead, for they could not bear to see their kinsfolk spend time in the netherworld with insufficient sustenance.

FUNERARY RITUALS AND CUSTOMS

Besides preparing a tomb and funerary objects, a proper funeral would not have been considered complete without a certain set of rituals to conclude the process and send off the departed. During the ritual, prayers would be recited and protective spells cast, sometimes written down and buried in the tomb.

Simply put, when a person died, the body was washed and dressed according to propriety. For a rich family such as that of the Marquis Dai, Lady Dai's body was wrapped in twenty layers of silk garments. Archaeological and textual evidence also shows that jade suits of various types could be supplied to the kings, princes, and high officials.

32 *Qianfu lun* 3: 137.
33 *Lunheng*: 461. For translation, Forke (1962, Vol. II: 369).

The coffin was to be placed at the front hall of the house so that family members and friends could come to pay their last respects, and to present their gifts of objects and money. A list of such gifts found in a Western Han tomb contains coins, silver, silk cloth, shoes, and garments that were worth a total of more than 50,000 cash.[34] This sum, although not a small amount, pales into insignificance compared with the records in the *History of Han*. It is said that "When the governor of a large commandery died, the funerary gifts in general would be more than tens of millions."[35] Despite possible exaggeration, funerary spending such as this must have been a burden to government finance, since it was customary that the gift money for the members of the imperial families and high officials was the responsibility of the imperial government. The amount of gift money was often astonishing: "Thirty million coins and thirty thousand rolls of clothes for a first generation prince who received a fiefdom and ten million coins and ten thousand rolls of clothes for the subsequent generations."[36]

After a certain period of time – the length of which varied according to the social status of the dead and special circumstances – the coffin was sent to the burial site with a procession of relatives and acquaintances, led by a "soul banner" that had the name of the deceased on it, in order to attract the soul of the deceased to attach itself to the banner, which eventually was to be buried in the tomb. The silk painting of the Mawangdui tombs was probably the earliest example and most elaborate version of such a banner, except that the name was replaced by a painting of the deceased. In any case, the funeral procession was an excellent opportunity to display the social status and family fortune of the deceased. Disregarding the funerals of the rich and powerful, where a large attendance was expected, it was interesting to note that sometimes the funeral of a famous scholar or the family member of a popular heroic figure would also attract a large crowd. When the popular hero Jumeng's (second century BCE) mother died, for example, 1,000 carriages came from afar to attend the funeral procession;[37] the famous scholar-official Huang Qiung's (86–164 CE) funeral attracted more than 6,000 people.[38] In such cases, the funerals became stages for a display of social power, often with political significance (Fig. 42).

The location of the tomb and the date of burial, however, were determined according to the principles of geomancy and calendars of auspicious dates. As Wang Chong remarked, people of his time took the choice of a burial site seriously, and a certain "Calendar for Burial" was circulating in society.[39]

[34] Yangzhou Bowuguan (1987).
[35] *HS* 92: 3714.
[36] *HHS* 42: 1450.
[37] *HS* 92: 3700.
[38] *HHS* 53: 1752.
[39] *Lunheng* 24: 989–90; Poo (1998: 141–46).

42. A funerary procession, Eastern Han tomb relief from Shandong. After Wang Sili 王思禮, "Shangdong Weishan xian Handai huaxiangshi diaocha baogao 山東微山縣漢代畫像石調查報告," *Kaogu* 考古 8(1989): 707

Another important aspect of customs related to funerals is the practice of observing a mourning period and the wearing of mourning garments. The *Book of Ceremonies* prescribed these in meticulous detail, and the length of the mourning period was regulated according to the hierarchy of kinship. Thus there were five kinds of mourning period: three years for parents, one year for a spouse, nine months for paternal cousins, five months for grandparents, and three months for maternal cousins. During the mourning period, the mourner was supposed to wear appropriate garments made of linen. There were five kinds of garments, each with different degrees of roughness to indicate the degree of closeness in the kinship system between the deceased and the mourner. As the Confucian philosopher Xunzi puts it, "Ritual is performed to divide and make difference, music is performed to unite and create unity."[40] The performance of rituals – funerals included – was therefore designed for the purpose of ensuring social hierarchy by literally arranging people of different social statuses into different physical positions. These practices lasted until modern times in various forms and became salient features of Chinese popular culture.

The rituals described in the *Book of Ceremonies* deal with a normal death when it occurred at home under ordinary circumstances. Ample time and preparations could be devoted to taking care of the dead. Yet often death came unexpectedly, and not in the comfort of home, such as those who died on the battlefield or during a long journey. No proper burial was provided, and no ritual performed. These are the circumstances that created the restless dead, whose unsettled existence was the burden of the collective social conscience.

[40] *Xunzi* 14: 382.

A famous parody told by the philosopher-cum-literary genius Zhuangzi tries to disentangle the possible reasons for an untimely death:

> On his way to the state of Chu, Zhuangzi saw a skull, with a distinct shape. He slashed it with horse whip and asked it, saying: "Was it because of your lust for life and the loss of your sense of justice that you arrived at this state? Was it because you have met with the destruction of state and execution by axe that you arrived at this? Was it because of your evil conduct and scandalous deeds that caused shame to your parents and wife that you arrived at this? Was it because you suffered from cold and hunger that you arrived at this? Was it because of your life span that you arrived at this?"[41]

However, it seems that what Zhuangzi was really driving at was not how the person died, but how one should conceive and accept death and what comes after it. In his typical fashion, Zhuangzi made the ghost of the skull say: "In death there is no sovereign above, no subjects below, neither are there the affairs of the four seasons, only nonchalantly taking heaven and earth as spring and summer. Not even the joy of being a king would exceed this."[42] Obviously such remarks about death and its benefit were counterintuitive to most people. For them, a proper ritual and incantation to appease relevant deities to take care of the deceased was necessary, even if no actual funeral could be held. Evidence shows that incantations were read at the occasion of a ceremony designed to appease the ghosts of the dead soldiers, whose bodies might have been hidden unrecognized on deserted battlefields.[43] The incantation, though brief, contains the essential elements: prayers, offerings, names of the deity and the dead, and the supplication for the return of the wandering souls of the dead to enjoy a good meal at home, or in the tomb, and hopefully be satisfied.

HOPE FOR A HAPPY AFTERLIFE

Thus the deceased was finally put to rest after the living had done what they considered appropriate, and all grief had to be put aside. The mourners hoped for the best, not only for the departed, but also for those who still remained on earth, as evidenced by a tomb inscription dated 151 CE that detailed the wishes of the living:

> May those who study rise to a high rank and receive an office seal, may those who do business earn ten thousand folds of money daily. He who descends to the dark region shall be separated [from the living], as the tomb pit once closed shall not be opened again.[44]

[41] *Zhuangzi* 6b: 617; for translation see Watson (1968, 6b: 5).

[42] *Zhuangzi* 6b: 617; for translation see Watson (1968, 6b: 5).

[43] Hubei sheng wenwu kaogu yanjiuso (1995: plate 113); see also Chen Songchang (1998); Hubeisheng wenwu kaogu yanjiuso and Beijing Daxue Zhongwenxi (2000:13, 50); Zhou Fengwu (2001: 943–45).

[44] Shandongsheng Bowuguan and Cangshanxian Wenhuaguan (1975).

Such kind of eager desire for a happy life for the living, moreover, can be seen in a special category of funerary objects, the inscribed bronze mirrors. The simpler type of mirror inscriptions of the Western Han period often contained shorter sentences: "May the family have lasting fortune and high prestige" or "Happiness lasting forever," or "Great happiness, having what one wishes, for ever and ever, and having longevity and extended lifetime." Thus happiness consisted of the gaining of fortune, social prestige, and longevity.[45] As the mirrors could be used by the deceased during their lifetime, we cannot exclude the possibility that, besides their practical function, they were meant to serve as a kind of auspicious object in people's daily lives. This is stated in a straightforward manner in an inscription carved around the edge of a mirror:

> He who buys this will become extremely rich, and have prolonged life, such as that of the King Father (of the East) and Queen Mother of the West. You shall attain a high rank, as high as a duke and a marquis. You shall have longevity and great fortune, and a long life as the Grand Master.[46]

Thus the mirror was regarded as a kind of lucky charm or magical talisman that could bring good fortune for the owner. However, the fact that mirrors were part of the funerary paraphernalia indicates that the happy life aspired to in the inscriptions could equally serve as hope for the future of the deceased in the netherworld.

Other than the mirror inscriptions, the most direct textual testimony to the imagining of the netherworld came from the so-called "tomb quelling text" or "exorcistic text" and related material found in the tombs.[47] Such texts were composed for the purpose of expelling bad luck and evil spirits, including the ghosts of the ancestors, for the living, and at the same time helping the dead to lead a peaceful and happy life in the netherworld. This mentality prevailed in most of the tomb quelling texts. To give an example, on a clay bottle dated to 173 CE, there are the following sentences:

> Today is an auspicious day. It is for no other reason but that the deceased Zhang Shujing, who sadly died prematurely, is scheduled to descend into the grave. The Yellow God, who created the Five Mountains, is in charge of the roster of the living, and recalling the *hun* and *po*, in charge of the list of the dead. The living may build a high tower; the dead returns and is buried deeply beneath. Eyebrows and beards having fallen, they drop and became dirt and dust. Now therefore I (the Messenger of Heavenly Emperor) present the medicine for removing poll-tax and corvée conscription, so that the descendants will not die. Nine pieces of ginseng (*renshen* 人蔘) from Shangdang substitute for the living. A lead figurine

[45] Lin Suqing (1999).
[46] Lin (1999: 283).
[47] Zhang and Bai (2006: 1–332).

> (*qianren* 鉛人) is intended to substitute for the dead. The soybeans and melon seeds are for the dead to pay taxes underground. The medicine of *lizhi* and *mouli* are to remove the earthly evil, so that no disaster will occur. When this decree arrives, restrict the officer of the Underworld, and do not disturb the Zhang family again. Doubly urgent as prescribed by the laws and ordinances.[48]

These extraordinary texts revealed a rich imagination of the netherworld. As indicated earlier, the bureaucratic nature of the netherworld was amply demonstrated in these texts.[49] On the one hand, the needs of the deceased in the netherworld, including daily sustenance or dealing with the bureaucracy about taxation and corvée conscription, were taken care of; on the other hand, the welfare of the living descendants was also protected by means of spells (the decree issued by the Heavenly Emperor) and magical objects such as ginseng. One persistent idea in these texts is that the dead should go his or her own way without any further engagement with the living. It has been suggested that these texts could have represented traces of rituals that were later incorporated into the early Heavenly Master Daoist religion founded by Zhang Daoling.[50] In this belief system the ghosts of the deceased are potentially dangerous to the living; thus they needed to be separated from the living by means of the exorcistic rituals, spells, and magical objects.

The purpose of the tomb quelling/exorcistic texts, in fact, was often pronounced at the outset as mainly for the benefit of the family members of the deceased; thus one can detect certain tension between the living and the dead: as descendants and as filial sons and daughters, the living should theoretically show deep compassion for their deceased parents or family members; yet for practical protection, the belief in the malicious nature of the revenants required them to use the exorcistic/tomb quelling texts to keep the deceased at a distance. To put it in a more blunt fashion, it can even be said that, despite the prevailing social value of filial piety, people who resorted to the use of the tomb quelling texts and the kind of magical funerary objects actually showed a stronger desire to acquire maximum benefit for the living and keep their ancestors at a distance than taking care of the need of the deceased. The conceptualization of the netherworld, and the measures that were prescribed to deal with it, therefore, seemed to have been conditioned by and evolved around the concern for the happiness of the living. The hope that the descendants would become rich and famous and attain high-ranking government positions may be unrealistic, yet it points at a popular mentality that manifests itself in the funerary arrangements.

[48] Zhang and Bai (2006: 160).
[49] Lai (2015: 154–56).
[50] Zhang and Bai (2006: 15–16).

IMMORTALITY

Behind the preparation of the funeral and the imagination of the next life, such as we have so far discussed, one cannot but sense that something more was expected, that is, an eternal life that could render all anxiety nil, so as to achieve true happiness and peace of mind. The wish to prolong life is arguably one of the primordial urges of human beings. In China, the concrete evidence for such a wish could be found in the Western Zhou documents. Commemorative inscriptions on ritual bronze vessels often wished the owner of the vessels "longevity," or else "never-aging." This means that people toyed with the idea that one could live to an extremely old age, and this had already become synonymous with the idea of happiness for the upper-class elite.[51]

The further and logical development of this idea came about during the Warring States period. A number of texts touched on the idea of a deathless life. The book of *Hanfeizi* mentions a charlatan who claimed that he could teach the king of Yan the art of achieving immortality. The king ordered a servant to learn from this "master," yet the latter suddenly died before he could teach his secret to the servant. The king was so infuriated that he executed the servant for being slow to learn the art of immortality, without realizing that since the "master" could not even save his own life, his method of achieving immortality must have been fraudulent.[52] The author of *Hanfeizi* used this story to demonstrate the king's lack of intelligence, though inadvertently the story also reveals that immortality was by then not an uncommon idea. According to another story, the duke of Qi once expressed the thought that it would be wonderful if one could live forever. The witty minister Yanzi promptly deflated his illusory wish by saying that if no one had ever died since ancient times, he, the duke of Qi, would still be toiling in the field as an ignorant farmer, because the ancient ruler, no matter who it might have been, would still be sitting on the throne.[53]

This idea of immortality was certainly becoming popular toward the end of the Warring States period. The author of *Lüshi chunqiu* once remarked that "None of the rulers and nobles in the world, no matter if they are capable or not, would not want to have a long life and not grow old."[54] Admitting a certain degree of exaggeration, this passage unwittingly reveals some of the social sentiment of the late Warring States period. This concept of the state of deathlessness, however, was not elaborated until the appearance of the terms *xian* and *xianren*, which are generally translated as immortality and immortal.

Ascending to heaven or living in the mountain, it seems that such an immortal was believed to have led a rather reclusive life, far away from human

[51] Poo (1998: 157–63).

[52] *Hanfeizi* 11: 270. *Zhanguoce* 17: 836.

[53] *Yanzi* 1: 65.

[54] *Lüshi Chunqiu* 1: 22.

misery. One of the most colorful descriptions of such an immortal was given in the book of *Zhuangzi*:

> In the mountains of far-off Guyi there lives a daemonic (divine) man, whose skin and flesh are like ice and snow, and who is gentle as a virgin. He does not eat the five grains but sucks in the wind and drinks the dew; he rides the vapor of the clouds, yokes flying dragons to his chariot, and roams beyond the four seas.[55]

It is commonly assumed that this passage tries to depict an immortal who roams about in the clouds and leads a life that is detached from the mundane world. Such an image, in the context of Zhuangzi's works, should be understood as a metaphorical expression aimed at representing an absolutely independent spirit that is not affected by ephemeral worldly desires, troubles, and distractions. It is a literary and philosophical rendering of an idea of immortality that was beginning to gain more currency in late Warring States society. However, Zhuangzi did not deal with the problems of if or how an ordinary person could become an immortal, or what the relationship between the immortal and the mundane world would be. The solutions to these problems would have to wait until a later stage.

When China was united by the Qin dynasty, the idea of immortality gained a prominent position at court. The stories of the First Emperor of Qin's search for immortals in the Eastern Sea and Emperor Wu's searching for the elixir of immortality have been told repeatedly by generations of Chinese writers. Sima Qian, the first historian to record these stories, obviously held a cynical view of the vain pursuits of the emperors. Yet this does not mean that these vain pursuits were dissuaded when no elixirs or immortals were found. The idea of immortality was so attractive that people would rather accept the existence of the immortals than deny it, since there was no inherent difference between the immortals and the deities – both are immortal. If one believes gods exist, why not immortals? A number of shrines dedicated to some immortals testified to this idea.[56] In fact, a term for immortal that prevailed throughout subsequent Chinese history is *shenxian*, literally "divine-immortal," which illustrates this popular idea that the immortals were not only deathless beings but also powerful demigods who could relieve the pain and sorrow of the common people. This belief must have been quite prevalent in Han society, so much so that the great Western Han scholar Liu Xiang (79–8 BCE) was said to have compiled an *Arrayed Biographies of the Immortals* (*Liexian zhuan* 列仙傳) that included sixty-eight biographical stories of immortals circulating in his time. Although the date of this work has been under scholarly scrutiny, as was another similar work, the *Biographies of the Immortals* (*Shenxian zhuan* 神仙傳) attributed to

[55] *Zhuangzi* 1a: 28; Watson (1968, Vol. 1: 10).

[56] *HS* 25b: 1250, 1258; 28a: 1555, 1585; Campany (2009).

Ge Hong (283–343? CE),[57] the content of the biographies taken as a whole reveal a clear social background of the immortals: except for a small number of legendary figures such as the Yellow Emperor or Laozi, the majority of them seem to be ordinary people of no wealth or power.[58] There are also female immortals, which at least suggests that immortality was not gender specific. Such stories about immortals, collected by the literati and then redistributed to the public by means of copies and oral communications, could presumably have the effect of reinforcing the idea's acceptance by the common people, even though few of them would dare to hope that they themselves might have the chance to become immortal.

A famous Han dynasty scholar, Gu Yong, once gave the following account about the popular conception of the immortals:

> People say that there are the so-called immortals in this world, who were able to take the elixir of immortality, and then their bodies became light and could fly up to the top of the cloud and watch the world from above. They could also float to the island of immortality, Penglai, where they planted the five elements in the morning and harvested in the evening. Their ages are as endless as the rock on the mountains.[59]

Gu Yong himself, according to his biography, was not a believer in immortality. His account merely reports what he knew of the common understanding of the immortals in his time. A type of bronze mirror often found in the Han tombs bears the following inscription:

> The Shangfang (imperial workshop) made this mirror and truly it is very fine. Upon it are immortal beings oblivious of old age. When they are thirsty they drink from the spring of jade, when they are hungry they feed on jujubes. They roam at large throughout the world, wandering between the four oceans. They rove at will on the well-known hills plucking the Herb of Life. Long life be yours, like that of metal and stone, and may you be protector of the land; eternal joy without end; as is fit for a nobleman or king.[60]

We are not sure if this inscription expresses the wish that the owner of the mirror might become an immortal, yet the state of immortality depicted certainly conveys a popular perception. Reliefs and paintings found among the tomb decorations, furthermore, often depict winged immortals, sometimes playing board games with exhilarating gestures, obviously in great enjoyment.[61]

[57] Campany (2002).
[58] Poo (1995).
[59] *HS* 25b: 1260.
[60] Loewe (1979: 198).
[61] Finsterbusch (1966, Vol. 2: 143).

It is interesting to speculate on how one might have become an immortal. The story in *Hanfeizi* has already provided an answer: by taking the elixirs of immortality. It is notable that the idea of drinking an elixir to become an immortal was an extremely materialistic method, as immortality was achieved through a change of the physiological composition, and, as far as it could be determined, had no necessary correlation with one's moral integrity or social status. Other methods include meditation, exercise, and the control of breathing. It was, therefore, not because of their moral or ethical values, nor because they had made any extraordinary contribution to society, such as in the case of Greek heroes, that they achieved immortality.

On the other hand, since the immortals possessed superior power, they were often expected to perform magical and beneficial acts for the people. The *Arrayed Biographies of the Immortals* provides the following example:

> Ping Changsheng of Gucheng village was of unknown origin. He died several times and came back to life. People thought this to be unlikely. Later there was a great flood that caused all manner of damage. Ping stood on top of mount Quemen and called out saying "Ping Changsheng is here!" He then said that the rain and flood would cease in five days. When the flood receded, people went up the mountain and sought to worship him, and saw Ping dressed in a coat with a leather belt. Several decades later he became the gate keeper of the city of Huayin.[62]

The story depicts Ping's magical deeds to help stop the flood, which betrays a collective yearning for a miracle when people are in grave distress. It should not be ignored, however, that a certain degree of moral integrity could still be required of the immortality seeker. According to the *Baopuzi* (*Master Who Embraces Simplicity*), in order to become a heavenly immortal, one has to perform 1,200 good deeds, in addition to physical practices and elixir intake. If one wishes to become an earthly immortal who stays in this world even though he or she is deathless, he or she has to perform 300 good deeds to qualify.[63] Although this sounds somewhat utilitarian or mechanical in that good deeds become mere numbers, which tends to obscure the true meaning of compassion, it is also true that the author intended to make moral integrity a necessary condition for immortality:

> Anyone who intends to seek immortality should base his efforts on loyalty, filial piety, friendliness, obedience, humanity, and trustworthiness. Those who do not tend to the cultivation of the virtues but only concentrate on the magical methods will not be able to achieve immortality in the end.[64]

[62] *Liexian zhuan* 5: 67.
[63] *Baopuzi* (1985: 53); Ware (1966: 66).
[64] Ware (1966: 66).

This emphasis on the "virtues" of the immortal seekers, interestingly, hinges heavily on Confucian virtue, which hints at some very interesting problems regarding the moral and ethical foundations of the Daoist religion and its relationship with Confucianism. When the earliest Daoist sect, the Way of Five Pecks of Rice, was first established in the latter days of Han rule, the leader Zhang Lu taught his followers to repent for their wrong doings when they suffered sickness. Although it was not meant to achieve immortality, the emphasis on the importance of moral value in pursuing the true Way was obvious. This sets the Daoist teaching apart from the contemporary shamanistic practices that mainly employed talismans and various exorcistic acts to treat the sick and the possessed.[65]

In the Daoist tradition, therefore, cultivating moral values, searching for elixirs, and practicing physical training received a different emphasis in different situations or traditions. Ge Hong's own writing, for example, makes it clear that he was not always consistent in explaining the conditions for achieving immortality.

What is remarkable is that while the wish to prolong life might be a universal human desire, to develop this wish into an elaborate system of physical and mental exercises is certainly unusual. In ancient Mesopotamia, people were perhaps more pessimistic as a group, as human beings were thought to be the creation of the gods to serve the divine community, and there was no independent meaning to human life.[66] It was only in the *Epic of Gilgamesh* that the problem of immortality was raised. The epic was built around the theme of the hero Gilgamesh's journey to find the plant of immortality. Yet in the end the plant was lost, and mankind was never to have access to immortality. This hard look at the reality of human life was perhaps what elevates the *Epic of Gilgamesh* from a heroic story to a philosophical meditation.[67] Any idea of immortality, therefore, was utterly shattered by the Gilgamesh story. In the Chinese case, the goal of immortality was to gain a "pure" form of existence that could last forever, and this hope lingered in society for a long time. This pure form of existence was fundamentally different from the mortal existence: the immortals were supposed to live indefinitely, with an indestructible body; have no physical impairments of any sort; and possess magical power. There is no need to worry about any social or political matters since the immortal is not bound by any human institution.

What remains to be asked is why the idea of immortality could have gained ground in the first place. Short of an ultimate answer, we can look at the religious condition of the Chinese people at the time and try to see what the idea of immortality had to offer that the current religious ideas and practices could

[65] See two opposing views: Stein (1979); Lai Chi-tim (1998).
[66] Bottéro (1992: 225–28).
[67] Jacobsen (1976: 193–219).

not. In the early Han period, religious activities in society could generally be divided into two categories: official cults and private worship. The official cults, being official, were established by the state mainly for promoting the welfare of the emperor and the imperial house, as well as the prosperity of the state, such as a good harvest, prosperous life, or peace in the land. These were basically political in nature. Private worship was concerned with the welfare of individuals and their family members. The object of worship was naturally the ancestors of the family, in addition to various ghosts and spirits. Neither official cults nor private worship, however, could guarantee an eternal life and unlimited happiness for the worshippers. This is amply demonstrated by the immortality-seeking emperors. If, despite all the state cults and all the sacrifices to Heaven and Earth and the deities, the emperors were still keen on seeking the elixir of immortality, the state cults must have lacked some quality that could satisfy the personal cravings of the emperors. The emperors' wish to gain immortality may be seen as a greed for everything good in life. Yet the very idea that immortality was possible must have been prevalent enough in society to support this wish. The emperors did not invent the idea of immortality. On the contrary, it was the existence of the idea of immortality that supplied such cravings.

That immortality was imaginable at all, moreover, must have also been inspired or supported by certain empirical or physical evidence, in addition to a primordial urge to prolong life. As a sign of immortality, longevity was obviously the basic feature that was shown in the *Arrayed Biographies of the Immortals*. Tales about people of extreme old age, which might not have been uncommon even for the ancient period when the average life expectancy must have been very low, could have reinforced the concept of immortality in the popular mentality. The way to achieve longevity, besides doing special exercises, was to rely on the help of an elixir, which had to do with the development of medicine since the Warring States period. The medical texts discovered in the Mawangdui tomb no. 3, though explicitly aimed at providing pharmaceutical recipes and physical therapies of various kinds, imply an effort to uphold life and strive for immortality. The terms employed in the texts, such as *yangshen* (Nourishing Life) and *quegu shiqi* (Eliminating Grain and Eating Vapour), are intimately related to the terminology used in the work of *Zhuangzi* in relation to the immortals. As the knowledge of human physiology and medicine advanced, it is imaginable that the effects of certain drugs in improving physical well-being could have become associated with immortality.[68]

The idea of immortality, then, provided new hope for people of every social stratum. If one could avoid the attack of death, an endless happy life would become possible. Still, one last question remains: what was the meaning of

[68] Poo (2005).

an immortal life? The fact that in the chapter on the making of elixirs in *The Master Who Embraces Simplicity* we often encounter such statements as "such and such a drug would make one live for hundreds of years" indicates that, in the mind of the immortality seekers, the so-called longevity was close to, or interchangeable with, immortality or deathless life. In other words, the concept of immortality was still conceived in terms of countable years. If this was the case, then immortality would be basically a quantitative and not a qualitative change of one's life. On the other hand, it is obvious that the status of the immortal was built on qualitative differences: an indestructible and youthful body, magical power, the ability to fly about on a cloud, and prophesying the future. Without this qualitative difference, the quantitative difference would be useless. The two, however, were not necessarily emphasized at the same time. Here the possible incongruence suggests that ideas were not entirely thought through.

In fact, all, or almost all, human desires are built around the hidden assumption that lifetime is limited and therefore precious. When the restraint of time is removed, as in the state of immortality, all worldly concerns would become baseless and therefore meaningless. Such a state of existence, however, did not seem to have been fully recognized and developed. In the imagination of the believers of immortality, there were still small cycles of the progression of time within eternity: even the immortals would feel hungry and thirsty and needed food and drink. These are processes in which time played a key factor: it is because of the passing of time that one passes from satiation to hunger and thirst and back to satiation again. If immortality means that which mortality is not, this "not-mortal" condition did not seem to have been conceived to perfection, since to employ time-bound human faculties to imagine a timeless situation could only be a vague approximation at best.

Finally, mundane thoughts inevitably infiltrated the concept of the immortal: people began to imagine that there were different types of immortals. There were the heavenly immortals, the earthly immortals, and the corpse-dissolving immortals. The heavenly immortals lived in the heavenly court, far away from the mundane world. However, this heavenly court was imagined according to the earthly court, with a hierarchy of court officials, beginning from the highest god Laojun (Laozi) and the Three Pure Ones (Yuanshi 元始, Lingbao 靈寶, Daode 道德), followed by an array of lesser heavenly officials and immortals.[69] Apparently this heavenly court was not suitable for all immortals; thus came about the idea of the earthly immortals, i.e., immortals who did not wish to ascend to heaven too soon but preferred to dwell in the world and therefore outside the jurisdiction of the heavenly court.[70] In other words, the earthly

[69] Robinet (1997).
[70] *Baopuzi* 52.

immortals were the "hermits" among the immortals who abhorred court life in heaven. With this aversion to the possible drawbacks of life in the "heavenly court," the purpose of achieving an absolutely free immortality seems to have been somewhat diminished. The "corpse-dissolving" immortals, finally, are the least "powerful," as they became immortals only after death, that is, death in human terms. For these immortals, death was only a process toward immortality. When that happens, their bodies will be dissolved and only their clothes and shoes shall be left in the coffin.[71] With the formation of these types of immortals, probably during the late Han and early Six dynasties periods, we see the emergence of a world of immortals that was, like the world of the deceased, modeled on the worldly bureaucratic state. The immortals were finally integrated into the omnipresent bureaucratic mindset of the mortals.

[71] Maspero (1981: 267–68); Schipper (1993: 166).

CONCLUSION: CONTINUATION AND TRANSFORMATION OF LIFE EXPERIENCE

After an attempt to portray different aspects of life during early imperial China, this final chapter gives a general account of the development of the Han state, how it disintegrated, how it fell again into the Warring States, and how a period of political division influenced the life of the people. In particular, the inroads of the nomadic people in northern China brought permanent change to many aspects in people's lives and customs. Refugees who migrated from the north into southern China also merged with the aborigines of the south to create new lifestyles. Thus, when the country was united again under the Sui–Tang dynasties, a new mode of daily life emerged both as a continuation as well as a transformation of the daily lives known to us during the Han period.

THE RISE AND FALL OF THE HAN STATE

Most of the historical period covered in this book falls in that of the Qin and Han dynasties. The Qin rule lasted only fifteen years (221–206 BCE), yet with the unprecedented energy and fortitude that was demonstrated, perhaps exaggeratedly, by the building of the Great Wall and the Mausoleum and clay army of the First Emperor, it set the path of imperial rule in China for the next 2,000 years. As we have seen in the previous chapters, its imprint was cast not only on the government structure, but also on many aspects that concerned the people's daily lives.[1]

[1] Pines (2014).

When Liu Bang was enthroned as the emperor of Han, he inherited more from the Qin institutions than he created or innovated; this was because the land was largely in disarray after years of war and destruction. Thus, the first few reigns of the Han, from Emperors Hui, Wen, to Jing, was a period of recuperation. By when Emperor Wu ascended the throne, the wealth accumulated by the government had reached its zenith. A more active and aggressive policy was implemented toward the strengthening of the government structure and the recruitment system, and toward dealing with the old rivaling nomadic neighbors to the north and west, and the burgeoning neighboring powers to the east, south, and southwest of the country's borders. Conflicts and compromises with these neighbors were a constant factor in "national security" throughout the Han period, even when it was divided into the Former or Western Han, and the Later or Eastern Han, by a brief interlude of the short-lived Xin dynasty (9–23 CE) established by the usurper Wang Mang. For Emperor Wu, the refurbished military power allowed his generals to launch a series of attacks on the Xiongnu, with some degree of success, and a number of fortresses were built along the roads toward the western desert. The Central Asian territory, which had never been part of the Chinese state, was now open to more frequent communications with the Han, both diplomatically and economically. However, even when the Han military was claiming success, signs of economic distress caused by the continuous warfare were already surfacing, which prompted the establishment of the government monopoly on the production of salt, wine, and iron in order to extract more revenue from the people. We have already read many times in the previous chapters about the Debate of Salt and Iron that took place during the reign of Emperor Zhao.[2] Yet although most political debates were formulated under the pretense of benefiting the state and the people, the real intention was probably the struggle for power and influence between the different factions at court. The common people could not have known anything different from what appeared to be an order from above to pay this or that tax.

After the disastrous case of witchcraft at the end of Emperor Wu's reign that caused major political persecution and cost thousands of lives, there was a brief period of recuperation during the reigns of the Emperors Zhao and Xuan; the latter was the grandson of Emperor Wu's unfortunate heir-apparent who lost his life and entire family during the witchcraft purge. Because of his personal experience and upbringing, Emperor Xuan made a particular point of caring for the welfare of the common people by employing capable ministers and governors who would ensure the smooth operation of government policy without unduly harsh measures. Some of his ministers were practically minded bureaucrats, although he could also appreciate people with a Confucian

[2] Von Glahn (2016: 120–26).

background and employed them for various important government positions. However, as with some previous reigns, such as those of Emperor Gaozu (Liu Bang) and Emperor Wu, Emperor Xuan could not or would not prevent the increasing role of the royal relatives of the empress and their infringement on royal power, which was to become a major factor that eroded the Han regime.

After the death of Emperor Xuan, Emperor Yuan, who from childhood was fond of Confucian ideals, adopted a different mode of governing by actively employing Confucian scholars for high posts in the government. Such a measure planted the seeds of conflict between the Confucian scholar-officials, the royal relatives, and, no less importantly, the eunuchs, who were always part of the political intrigues, since they were the people who could easily walk between the inner court where the emperor and empress lived and the outer court where the government officials worked. After the death of Emperor Yuan, Emperor Cheng, nineteen years of age and self-indulgent in wine and women, relied on the help of his uncle Wang Feng, brother of Empress Dowager Wang, who successively took hold of the major forces who controlled court politics. The following reigns, those of Emperors Ai and Ping, were short lived. The Grand Marshal (*dasima*) Wang Mang, nephew of Empress Dowager Wang, a person versed in Confucian classics and a careful plotter who cultivated his reputation as a true follower of Confucian teaching, finally gained absolute power by eliminating all opposition, including the eunuchs, other Confucian officials, and his own relatives; also, he murdered the young Emperor Ping and then created a puppet Emperor Zi Ying, only two years old. His ambition was no longer hidden, and soon he took over the throne under the pretext that numerous portents sent by heaven had indicated his legitimacy to receive the Mandate of Heaven.

For the general public, Wang Mang's Xin (i.e., New) dynasty (8–23 CE) was a period of unsettling institutional changes that deeply disturbed the people's livelihoods. A new system of coinage was introduced to replace the "*wuzhu*" coin issued by Emperor Wu, a coin that was generally accepted by the population without too much trouble. The new system contains six categories of currencies: gold, silver, turtle, shell, coin, cloth, with twenty-eight value units. As can be imagined, such a complicated system would inevitably cause great confusion to the common people. To his credit, though, he had certain "good" intentions to take care of the large majority of farmers, including the implementation of the well-field (*jingtian* 井田) system. With this he made all the land in the country government land, and redistributed it to the people, with each male member of the household entitled to 100 *mu* of land.[3] This well-field system was actually an ancient Confucian ideal that was never implemented, and Wang Mang's new measure met a disastrous end. Furthermore, he used a

[3] Von Glahn (2016: 136–37).

double-sided way to encourage people to work: on the one hand, he increased the categories of government monopoly, and increased taxes for the people; on the other hand, he implemented interest-free government loans to people in need, and to people who intended to do small business, with 10 percent annual interest of the net profit. Obviously, these drastic reforms caused opposition from the privileged classes, and the common people were driven by all sorts of pressures into taking the road of insurgence. Natural disasters during the years after 17 CE, moreover, forced the distressed hunger-stricken people of a vast area between the Yellow River and the Yangtze River (roughly today's Shandong, Jiangsu, Hubei, and Hunan Provinces) to evolve from spontaneous refugees to organized rebel forces. It was one of these forces that finally brought down the regime of Wang Mang in the year 23 CE.

In the ensuing civil wars, the country was in a fragmented state, with first the rivalry between the descendants of the Liu royal house, and then between the victor Liu Xiu, who enthroned himself as Emperor Guangwu (25–57 CE), and the other warlords. Finally, after more than a decade of warfare, Liu Xiu succeeded in reuniting the country in the year 37 CE, under the name of Han. Little is known about the livelihood of the people during these turbulent years, but if we count the years from the beginning of the rebellion after 17 CE, it was twenty years of continuous and rampant civil wars – far surpassing the period of warfare after the fall of the Qin dynasty (209–202 CE) – which no normal society could have endured without suffering great hardship. Because it took the Western Han seventy years to recover from the civil war, it is only expected that the Eastern Han would have suffered any less.

Nevertheless, a period of relative peace followed the reign of Emperor Guangwu, despite the personal flaws of the rulers: Emperor Ming (57–75 CE) was prone to a Legalist approach in his rule, while Emperor Zhang (75–88 CE) was a promotor of Confucian leniency toward his subjects, and both were somewhat off balance, which caused widespread discontent among the subjects in the former case, and increasing corruption among the royal relatives in the latter. Despite the personal shortcomings of Emperors Ming and Zhang, they were praised in later Chinese history as the "good emperors," in contrast to those who followed them, some of whom were either minors when they were enthroned and died young, or ineffectual persons who could not really bring themselves to rule in a just and efficient manner. The latter half of the Eastern Han, therefore, was a period marred by rampant corruption, struggles between the maternal royal relatives and the eunuchs, and scholar-officials who tried to sustain what little achievement their predecessors had gained in the government institutions and just laws.

Power struggles in the capital and in the local governments inevitably affected the lives of the common people, since the corruption carried out by the unrestrained partisans of the powerful eunuchs directly infringed on the people's livelihoods in the form of extortion, bribery, overtaxation, forced labor, even blatant robbery, etc. Thus just as natural disasters drove the people away from their homes to seek survival wherever they could, human disasters such as those mentioned earlier also forced people away from their villages and towns in search of a livable life. By about 184 CE, distressed refugees, numbered in tens of thousands, were recruited by a sectarian leader, Zhang Jiao, to form a rebellious group called "The Way of Great Peace" (Taipingdao), which quickly spread to many provinces along the mid-to-lower Yellow River valley and in the Central Plain, and some even to Sichuan and Hunan. Although Zhang Jiao was defeated and killed, and his followers dispersed when attacked by government forces, the fabric of social cohesion was destroyed, as rampant rebellions and banditries surged in many parts of the empire. This was both the cause and the consequence of the final demise of the Han dynasty, because the quelling of local rebellions required the increase of local military power, and the increased local military power in turn forged the growth of the ambition of local military/political leaders. One kind of local military and political leader were the generals or governors who were given autonomous military power to defend the northern, western, and southern border areas, either by recruiting from the farming communities, or by adopting the mercenary nomadic soldiers who were the fiercer fighters. If we remember how many bows and arrows were stored in the armory at the Donghai Commandery mentioned in Chapter 2, it would not be surprising that, given the right circumstances, a local army could easily be assembled.

While local rebellions were ripping apart the social fabric of the country, political struggles at court severely impaired the normal operation of the government institutions and the procurement of resources that usually supported such an operation. Factional fights between the maternal royal relatives and the eunuchs, both groups that were in cooperation with certain scholar-officials at one time or another, finally dealt a death blow to the Han regime, and whatever hope that was left for the house of Liu that had lasted for 400 years was utterly shattered when a group of nomadic soldiers led by the notorious general Dong Zhuo entered and raided the capital Luoyang in the year 190 CE. Emperor Xian (189–220 CE), merely seven years of age, was taken captive by Dong Zhuo and removed from the ruined city of Loyang to the old capital Chang'an. The terror and devastation that the people yet again experienced was captured in the poem that was purportedly written by Cai Yan, whom we met in Chapter 9:

> Dong Zhuo's hordes descended on the east,
>   metal armor gleamed in the rays of the sun.
> The people of the plains were weaker,
>   the troops that came were all Hu and Qiang.
> They coursed the wilds, surrounded the cities,

wherever they went, all were destroyed.
They butchered and beheaded, left not one person behind,
corpses were propped up against one another.
Men's heads were strung from the horses' sides,
women and girls, brought behind the horses.[4]

THE END OF THE HAN AND THE BEGINNING OF THE ERA OF DIVISION

The attempt of Dong Zhuo to hold the ultimate political power by using the Emperor as a puppet, however, was an all-too-familiar plot shared by many ambitious generals. As a figurehead, Emperor Xian was in the custody of various warlords, and was finally in the control of Cao Cao from 196 onward until 220 CE, when Cao died. His son Cao Pi promptly forced Emperor Xian to abdicate and passed the Mandate to himself, the first Emperor of the Wei dynasty (220–266 CE). By this time, China was no longer a unified country, as a distant relative of the Liu House, Liu Bei, established his power base in the province of Shu (modern Sichuan), known as Shu-Han (221–263 CE), and another general, Sun Quan, took hold of the area south of mid-to-lower Yangtze valley (modern Zhejiang, Fujian, Jiangxi, Guangdong, Hunan, etc.), known as Wu (229–280 CE). The tripartite division of the Han Empire finally came to an end when the throne of Wei was usurped by the Jin dynasty (266–420 CE) and Wu succumbed to Jin in 280 CE.

After twenty years of peace, however, civil war broke out again amongst the members of the royal house, and the fighting lasted for sixteen years. Predictably, such prolonged civil war hurt the livelihood of the people and weakened the normal operation of the government institutions. One of the most significant results of the civil war was the invasion by the nomadic tribes from the north who had been lurking around the borders ever since the Eastern Han, and this invasion finally caused the collapse of the Jin military power and the death of the Emperor. The Jin court was nevertheless able to regroup under the leadership of the self-made Emperor Yuan (317–323 CE), who established a new capital south of the Yangtze River, in the city of Jianye (modern Nanjing). Numerous people fled from the attacks of the nomadic groups and crossed the Yangtze to the south. This massive movement of people was culturally very significant, since this would be the first time that the people of the Central Plain area, with their cultural roots traceable back for 2,000 years since the Shang dynasty, migrated en masse to the area south of the Yangtze. A new kind of culture would be formed in the course of time in this area, as the newcomers began to encounter and adjust to the new situation, culturally and environmentally.

[4] For the full translation, see Owen (2006: 234–37).

For those who could not or would not migrate to the south, the next 200 years were also a period of tumultuous cultural change, as various nomadic groups – the Xiongnu, Xianbi, Jie, Chiang, and Di – to name the most prominent and powerful ones, incessantly invaded and ravaged the Central Plain area, and westward to the Wei River basin where the core of the Qin-Han dynasties was located. Simply put, the regions to the north of the Yangtze River fell into chaos and were ruled by a series of short-lived regimes established by various nomadic tribes, a period traditionally referred to as that of the Sixteen Kingdoms (304–439 CE). In fact, there were more than sixteen kingdoms, and some were established by Han Chinese. The inevitable confrontations and mutual adjustments between the nomadic and the agricultural people were difficult to resolve, and it would take hundreds of years to forge a balance and nurture a new breed of population in northern China.[5]

THE NOMADIC INROADS AND CULTURAL TRANSFORMATION

Throughout the Han dynasty, the nomadic Xiongnu people posed a continuous threat to the security of China – according to Chinese sources, and the nomadic customs were seen as the epitome of the opposite of Chinese culture.[6] Because one side could not defeat the other in a decisive manner, the relationship between the Han and the Xiongnu vacillated constantly between war and peace. One of the official policies, when the situation required it, was to forge marriage alliances with the nomadic peoples. This was an ancient tradition that can be traced back as far as the Spring and Autumn period. During the Han dynasty, marriage alliance was a strategy used by the Han government in its efforts to stop the invasion of the Xiongnu. It was only when the balance of power and mutual exchange relationship was disparate that wars broke out.[7] The Han government bestowed high noble titles on defected Xiongnu leaders and gave them Chinese names.[8] However, it was not uncommon for some Chinese, for one reason or another, to defect to the Xiongnu side.[9] In fact, a daily exchange of people and goods at the borders was the norm rather than the exception.

Documents from the Han period regarding the Xiongnu's identity are, noteworthily, written in Chinese. Nevertheless, there should be no doubt that the nomadic lifestyle was strongly upheld as being at the core of Xiongnu

5 Part of the material in this chapter has been adopted from Poo (2013).

6 The classic description of Xiongnu custom is in *SJ* 110:2879. See Barfield (1989: 32–84); Di Cosmo (2002: 161–204).

7 For the history of Han and Xiongnu intercourse, see *SJ* 110. Also *SJ* 108: 2861; Di Cosmo (2002: 161–204); Barfield (1989: 32–84). See also a general survey, Jagchid and Symons (1989). An older classic, still useful, is Lattimore (1951).

8 *SJ* 20: 1059; 57: 2078.

9 *SJ* 93: 2638.

cultural identity. According to a report by the Chinese historian Sima Qian, the Xiongnu people were once attracted to fancy silk dresses and Chinese food, but were later dissuaded by a loyal subject, Zhonghang Yue, who happened to be a defected Chinese. He argued that their indulgence in Chinese luxuries would result in the destruction of the Xiongnu people.[10] The same person also told a Han messenger that Xiongnu customs, such as not giving the elders the best food, or consanguineous marriage, although unimaginable to the Chinese, were perfectly reasonable in their own cultural context.[11] Throughout the Han dynasty, the distinction between Han and non-Han was tied, according to this official ideology, to the two different lifestyles and value systems. The term "Han," although originally the name of the dynasty, had by then become the generic name for the people of the former Han territory. It was used as the equivalent of Hua or Xia, terms used for the people of the Central Plain area since the Spring and Autumn period, or the people of Zhongguo – the "Middle Kingdom," and eventually it became the synonym for "China."[12]

In 436 CE, the Northern Wei dynasty (398–543 CE) established by the Toba clan of the Xianbei tribe unified northern China under one flag. Thus began the Northern Dynasties, which included the Northern Wei, its successors the Eastern Wei (534–550 CE) and the Western Wei (535–557 CE), and their successors, the Northern Qi (550–577 CE) and Northern Zhou (556–581 CE). It was a general of the Northern Zhou by the name of Yang Jian, a Han Chinese, who took the opportunity afforded by internal weakness, usurped the Zhou regime, and established the Sui dynasty (581–617 CE), which eventually united the whole country. However, the Sui was short lived and it was then replaced by the Tang (618–907 CE), much like the Han replaced the Qin.

CONTINUATION AND TRANSFORMATION OF LIFE EXPERIENCE

It was in the historical context described earlier that the various types of life experience discussed in the previous chapters were taking place. Apparently, the political events and government policies of the four centuries of the Han rule did exert a considerable impact on the lives of the people. The formation of the bureaucratic state, with the various levels of governing apparatus, and the application of household registration, had intended to place people under the control of the government. There was also the legal system that extended to the management of activities that people engaged in on a daily basis, such as farming, hunting, fishing, traveling, managing small businesses, and no less pervasively, the registration of household property, marriage, and inheritance, always with the prospect of taxation. Government policies, such

10 *SJ* 110: 2899.

11 *SJ* 110: 2899.

12 For a general background of this period, see Eberhard (1965); Dien (2007).

as the implementation of the monopoly of salt and iron, or the issuing of new currency, made a direct impact on the economic life of the population in the country. Civil wars also caused mass destructions to the society at large, especially during the intervening years between the Western Han and Eastern Han, as well as at the end of the Eastern Han. From the limited evidence we can gather on the income and expenditure of ordinary households, it appears that the average farming family had led a rather difficult life, and it was always a struggle for a family to balance the two throughout the year.[13]

Yet despite this grim picture, there must also have been a persistent force in society at large that allowed the lives of the people to continue, as there were always times of famine and times of feast. During the first half of the reign of Emperor Wu, for example, owing to the less aggressive management adopted by the central government, the society was in a state of well-supplied prosperity. This was the reason why Emperor Wu was able to expand the territory and wage wars against the Xiongnu. The continuous development of farming technology improved agricultural product, and the spread of cities gradually changed the quality of life in a minute way. There must have been, moreover, a number of ways for people to get around the government control and create their small niche of sustainable life.

There was, to be sure, a great discrepancy between the rich and the poor, between the small groups of elites who helped the imperial government to rule and accumulate wealth, and the vast majority of farmers who sustained the operation of the economy and the bureaucracy. The society would have collapsed if the balance between the two could not be maintained. And it indeed collapsed when the government fell into dysfunction by the hands of the eunuchs and the warlords, as described earlier. Whether the disintegration of the government brought relief to the life of people, of course, depended on the areas where they lived. Where warlords reigned, a certain degree of hardship was expected. Yet people could also seek protection in the manors or fortresses that some of the warlords and local magnates built to attract people and increase their power.[14]

Thus when we talk about daily life in this remote era, we are not retracing the actual everyday activities of any person, knowing that the life of a farmer was very different from that of a county magistrate or an official at court. They each would have had their obligations to fulfill, and needs to satisfy. What we have chosen to do in this volume was to describe the various contexts – political, legal, economic, technological – in which people of various walks of life formed their patterns of behavior, and passed those patterns from one

[13] See von Glahn (2016: 136).
[14] See von Glahn (2016: 160–67).

generation to the next. Within this context, life evolved as time passed by, and there were continuations and changes along different levels with different speed.

There were continuations of patterns of lifestyle, notably the general acceptance of a set of ideal ethics that manifested in social relations, family structure, legal statutes, which also contains several layers of patterns: those for the ruling elites; those for the government bureaucrats; and those for the general public such as the farmers, artisans, and merchants. That people at each level conducted their lives following the patterns but with deviations and revisions is only to be expected.

In terms of dietary habit, millet, barley, and other crops that pre-Qin people consumed continued to be the major staple food source during the Han. Yet changes did happen. With the active policy to expand the territory during Emperor Wu's time, new crops and vegetation were brought into China.[15] The actual process of the dietary assimilation of new foodstuffs into Chinese daily life was of course a long and slow one. Among the new items that were imported into China at one time or another after the Western Han, one can list grapes, alfalfa, pomegranates, walnuts, sesame, onions, caraway, peas, coriander, cucumbers, etc. By the end of the Han, food of nomadic or foreign origin became normal consumption items in people's households. The term "*hu* 胡," a designation of the nomadic people, was also used to name many newly imported objects and foodstuffs. Emperor Ling of Han was said to love the "*hu*-food," perhaps grain food cooked with flavorful sesame.[16] Emperor Ling, in fact, loved all sorts of imported items. According to the *History of Later Han*, "Emperor Ling was found of *hu*-garments, *hu*-tents, *hu*-bed, *hu*-seat, *hu*-food, *hu*-pipe, *hu*-flute, and *hu*-dance. The nobles in the capital all vied to imitate. This is called the "garment-portent." Later on Dong Zuo gathered many *hu*-soldiers. They filled the streets, ravaged the palace, and excavated the mausoleums."[17] This anecdote indicates that well before the onslaught of the nomadic invasion after the fall of the Western Jin that set apart the north and the south, foreign customs and cultural elements were already fairly familiar to those of the late Eastern Han people, but unimaginable in the Western Han.

There was also the continuation of belief systems. The veneration of natural deities and all sorts of spirits continued from the pre-Qin and Han periods and remained the same in terms of structure and characteristics. Various local deities and spirits kept appearing or disappearing, as was always the case. Yet there was also change, that is, a more articulated view of the afterlife seemed to have been developed in society and became more visible during the course of the Han dynasty. The change in tomb styles from vertical pit wooden casket tomb to horizontal brick tomb, for another example, also indicated the

15 Chang (1977: 53–83).

16 *HHS* 13: 3272; Chang (1977: 80).

17 *HHS* 13: 3272.

changing perception of the tomb as the abode of the deceased. From the tomb decorations one can see that a plethora of daily life scenes, real or imagined, was depicted, demonstrating the desire to remember the life on earth, and anticipating the life to come. It is true that the scenes did not appear in the tombs of the ordinary farmers, yet one can also argue that these scenes were the model of life that the society in general aspired to, just like the model houses and estates were.

One should of course mention that by the end of the Eastern Han, a more drastic change in the realm of religious belief began to take shape. This was the formation of the religious Daoist movement and the development of Buddhism. The Daoist movement grew out of the indigenous religious practices and beliefs by incorporating the pre-Qin Daoist philosophy of Laozi and Zhuangzi. Buddhism, on the other hand, offered the Chinese people a whole new eschatology and a new way to understand the relationship between the world and human fate, which challenged the traditional, mainly Confucian, social norm that passed down from the preimperial period through the Eastern Han. Both, however, had to find their foothold in people's lives by helping to resolve the eternal problems of the origin and destination of life, and how to lead a happy life on earth before moving on to the next.[18]

[18] Ch'en (1964); Robinet (1997); Zürcher (2007); Kleeman (2016).

BIBLIOGRAPHY

PRIMARY SOURCES

Baopuzi 抱朴子. By Ge Hong 葛洪.

Baopuzi neipian jiaoshi 抱朴子內篇校釋. By Wang Ming 王明. Beijing: Zhonghua shujue, 1985.

Changyan 昌言. By Zhongchang Tong 仲長統. Beijing: Zhonghua shuju, 2012.

Chunqiu fanlu 春秋繁露. By Dong Zhongshu 董仲舒. Taipei: Zhonghua shuju, 1984.

Dongguan hanji jiaozhu 東觀漢紀校注. By Liu Zhen 劉珍. Beijing: Zhonghua shuju, 2008.

Fan Shengzhi shu jinyi 氾勝之書今譯. By Shi Shenghan 石聲漢. Beijing: Kexue chubanshe, 1956.

Guanzi jiaozhu 管子校注. By Li Xiangfeng 黎翔鳳. Beijing: Zhonghua shuju, 2004.

Hanfeizi jijie 韓非子集解. By Wang Xianshen 王先慎. Beijing: Zhonghua shuju, 1998.

Hanguan liuzhong 漢官六種. By Sun Xingyan 孫星衍. Taipei: Zhonghua shuju, 1985.

Hanshu (HS) 漢書. By Ban Gu 班固. Beijing: Zhonghua shuju, 1962.

Houhanshu (HHS) 後漢書. By Fan Ye 范曄. Beijing: Zhonghua shuju, 1965.

Huainanzi jishi 淮南子集釋. By He Ning 禾寧. Beijing: Zhonghua shuju, 1995.

Jinshu 晉書. By Fang Xuanling 房玄齡. Beijing: Zhonghua shuju, 1974.

Laozi jiaoshi 老子校釋. By Zhu Qianzhi 朱謙之. Beijing: Zhonghua shuju, 2000.

Li Taibai ji 李太白集. By Li Bai 李白. Ed. by Yang Lian 楊鐮. Shenyang: Liaoning jiaoyu cubanshe, 1997.

Liexian zhuan 列仙傳. By Liu Xiang 劉向. Shanghai: Shangai guji chubanshe, 1987.

Liji zhengyi 禮記正義. In *Shisanjing zhushu* 十三經注疏. By Ruan Yuan 阮元. Taipei: Yiwen chubanshe, 1976.

Lunheng 論衡. By Wang Chong 王充. See *Lunheng jijie*. 論衡集解. By Liu Pansui 劉盼遂. Taipei: Shijie shuju, 1990.

Lunyu zhushu 論語注疏. In *Shisanjing zhushu* 十三經注疏. By Ruan Yuan 阮元. Taipei: Yiwen chubanshe, 1976.

Lüshi chunqiu jishi 呂氏春秋集釋. By Xu Weiju 許維遹. Beijing: Zhonghua shuju, 2009.

Maoshi zhengyi 毛詩正義. In *Shisanjing zhushu* 十三經注疏. By Ruan Yuan 阮元. Taipei: Yiwen chubanshe, 1976.

Mengzi zhushu 孟子注疏. In *Shisanjing zhushu* 十三經注疏. By Ruan Yuan 阮元. Taipei: Yiwen chubanshe, 1976.

Qianful un 潛夫論. By Wang Fu 王符. See *Qianfu lun jian jiaozheng* 潛夫論箋校正. By Wang Fu王符. Beijing: Zhonghua shuju, 1997.

Qimin yaoshu 齊民要術. By Jia Sixie 賈思勰. See *Qimin yaoshu jinshi* 齊民要術今釋. By Shi Shenghan 石聲漢. Beijing: Kexue chubanshe, 1957.

Quanshanggu Sandai Qin·Han Sanguo Liuchao wen 全上古三代秦漢三國六朝文. Yan Kejun 嚴可均. 6 vols. Beijing: Zhonghua shuju, 1958.

Shangjun shu jiegu 商君書解詁. By Zhu Shiche 朱師轍. Taipei: Shijie shuju, 1973.

Shangshu zhengyi 尚書正義. In *Shisanjing zhushu* 十三經注疏. By Ruan Yuan 阮元. Taipei: Yiwen chubanshe, 1976.

Shiji (SJ) 史記. By Sima Qian 司馬遷. Beijing: Zhonghua shuju, 1962.

Simin yueling 四民月令. By Cui Shi 崔寔. See *Simin yueling jiaozhu* 四民月令校注. By Shi Shenghan 石聲漢. Beijing: Zhonghua shuju, 1965.

Taiping yulan 太平御覽. By Li Fang 李昉 et al. Beijing: Zhonghua shuju, 1960.

Xijing zaji 西京雜記. By Liu Xin 劉歆. Changchun: Jilin daxue chubanshe, 1992.

Xin shu 新書. By Jia Yi 賈誼. Beijing: Zhonghua shuju, 1987.

Yantie lun 鹽鐵論. By Huan Kuan 桓寬. See *Yantie lun jiaozhu* 鹽鐵論校注. By Wang Liqi 王利器. Beijing: Zhonghua shuju, 1992.

Yanzi chunqiu jishi 晏子春秋集釋. By Wu Zeyu 吳則虞. Beijing: Zhonghua shuju. 2010

Yili zhushu 儀禮注疏. In *Shisanjing zhushu* 十三經注疏. By Ruan Yuan 阮元. Taipei: Yiwen chubanshe, 1976.

Yiwen leiju 藝文類聚. By Ouyang Xun 歐陽詢. 4 vols. Shanghai: Shanghai guji chubanshe, 1982.

Yuefu shiji 樂府詩集. By Guo Maoqian 郭茂倩. 4 vols. Beijing: Zhonghua shuju. 1979.

Zhanguoce jizhu huikao 戰國策集注彙考. By Zhu Zugeng 諸祖耿. Nanjing: Jiangsu guji chubanshe, 1985.

Zhenglun 政論. By Cui Shi 崔寔. Beijing: Zhonghua shuju, 2012.

Zhouli zhushu 周禮注疏. In *Shisanjing zhushu* 十三經注疏. By Ruan Yuan 阮元. Taipei: Yiwen chubanshe, 1976.

Zhuangzi jishi 莊子集釋. By Guo Qingfan 郭慶藩. Beijing: Zhonghua shuju, 1985.

Zuozhuan zhengyi 左傳正義. In *Shisanjing zhushu* 十三經注疏. By Ruan Yuan 阮元. Taipei: Yiwen chubanshe, 1976.

MODERN SOURCES

Alexiou, Margaret. 1974. *The Ritual Lament in Greek Tradition*. London: Cambridge University Press.

Bakhtin, M. M. 1984. *Rabelais and His World*. (trans. H. Iswolsky). Bloomington, IN: Indiana University Press.

Barbieri-Low, Anthony. 2007. *Artisans in Early Imperial China*. Seattle, WA: University of Washington Press.

Barbieri-Low, A. J., and Robin D. S. Yates. 2015. *Law, State, and Society in Early Imperial China: A Study with Critical Edition and Translation of the Lagal Texts from Zhangjiashan Tomb no. 247*. Leiden: Brill.

Barfield, Thomas J. 1989. *The Perilous Frontier: Nomadic Empires and China*. Cambridge: Basil Blackwell.

Benn, Charles D. 2002. *Daily Life in Traditional China: The Tang Dynasty*. Westport, CT: Greenwood Press.

Bielenstein, Hans. 1947. "The census of China during the period 2–742 A.D." *BMFEA* 19: 135–45.

Bodde, Derk. 1975. *Festivals in Classical China*. Princeton, NJ: Princeton University Press.

Boltz, William G. 1999. "Language and writing." In *The Cambridge History of Ancient China*, eds. Micheal Loewe and Edward L. Shaughnessy, 74–123. Cambridge: Cambridge University Press.

Bottéro, Jean. 1992. *Mesopotamia: Writing, Reasoning, and the Gods*. Chicago, IL: University of Chicago Press.

Bottéro, Jean. 2001. *Religion in Ancient Mesopotamia*. Chicago, IL: University of Chicago Press.

Brashier, Kenneth. 2011. *Ancestral Memory in Early China*. Cambridge, MA: Harvard University Asia Center for the Harvard-Yenching Institute.

Bremmer, Jan N. 1983. *The Early Greek Concept of the Soul*. Princeton, NJ: Princeton University Press.

Brown, Miranda. 2015. *The Art of Medicine in Early China: The Ancient and Medieval Origins of a Modern Archive*. Cambridge: Cambridge University Press.

Burke, Peter. 1994. *Popular Culture in Early Modern Europe*. Burlington, VT: Ashgate.

Cai, Liang. 2014. *Witchcraft and the Rise of the First Confucian Empire*. Albany, NY: State University of New York Press.

Campany, Robert F. 2002. *To Live as Long as Heaven and Earth: A Translation and Study of Ge Hong's Traditions of Divine Transcendents*. Berkeley, CA: University of California Press.

Campany, Robert. F. 2009. *Making Transcendents: Ascetics and Social Memory in Early Medieval China*. Honolulu, HI: University of Hawai'i Press.

Carr, E. H. 1986. *What Is History?*, 2nd edn. London: Palgrave.

Chang, Kwang-Chih, ed. 1977. *Food in Chinese Culture*. New Haven, CT: Yale University Press.

Chang, Kwang-Chih. 1980. *Shang Civilization*. New Haven, CT: Yale University Press.

Chang, Kwang-Chih. 1983. *Art, Myth, and Ritual: The Path to Political Authority in*

Ancient China. Cambridge, MA: Harvard University Press.

Chang, Kwang-Chih. 1986. *The Archaeology of Ancient China*, 4th edn. New Haven, CT: Yale University Press.

Chavannes, Édouard. 1910. *Le T'ai Chan*. Paris: Ernest Leroux.

Ch'en, Kenneth K. S. 1964. *Buddhism in China*. Princeton, NJ: Princeton University Press.

Chen Songchang 陳松長. 1998. "Zhanguo shidai bingsizhe de daoci 戰國時代兵死者的禱辭." *Jianbo yanjiu yicong* 2: 30–42.

Cheng Youwei 程有為. 2008. "Neihuang Sanyangzhuang shuizai yizhi yu Huanghe shuihuan 內黃三楊莊水災遺址與黃河水患." *Zhongzhou xuekan* 4: 172–76.

Childs-Johnson, Elizabeth. 1998. "The metamorphic image: A predominant theme in the ritual art of Shang China." *Bulletin of the Museum of Far Eastern Antiquities* 70: 5–171.

Ch'ü, Tung-Tsu. 1972. *Han Social Structure*. Seattle, WA: University of Washington Press.

Cui Mingde 崔明德. 2005. *Zhongguo gudai heqin shi* 中國古代和親史. Beijing: Renmin chubanshe.

Di Cosmo, Nicola. 2002. *Ancient China and Its Enemies: The Rise of Nomadic Power in East Asian History*. Cambridge: Cambridge University Press.

Dien, A. E. 2007. *Six Dynasties Civilization*. New Haven, CT: Yale University Press.

Dikötter, Frank. 2007. *Things Modern: Material Culture and Everyday Life in China*. London: C. Hurst & Co.

Dubs, Homer H., trans. 1938. *The History of the Former Han Dynasty*, a critical translation, with annotations by Homer H. Dubs, with the collaboration of Jen Tai and Pan Lo-Chi. 3 vols. Baltimore, MD: Waverly.

Duyvendak, J. J. L., trans. 1929. *Book of Lord Shang: A Classic of the Chinese School of Law*. Chicago, IL: University of Chicago Press.

Eberhard, Wolfram. 1965. *Conquerors and Rulers: Social Forces in Medieval China*. Leiden: Brill.

Ebrey, Patricia B. 1974. "Estate and family management in the later Han as seen in the monthly instructions for the four classes of people." *Journal of Economic and Social History of Orient* 17: 173–205.

Ebrey, Patricia Buckley. 1978. *The Aristocratic Families of Early Imperial China*. Cambridge: Cambridge University Press.

Elvin, Mark. 2004. *The Retreat of the Elephants: An Environmental History of China*. New Haven, CT: Yale University Press.

Eno, Robert. 2009. "Shang state religion and the pantheon of the oracle texts." In *Early Chinese Religion. Part 1, Shang through Han (1250 BC-220 AD)*, eds. John Lagerwey and Marc Kalinowski, 41–102. Leiden: Brill.

Eyre, Christopher J. 2009. "Belief and the dead in Pharaonic Egypt." In *Rethinking Ghosts in World Religions*, ed. Mu-chou Poo, 33–46. Leiden: Brill.

Falkenhausen, Lothar von. 2006. *Chinese Society in the Age of Confucius (1000–250 BC): The Archaeological Evidence*. Los Angeles, CA: Cotsen Institute of Archaeology, University of California.

Finsterbusch, Käte. 1966. *Verzeichnis und motivindex der Han darstellungen*, 4 vols. Wiesbaden: Otto Harrassowitz.

Finucane, R. C. 1996. *Ghosts, Appearances of the Dead in Cultural Transformation*. Amherst, NY: Prometheus Books.

Flad, Rowan. 2011. *Salt Production and Social Hierarchy in Ancient China: An Archaeological Investigation of Specialization in China's Three Gorges*. Cambridge: Cambridge University Press.

Forke, Alfred. 1962. *Lun Heng*, 2 vols. New York, NY: Paragon Book Gallery.

Gansu sheng wenwu kaogu Yanjiusuo 甘肅省文物考古研究所, et al. 1990. *Juyan xinjian: Jiaqu houguan yu disisui* 居延新簡: 甲渠候官與第四燧. Beijing: Wenwu chubanshe.

Gansu sheng wenwu kaogu Yianjiuso 甘肅省文物考古研究所. 1989. "Gansu tianshui fangmatan zhanguo Qin Han muqun de fajue 甘肅天水放馬灘戰國秦漢墓群的發掘." *WW* 2: 1–11.

Geertz, Clifford. 1973. "Deep play: Notes on the Balinese cockfight." In *The Interpretation of Cultures*, 412–53. New York, NY: Basic Books.

Gernet, J. 1962. *Daily Life in China on the Eve of the Mongol Invasion, 1250–1276*. London: George Allen & Unwin (tr. of *La vie quotidienne en Chine à la veille de l'invasion mongole, 1250–1276*, Paris: Hachette, 1959).

Goldin, Paul. 2001. *The Culture of Sex in Ancient China*. Honolulu, HI: University of Hawai'i Press.

Graham, Angus C. 1986. *Yin-Yang and the Nature of Correlative Thinking*. Singapore: Institute of East Asian Philosophies.

Granet, Marcel. 1932. *Festivals and Songs in Ancient China*. London: George Routledge and Sons.

Guan Dexiang 官德祥. 2001. "Liang Han shiqi huangzai shulun 兩漢時期蝗災述論." *Zhongguo nongshi* 3: 8–15.

Guizhou sheng Bowuguan 貴州省博物館. 1959. "Guizhou Qingzhen Pingba Hanmu fajue baogao 貴州清鎮平壩漢墓發掘報告." *Kaogu xuebao* 1: 99–110.

Harper, Donald. 1994. "Resurrection in Warring States popular religion." *TR* 5.2: 13–28.

Harper, Donald. 1998. *Early Chinese Medical Literature: The Mawangdui Medical Manuscripts*. London: Kegan Paul International.

Harper, Donald. 2004. "Contracts with the spirit world in Han common religion: The Xuning prayer and sacrifice documents of A.D. 79." *CEA* 14: 227–67.

Harper, Donald, and Kalinowski, Mark, eds. 2017. *Books of Fate and Popular Culture in Early China: The Daybook Manuscripts of the Warring States, Qin and Han*. Leiden: Brill.

He Shuangquan 何雙全. 1989. "Tianshui fangmatan Qi mu chutu ditu chutan 天水放馬灘秦墓出土地圖初探." *WW* 2: 12–22.

Hinsch, Bret. 2002. *Women in Early Imperial China*. Lanham, MD: Rowan & Littlefield.

Hou Liang 侯良. 1994. *Mawangdui chuanqi* 馬王堆傳奇. Taipei: Dongda.

Hou Xudong 侯旭東. 2010. "Yucai shoulie yu Qin-Han beifang minzhong shengji: jianlun yinong liguo chuantong de xingcheng yu nongmin de pubianhua 漁採狩獵與秦漢北方民眾生計—兼論以農立國傳統的形成與農民的普遍化." *Lishi yanjiu* 5: 4–26.

Hou Xudong 侯旭東. 2011. "Cong chaosu zhi she dao shangpu: Handai Junguodi yu Liuchao didian kaolun 從朝宿之舍到商鋪—漢代郡國邸與六朝邸店考論." *Qinghua daxue* 5: 32–43.

Hsiung, Ping-Chen. 1994. "Constructed emotions: The bond between mothers and sons in late mperial China." *Late imperial China* 15.1: 87–117.

Hsiung, Ping-Chen. 2005. *A Tender Voyage*. Stanford, CA: Stanford University Press.

Hsu, Cho-Yun 許倬雲. 1965. *Ancient China in Transition*. Stanford, CA: Stanford University Press.

Hsu, Cho-Yun. 1980. *Han Agriculture*. Seattle, WA: University of Washington Press.

Hsu, Cho-Yun. 1982. "Handai jiating de daxiao 漢代家庭的大小." In *Qiougu bian* 求古編, 515–41. Taipei: Lianjing chubanshe 聯經出版社.

Hu Pingsheng 胡平生, and Zhang Defang 張德芳, eds. 2001. *Dunhuang Xuanquan Hanjian shicui* 敦煌懸泉漢簡釋粹. Shanghai: Shanghai guji chubanshe.

Huang Jin-Yan 黄今言. 1984. "Handai de zisuan 漢代的訾算." *Zhongguo shehui jingjishi yanjiu* 1: 77–82.

Huang Jinyan 黄今言. 2005. *Qin-Han shangpin jingji yanjiu* 秦漢商品經濟研究. Beijing: Renmin chubanshe.

Huang Jinyan 黄今言. 2006. "Handai nongmin 'Beiben qumo' de lishi kaocha 漢代農民'背本趨末'的歷史考察." *Zhongguo jingjishi yanjiu* 4: 118–27.

Huang Jinyan 黄今言, and Wen Leping 溫樂平. 2000. "Handai ziran zaihai yu zhengfu de zhenzhai xingji nianbiao 漢代自然災害與政府的賑災行跡年." *Nongye kaogu* 3: 242–52.

Huang Xiaofen 黄曉芬. 2003. *Hanmu de kaoguxue yanjiu* 漢墓的考古學研究. Changsha: Yuelu shushe.

Huang, Xuehui, et al. 2012. "A map of rice genome variation reveals the origin of cultivated rice." *Nature* 490.7421: 497–501.

Hubei sheng wenwu kaogu Yanjiuso 湖北省文物考古研究所, and Beijing daxue zhongwenxi 北京大學中文系. 2000. *Jiudian Chujian* 九店楚簡. Beijing: Zhonghua shuju.

Hubei sheng wenwu kaogu Yanjiusuo 湖北省文物考古研究所. 1995. *Jiangling Jiudian Dong-Zhou mu* 江陵九店東周墓. Beijing: Kexue chubanshe.

Huizinga, Johan. 1950. *Homo ludens*. Boston, MA: Beacon Press.

Hulsewé, A. F. P. 1985. *Remnants of Ch'in Law*. Leiden: Brill.

Hulsewé, A. F. P. 1990. "Fragments of Han law." *TP* LXXVI: 208–35.

Hunan sheng Bowuguan 湖南省博物館, and Zhongguokexueyuankaoguyenjiuso 中國科學院考古研究所 eds. 1973. *Changsha mawangdui ihao hanmu* 長沙馬王堆一號漢墓. Beijing: Wenwu chubanshe.

Instituta vostokovedeniia (Rossiiskai akademii nauk), Sankt-peterburgskoe otdelenie, ed. 2001. *Ecang Dunhuang wenxian* 俄藏敦煌文獻, 17 vols. Shanghai: Shanghai guji chubanshe; Moscow: Eluosi kexue chubanshe dongfang wenxuebu.

Jacobsen, Thorkild. 1976. *The Treasures of Darkness: A History of Mesopotamian Religion*. New Haven, CT: Yale University Press.

Jagchid, Sechin, and Van J. Symons. 1989. *Peace, War and Trade along the Great Wall*. Bloomington, IN: Indiana University Press.

James, Jean. 1996. *A Guide to the Tomb and Shrine Art of the Han Dynasty 206 B.C.-A.D. 220*. Lewiston, NY: E. Mellen Press.

Kaltenmark, Maxime. 1966. "Notes à propos du Kao-mei." *Annuaire de l'Ecole Pratique des Hautes Etude, V^e^ section, science religeuses* 3–34.

Keightley, David N. 1978. *Sources of Shang History: The Oracle-Bone Inscriptions of Bronze Age China*. Berkeley, CA: University of California Press.

Keightley, David. 2000. *The Ancestral Landscape: Time, Space, and Community in Late Shang China (ca. 1200–1045 B.C.)*. Berkeley, CA: Institute of East Asian Studies, University of California, Berkeley, Center for Chinese Studies.

Keightley, David N. 2012. *Working for His Majesty*. Berkeley, CA: University of California Press.

Kieschnick, John. 2003. *The Impact of Buddhism on Chinese Material Culture*. Princeton, NJ: Princeton University Press.

Kinney, Anne B., ed. 1995. *Chinese Views of Childhood*. Honolulu, HI: University of Hawai'i Press.

Kinney, Anne B. 2014. *Exemplary Women of Early China: The Lienü zhuan of Liu Xiang*. New York, NY: Columbia University Press.

Kleeman, Terry F. 2016. *Celestial Masters: History and Ritual in Early Daoist Communities*. Cambridge, MA: Harvard University Asia Center.

Knapp, Keith. 2005. *Selfless Offspring: Filial Children and Social Order in Medieval China*. Honolulu, HI: University of Hawai'i Press.

Knechtges, David R., trans. 1982. *Wen Xuan* 文選, or, *Selections of Refined Literature/Xiao Tong*, with annotations and introduction, 3 vols. Princeton, NJ: Princeton University Press.

Kuhn, Dieter, ed. 2012. *Chinese Silks*. New Haven, CT: Yale University Press.

Lagerwey, John, and Marc Kalinowski, eds. 2009. *Early Chinese Religion. Part 1, Shang through Han (1250 BC-220 AD)*. Leiden: Brill.

Lai Chi-Tim. 1998. "The opposition of celestial master Taoism to popular cults during the Six Dynasties." *Asia Major (3rd series)* 11.1: 1–20.

Lai, Guolong. 2015. *Excavating the Afterlife: The Archaeology of Early Chinese Religion*. Seattle, WA: University of Washington Press.

Lattimore, Owen. 1951. *Inner Asian Frontiers of China*. New York, NY: American Geographic Society.

Lau, D. C. 2001. *Tao te ching. A Bilingual Edition*. Hong Kong: The Chinese University Press.

Lau, D. C. 2003. *Mencius. A Bilingual Edition*. Hong Kong: The Chinese University Press.

Le Roy Ladurie, E. 1979. (Trans. Feeney, M.) *Carnival in Romans*. New York, NY: George Braziller.

Legge, James. 1960. *The Chinese Classics*, 5 vols. Hong Kong: Hong Kong University Press.

Lewis, Mark Edward. 2006. *The Flood Myths of Early China*. Albany, NY: State University of New York Press.

Lewis, Mark Edward. 2007. *The Early Chinese Empires: Qin and Han*. Cambridge, MA: Harvard University Press.

Li, Feng. 2008. *Bureaucracy and the State in Early China: Governing the Western Zhou*. Cambridge: Cambridge University Press.

Li, Feng. 2013. *Early China: A Social and Cultural History*. Cambridge: Cambridge University Press.

Li, Feng, and David P. Branner, eds. 2011. *Writing and Literacy in Early China*. Seattle, WA: University of Washington Press.

Li Jinghua 李京華, and Chen Changshan 陳長山. 1995. *Nanyang Handai yetie* 南陽漢代冶鐵. Zhengzhou: Zhongzhou guji chubanshe.

Li Junming 李均明, and He Shuangquan 何雙全, eds. 1990. *Sanjian jiandu heji* 散見簡牘合輯. Beijing: Wenwu chubanshe.

Li Mingxiao 李明曉, and Zhao Jiuxiang 趙久湘. 2011. *Sanjian Zhanguo Qin-Han jianbo falü wenxian zhengli yu yanjiu* 散見戰國秦漢簡帛法律文獻整理與研究. Chongqing: Xinan Shifan daxue chubanshe.

Li Mingzhao (Lai Mingchiu) 黎明釗. 2012. "Jinguanling yu jianghu daozei" 津關令與江湖盜賊. In *Han diguo de zhidu yu shehui zhixu* 漢帝國的制度與社會秩序, ed. Li Mingzhao 黎明釗, 365–408. Hong Kong: Oxford University Press.

Liang Fangzhong 梁方仲. 2008. *Zhongguo lidai hukou, tiandi, tianfu tongji* 中國歷代戶口、田地、田賦統計. Beijing: Zhonghua shuju.

Lianyungang Bowuguan 連雲港博物館, ed. 1997. *Yinwan Han mu jiandu* 尹灣漢墓簡牘. Beijing: Zhonghua shuju.

Lin, Fu-Shih. 2009. "The image and status of Shamans in ancient China." In *Early Chinese Religion*. Part 1, *Shang through Han (1250 BC-220 AD)*, Vol. 1, eds. John Lagerwey and Marc Kalinowski, 397–458. Leiden: Brill.

Lin Suqing 林素清. 1999. "Liang-Han jingming huibian 兩漢鏡銘彙編." In *Gu wenzixue lunwenji* 古文字學論文集, eds. Zhou Fengwu 周鳳五 and Lin Suqing 林素清, 235–312. Taipei: Guoli bianyiguan.

Liu Haiwang 劉海旺. 2006. "Shouci faxian de Handai nongye lüli yizhi: Zhongguo Henan Neihuang Sanyangzhuang Handai juluo yizhi chushi 首次發現的漢代農業閭里遺址—中國河南內黃三楊莊漢代聚落遺址初識." In *Kaogu fajue yu lishi fuyuan* 考古發掘與歷史復原, eds. Chen Xingcan 陳星燦 and Mi Gaila 米蓋拉, 64–78. Beijing: Zhonghua shuju.

Liu Jiagui 劉家貴. 2008. "Chongping Xi-Han yantie huiyi ji xianliang wenxue de jingji sixiang 重評西漢鹽鐵會議及賢良文學的經濟思想." *Zhongguo jingjishi yanjiu* 4: 135–43.

Liu, Li. 2012. *The Archaeology of China: From the Late Paleolithic to the Early Bronze Age*. Cambridge: Cambridge University Press.

Liu Tseng-Kuei 劉增貴. 1980. *Handai hunyin zhidu* 漢代婚姻制度. Taipei: Huashi chubanshe.

Liu Tseng-Kuei 劉增貴. 1997. "Handai de Taishan xinyang 漢代的泰山信仰." *Dalu zazhi* 94.5: 193–205.

Liu Yanchi. 1988. *The Essential Book of Traditional Chinese Medicine*, 2 vols. New York, NY: Columbia University Press.

Liu Yunyong 劉運勇. 1992. "Zailun Xi-Han Chang'an buju ji xingcheng yuanyin 再論西漢長安佈局及形成原因." *KG* 7: 640–45.

Loewe, M. 1967. *Records of Han Administration*, 2 vols. London: Cambridge University Press.

Loewe, M. 1968. *Everyday Life in Early Imperial China during the Han Period, 202 BC-AD 220*. London: Putnam.

Loewe, M. 1974. *Conflict and Crisis in Han China (104 BC to AD 9)*. London: George Allen & Unwin.

Loewe, M. 1979. *Ways to Paradise: The Chinese Quest for Immortality*. London: Allen & Unwin.

Loewe, M. 1982. *Chinese Ideas of Life and Death: Faith, Myth and Reason in the Han Period (202 BC–AD 220)*. London: Allen & Unwin.

Loewe, M., ed. 1993. *Early Chinese Texts: A Bibliographical Guide*. Berkeley, CA: University of California Press.

Loewe, M. 1994. *Divination, Mythology and Monarchy in Han China*. Cambridge: Cambridge University Press.

Loewe, M. 2006. *The Government of the Qin and Han Empires: 221 BCE-220 CE*. Indianapolis: Hackett.

Loewe, M. 2011. *Dong Zhongshu, a "Confucian" Heritage and the Chunqiu Fanlu*. Leiden: Brill.

Loewe, M., and Shaungnessy, E., eds. 1999. *The Cambridge History of Ancient China: From the Origins of Civilization to 221 B.C.* Cambridge: Cambridge University Press.

Loewe, M., and Twitchett, D., eds. 1986. *The Cambridge History of China*, Vol. I: *The Ch'in and Han Empires, 221 B.C – A.D. 220*. Cambridge: Cambridge University Press.

Lü Zongli 呂宗力. 2011. *Handai de yaoyan* 漢代的謠言 Hangzhou: Zhejiang daxue chubanshe.

Ma Maoyuan 馬茂元. 1969. *Gushi shijiushou tansuo* 古詩十九首探索. Hong Kong: Wenhan chubanshe.

Maspero, Heri. 1981. *Taoism and Chinese Religion*, trans. F. A. Kierman, Jr. Amherst, MA: University of Massachusetts Press.

Mote, F. 1989. *Intellectual Foundations of China*, 2nd edn. New York, NY: Knopf.

Munslow, Alun. 1997. *Deconstructing History*. London: Rutledge.

Nagata Hidemasa 永田英正. 1954. *Kandai setsukoku shūsei* 漢代石刻集成, *Honbun hen* 本文篇. Kyōto: Dōhōsha.

Needham, Joseph. 2004. *Science and Civilisation in China*. 7 vols. Cambridge: Cambridge University Press.

Nylan, Michael. 2001. *The Five "Confucian" Classics*. New Haven, CT: Yale University Press.

Nylan, Michael, and Griet Vankeerberghen, eds. 2015. *Chang'an 26 BCE: An Augustan Age in China*. Seattle, WA: University of Washington Press.

Owen, Stephen. 2006. *The Making of Early Chinese Classical Poetry*. Cambridge, MA: Harvard University Press.

Pankenier, David. 2013. *Astrology and Cosmology in Early China: Conforming Earth to Heaven*. Cambridge: Cambridge University Press.

Peng Wei 彭衛. 2010. *Handai hunyin xingtai* 漢代婚姻形態. Beijing: Renmin University Press.

Peng Wei 彭衛, and Yang Zhenhong 楊振紅. 2001. *Zhongguo fengsu tongshi (Qin Han Juan)* 中國風俗通史 (秦漢卷). Shanghai: Wenyi chubanshe.

Pines, Yuri. 2002. *Foundations of Confucian Thought: Intellectual Life in the Chunqiu Period (722–453 B.C.E.)*. Honolulu, HI: University of Hawai'i Press.

Pines, Yuri, et al., eds. 2014. *The Birth of an Empire: The State of Qin Revisited*. Berkeley, CA: University of California Press.

Poo, Mu-Chou. 1990. "Ideas concerning death and burial in pre-Han and Han China." *Asia Major* (3rd series) 3.2: 25–62.

Poo, Mu-Chou. 1995. "The images of immortals and eminent monks: Religious mentality in early medieval China." *Numen* 42: 172–96.

Poo, Mu-Chou. 1998. *In Search of Personal Welfare: A View of Ancient Chinese Religion*. Albany, NY: State University of New York Press.

Poo, Mu-Chou. 1999. "The use and abuse of wine in ancient China." *Journal of the Economic and Social History of the Orient* 42.2: 123–51.

Poo, Mu-Chou. 2004. "The concept of ghost in ancient Chinese religion." In *Chinese Religion and Society*, Vol. 1, ed. John Lagerwey, 173–91. Hong Kong: Chinese University Press.

Poo, Mu-Chou. 2005. "A taste of happiness: Contextualizing elixirs in Baopuzi." In *Of Tripod and Palate: Food, Politics, and Religion in Traditional China*, ed. Roel Sterckx, 123–39. New York, NY: Palgrave.

Poo, Mu-Chou. 2007. "The formation of the conception of antiquity in early China." In *Perceptions of Antiquity in Chinese Civilization*, eds. Dieter Kuhn and Helga Stahl, 85–101. Heidelberg: Edition Forum.

Poo, Mu-Chou. 2010. "Preparation for the after-life in Ancient China." In *Mortality in Traditional China*. eds. Amy Olberding and P.J. Ivanhoe, 13–36. Honolulu, HI: University of Hawai'i Press.

Poo, Mu-Chou. 2013. "To become a Chinese: Cultural consciousness and political legitimacy in early Medieval China (220–681)." In *Migration and Membership Regimes in Historical Perspective*, eds. Ulbe Bosma, Gijs Kessler, and Leo Lucassen, 169–89. Leiden: Brill.

Poo, Mu-Chou, Harold Drake, and Lisa Raphals, eds. 2017. *Old Society, New Belief: Religious Transformation of China and Rome, ca. 1st-6th Centuries*. Oxford: Oxford University Press.

Pu Muzhou (Poo, Mu-chou). 2008. *Muzang yu shengsi: Zhongguo gudai zongjiao zhi xingsi* 墓葬與生死: 中國古代宗教之省思. Taipei: Lianjing chuban, 1993; Beijing: Zhonghua shuju.

Qu Liuyi 曲六乙, and Qian Fu 錢茀. 2003. *Zhongguo nuo wenhua tonglun* 中國儺文化通論. Taipei: Xuesheng shuju.

Queen, Sarah. 1996. *From Chronicle to Canon: The Hermeneutics of the Spring and Autumn According to Tung Chung-shu*. New York, NY: Cambridge University Press.

Raphals, Lisa. 1998. *Sharing the Light: Representations of Women and Virtue in Early China*. Albany, NY: State University of New York Press.

Raphals, Lisa. 2013. *Divination and Prediction in Early China and Ancient Greece*. Cambridge: Cambridge University Press.

Rickett, W. Allyn. 1985. *Guanzi: Political, Economic, and Philosophical Essays from Early China: A Study and Translation*. Princeton, NJ: Princeton University Press.

Robinet, Isabell. 1997. *Taoism: Growth of a Religion*. Stanford, CA: Stanford University Press.

Sanft, Charles. 2009. "Edict of monthly ordinances for the four seasons in fifty articles from 5 C.E.: Introduction to the wall inscription discovered at Xuanquanzhi, with annotated translation." *Early China* 32: 125–208.

Sato, Taketoshi 佐藤武敏. 1993. *Chūgoku saigaishi nenpyō* 中国災害史年表. Tōkyō: Kokusho kankōkai.

Schaberg, David. 2001. *A Patterned Past: Form and Thought in Early Chinese Historiography*. Cambridge, MA: Harvard University Asia Center. Distributed by Harvard University Press.

Schipper, Krstofer. 1993. *The Taoist Body*. Berkeley, CA: University of California Press.

Schwartz, Benjamin I. 1985. *The World of Thought in Ancient China*. Cambridge, MA: Harvard University Press.

Shandong sheng Bowuguan 山東省博物館, and Cangshanxian wenhua Guan 蒼山縣文化館. 1975. "Shandong Cangshan Yuanjia yuannian huaxiangshi mu 山東蒼山元嘉元年畫像石墓." *KG* 2: 124–34.

Shaughnessy, E. 1988. "The historical significance of the introduction of the chariot into China." *Harvard Journal of Asiatic Studies* 48.1: 189–237.

Shaughnessy, Edward, ed. 1997. *New Sources of Early Chinese History: An Introduction to the Reading of Inscriptions and Manuscript*. Berkeley, CA: Society for the Study of Early China and the Institute of East Asian Studies, University of California, Berkeley.

Shi Sheng-Han 石聲漢. 1957. *Qimin Yaoshu jinshi* 齊民要術今釋. Bejing: Kexue chubanshe.

Shi Sheng-Han 石聲漢. 1956. *Fanshengzhi Shu jinyi* 氾勝之書今釋. Beijing: Kaxue chubanshe.

Shi Sheng-Han 石聲漢. 1965. *Simin Yueling jiaozhu* 四民月令校注. Beijing: Zhonghua shuju.

Shuihudi qinmu zhujian zhengli Xiaozu 睡虎地秦墓竹簡整理小組. 1990. *Shuihudi Qin-mu zhujian* 睡虎地秦墓竹簡. Beijing: Wenwu chubanshe.

Sivin, Nathan. 1968. *Chinese Alchemy: Preliminary Studies*. Cambridge, MA: Harvard University Press.

Sivin, Nathan. 1969. "Cosmos and computation in early Chinese mathematical astronomy." *TP* 55.1: 1–73.

Sivin, Nathan. 1993. "Huang Ti Nei Ching." In *Early Chinese Texts: A Bibliographic Guide*, ed. Michael Loewe, 196–215. Berkeley, CA: Society for the Study of Early China and Institute of East Asian Studies.

Song Huiqun 宋會群, and Miao Xuelan 苗雪蘭. 2010. *Zhongguo boyi wenhuashi* 中國博弈文化史. Beijing: Shehui kexue wenxian chubanshe.

Song Jie 宋杰. 1987. "'Jiuzhang Suanshu' suo fanying de Handai jiaotong zhuangkuang '九章算術' 所反映的漢代交通狀況." *Shoudu shifan* 2: 43–53.

Stein, Rolf A. 1979. "Religious Taoism and popular religion from the second to seventh centuries." In *Facets of Taoism*, eds. H. Welch and A. Seidel, 53–81. New Haven, CT: Yale University Press.

Steinhardt, Nancy S. 1990. *Chinese Imperial City Planning*. Honolulu, HI: University of Hawai'i Press.

Sterckx, Roel. 2011. *Food, Sacrifice, and Sagehood in Early China*. Cambridge: Cambridge University Press.

Sun Chang, Kang-I and Haun Saussy, eds. 1999. *Women Writers of Traditional China: An Anthology of Poetry and Criticism*. Stanford, CA: Stanford University Press.

Sun Hongfei 孫紅飛. 2012. "Liang Han ducheng guihua buju tanxi 兩漢都城規劃布局探析." *Zhongyuan wenwu* 5: 22–28.

Swann, Nancy Lee. 1932. *Pan Chao: Foremost Woman Scholar of China*. New York, NY: Century Co.

Swann, Nancy Lee. 1950. *Food and Money in Ancient China, the Earliest Economic History of China to A.D. 25: Han shu 24, with Related Texts, Han shu 91 and Shih-chi 129*. Princeton, NJ: Princeton University Press.

Teiser, Stephen E. 1994. *The Scripture on the Ten Kings and the Making of Purgatory in Medieval Chinese Buddhism*. Honolulu, HI: University of Hawai'i Press.

Tseng, Lillian L. Y. 2011. *Picturing Heaven in Early China*. Cambridge, MA: Harvard University Asia Center.

Tsien, Tsuen-Hsuin. 1962. *Written on Bamboo and Silk: The Beginnings of Chinese Books and Inscriptions*. Chicago, IL: University of Chicago Press.

Unschuld, Paul. 2003. *Huang Di Nei Jing Su Wen: Nature, Knowledge, Imagery in an Ancient Chinese Medical Text: With an Appendix: The Doctrine of the Five Periods and Six Qi in the Huang Di Nei Jing Su Wen*. Berkeley, CA: University of California Press.

Von Glahn, Richard. 2016. *The Economic History of China*. Cambridge: Cambridge University Press.

Wagner, Donald B. 1993. *Iron and Steel in Ancient China*. Leiden: Brill.

Wagner, Donald B. 2001. *The State and the Iron Industry in Han China*. Copenhagen: Nordic Institute of Asian Studies.

Wang, Yü-Ch'üan. 1951. *Early Chinese Coinage*. New York, NY: American Numismatic Society.

Wang Zhengzhong 王震中. 2013. *Zhongguo gudai guojia de qiyuan yu wangquan de xingcheng* 中國古代國家的起源與王權的形成. Beijing: Zhongguo shehui kexue chubanshe.

Wang Zhongshu. 1982. *Han Civilization*. New Haven, CT: Yale University Press.

Wang Zijin 王子今. 1994. *Qin-Han jiaotong shigao* 秦漢交通史稿. Beijing: Zhonggong Zhongyang Dangxiao chubanshe.

Ware, James R. 1966. *Alchemy, Medicine, Religion in the China of A.D. 320: The Nei P'ien of Ko Hung (Pao P'u Tzu)*. Cambridge, MA: MIT Press.

Watson, Burton, trans. 1964. *Chuang Tzu: Basic Writings*. New York, NY: Columbia University Press.

Watson, Burton, trans. 1968. *The Complete Works of Chuang Tzu*. New York, NY: Columbia University Press.

Watson, Burton. 1993. *Records of the Grand Historian of China, Ssu-ma Ch'ien*. 2 vols. New York, NY: Columbia University Press.

Winkler, Marjorie G., and Pao K. Wang. 1994. "The Late Quaternary vegetation and climate of China." In *Global Climates since the Last Glacial Maximum*, eds. H. E. Wright, et al., 221–64. Minneapolis, MN: University of Minnesota Press.

Wu Hung. 1992. "Art in a ritual context: Rethinking Mawangdui." *Early China* 17: 111–44.

Wu Hung. 2010. *The Art of the Yellow Springs: Understanding Chinese Tombs*. Honolulu, HI: University of Hawai'i Press.

Xiao Fan 蕭璠 1986. "Guanyu liang Han Weijin shiqi yangzhu yu jifei wenti de ruogan jiantao 關於兩漢魏晉時期養豬與積肥問題的若干檢討." *BIHP* 57.4.

Xie Guihua 謝桂華, Li Junming 李均明, and Zhu Guozhao 朱國炤, eds. 1987. *Juyan Hanjian shiwen hejiao* 居延漢簡釋文合校. Beijing: Wenwu chubanshe.

Xing Yitian (Hsing I-tien) 邢義田. 1986. "Handai bihua de fazhan he bihua mu 漢代壁畫的發展和壁畫墓." *BIHP* 57.1: 139–70.

Xing Yitian (Hsing I-tien) 邢義田. 2004. "Han huaxiang Kongzi jian Laozi tu guoyanlu: Riben pian 漢畫象孔子見老子圖過眼錄—日本篇." *Jiuzhou xuelin* 九州學林 2.2: 313–25.

Yan Gengwang 嚴耕望. 1952. "Qin-Han langli zhidu kao 秦漢郎吏制度考." *BIHP* 23: 122.

Yang Jiping 楊際平. 2007. "Qin-Han huji guanli zhidu yanjiu 秦漢戶籍管理制度研究." *Zhonghua wenshi luncong* 1: 1–35.

Yangzhou Bowuguan 揚州博物館. 1987. "Jiangsu Yizheng Xupu 101 hao Xi-Hanmu 江蘇儀征胥浦101號西漢墓." *WW* 1: 1–19.

Yates, Robin D. S. 1994. "Body, space, time and bureaucracy: Boundary creation and control mechanisms in early China." In *Boundaries in China*, ed. John Hay, 1–55. London: Reaktion Books.

Yates, Robin D. S. 1997. *The Five Lost Classics: Tao, Huanglao, and Yin-yang in Han China*, translated, and with an introduction by Robin Yates. New York, NY: Ballantine Books.

Yates, Robin D. S. 2001. "Cosmos, central authority, and communities in the early Chinese empire." In *Empires: Perspectives from Archaeology and History*, eds. Susan E. Alcock, et al., 351–68. Cambridge: Cambridge University Press.

Yates, Robin D. S. 2011. "Soldiers, scribes and women: Literacy among the lower orders in early China." In *Writing and Literacy in Early China,* eds. Li Feng and David P. Branner, 339–69. Seattle, WA: University of Washington Press.

Yates, Robin D. S. 2014. "The changing status of slaves in the Qin-Han transition." In *The Birth of an Empire: The State of Qin Revisited*, eds. Yuri Pines, et al. 206–23. Berkeley, CA: University of California Press.

Yin Zaishuo 尹在碩. 2012. "Qin-Han hukou tongji zhidu yu hukou bu 秦漢戶口統計制度與戶口簿." In *Han diguo de zhidu yu shehui zhixu* 漢帝國的制度與社會秩序, ed. Li Mingzhao 黎明釗, 68–69. Hong Kong: Oxford University Press.

Yü Ying-Shih. 1967. *Trade and Expansion in Han China*. Berkeley, CA: University of California Press.

Yü Ying-Shih. 1987. "O soul come back! A study in the changing conceptions of the soul and afterlife in pre-Buddhist China." *Harvard Journal of Asiatic Studies* 47.2: 363–95.

Yunmeng Shuihudi Qin-Mu Bianxiezu 雲夢睡虎地秦墓編寫組. 1981. *Yunmeng Shuihudi Qinmu* 雲夢睡虎地秦墓. Beijing: Wenwu chubanshe.

Zhang Pu 張溥 ed. 1990. *Han-Wei liuchao baisan mingjia ji* 漢魏六朝百三名家集, 5 vols. Rpt. Yangzhou 揚州: Jiangsu Guangling guji keyinshe.

Zhang Xunliao 張勛燎, and Bai Bin 白彬. 2006. *Zhongguo daojiao kaogu* 中國道教考古, 6 vols. Beijing: Xianzhuang shuju.

Zhangjiashan ersiqi hao Hanmu zhujian zhengli Xiaozu 張家山二四七號漢墓竹簡整理小組. 2006. *Zhangjiashan Hanmu zhujian [ersiqihao mu]: shiwen xiudingben* 張家山漢墓竹簡[二四七號墓]: 釋文修訂本. Beijing: Wenwu chubanshe.

Zhongguo shehui kexueyuan kaogu yanjiusuo Hancheng Gongzuodui 中國社會科學院考古研究所漢城工作隊. 1978. "Han Chang'an cheng Wuku yizhi fajue de chubu shouhuo 漢長安城武庫遺址發掘的初步收獲." *KG* 4: 261–69.

Zhou Changshan 周長山. 2001. *Handai chengshi yanjiu* 漢代城市研究. Beijing: Renmin chubanshe.

Zhou Changshan 周長山 2005. "Hebei diqu Handai chengshi de lishi kaocha 河北地區漢代城市的歷史考察." *Zhongguo lishi dili luncong* 中國歷史地理論叢 20.2: 33–40.

Zhou Fengwu 周鳳五. 2001. "Jiudian Chujian 'Gao Wuyi' chongtan 九店楚簡 '告武夷' 重探." *BIHP* 72.4: 941–59.

Zhou Yimou 周一謀, and Xiao Zuotao 蕭佐桃, eds. 1989. *Mawangdui yishu kaozhu* 馬王堆醫書考注. Taipei: Lequn.

Zürcher, Erik. 2007. *The Buddhist Conquest of China: The Spread and Adaptation of Buddhism in Early Medieval China*, 3rd edn. Leiden: Brill.

INDEX